Food Supply Protection and Homeland Security

FRANK R. SPELLMAN

GOVERNMENT INSTITUTES
An imprint of
The Scarecrow Press, Inc.
Lanham, Maryland • Toronto • Plymouth, UK
2008

 **Government Institutes**

Published in the United States of America
by Government Institutes, an imprint of The Scarecrow Press, Inc.
A wholly owned subsidiary of
The Rowman & Littlefield Publishing Group, Inc.
4501 Forbes Boulevard, Suite 200
Lanham, Maryland 20706
http://www.govinstpress.com/

Estover Road
Plymouth PL6 7PY
United Kingdom

British Library Cataloguing in Publication Information Available

Library of Congress Cataloging-in-Publication Data

Spellman, Frank R.
  Food supply protection and homeland security / Frank R. Spellman.
    p. cm.
  ISBN-13: 978-0-86587-177-9 (pbk. : alk. paper)
  ISBN-10: 0-86587-177-9 (pbk. : alk. paper)
  1. Agroterrorism—United States—Prevention. 2. Food contamination—United States—
Prevention. 3. Food supply—Security measures—United States. 4. National security—
United States. I. Title.
  HV6433.5.S64 2007
  363.325'93638—dc22   2007041471

∞™ The paper used in this publication meets the minimum requirements of
American National Standard for Information Sciences—Permanence of Paper for
Printed Library Materials, ANSI/NISO Z39.48-1992.
Manufactured in the United States of America.

For Revonna

Contents

Acronyms

AEOC	APHIS Emergency Operations Center
AFDO	Association of Food and Drug Officials
AI	Avian influenza
	Low-pathogenicity avian influenza (LPAI)
	High-pathogenicity avian influenza (HPAI)
ALF	Animal Liberation Front
AMR	Advance meat recovery
AMS	Agricultural Marketing Service
ANFO	Ammonium nitrate–fuel oil
AOAC	Association of Official Analytical Chemists
APHIS	Animal and Plant Health Inspection Service
APSnet	American Phytopathological Society
ARS	Agricultural Research Service
ASSE	American Society of Sanitary Engineers
ASTHO	Association of State and Territorial Health Officials
ATRI	American Transportation Research Institute
BWC	Biological Weapons Convention
CAFOs	Concentrated Animal-Feeding Operations
CBO	Congressional Budget Office
CCMS	Consumer Complaint Monitoring System
CCTV	Closed-Circuit Television
CDC	Centers for Disease Control and Prevention
CNPP	Center for Nutrition Policy and Promotion
COOP	Continuity of operations
CREES	Cooperative State Research, Education, and Extension Service
CRS	Congressional Research Service

DA   Departmental Administration
DHHS   Department of Health and Human Services
DHS   Department of Homeland Security
DoD   Department of Defense
ED   emergency department
EDEN   Extension Disaster Emergency Network
eLEXNET   Electronic Laboratory Exchange Network
EPA   Environmental Protection Agency
ERS   Economic Research Service
FAD   Foreign Animal Disease
FAS   Foreign Agricultural Service
F-BAT   Food Bio-security Action Team
FBI   Federal Bureau of Investigation
FDA   Food and Drug Administration
FERN   Food Emergency Response Network
FIS   Islamic Salvation Front
FMD   Foot-and-mouth disease
FNS   Food and Nutrition Service
FS   Forest Service
FSA   Farm Service Agency
FSAT   Food Security Advisory Team
FSIS   Food Safety and Inspection Service
GAO   Government Accountability Office
GIA   Armed Islamic Group
GIPSA   Grain Inspection, Packers, and Stockyards Administration
GNP   Gross national product
HACCP   Hazard Analysis Critical Control Points
HSPD-7   Homeland Security Presidential Directive
                       "Critical Infrastructure Identification, Prioritization,
                       and Protection"
IAG   Inter-agency Agreement
IFT   Institute of Food Technologists
ISP   Import Strategic Plan
LRN   Laboratory Response Network
MBM   Meat and bone meal
MDA   Michigan Department of Agriculture
NAIS   National Animal Identification System
NAL   National Agricultural Library
NASDA   National Association of State Departments of Agriculture

NASS	National Agricultural Statistics Service
NIIMS	National Interagency Incident Management System
NIMS	National Incident Management System
NPIP	National Poultry Improvement Plan
OASIS	Operational and Administrative System for Import Support
OCM	Office of Crisis Management
ODU	Old Dominion University
OFSEP	Office of Food Security and Emergency Preparedness
OIE	Office International des Epizooties; aka World Organization for Animal Health
OPHEP	Department of Health and Human Services/Office of Public Health Emergency Preparedness
ORA	FDA's Office of Regulatory Affairs
ORM	Operations Risk Management
SCC	Secretary's Command Center (of DHHS)
SITC	Safeguarding, Interdiction, and Trade Compliance
SPS WTO	Sanitary and Phytosanitary Agreement (SPS) of the World Trade Organization (WTO)
TSE	Transmissible spongiform encephalopathy
USC	U.S. Code
USDA	U.S. Department of Agriculture
VTA	Vulnerability and Threat Assessment Tool
WHO	World Health Organization

Preface

In the post–September 11 world, the possibility of agroterrorism, the malicious use of plant or animal pathogens or chemicals to cause devastating disease or damage in and to the agricultural sector, is real—very real. As the BBC reported on the topic: "When Tommy Thompson stood down as U.S. health secretary in 2004, he delivered a stark warning: 'I, for the life of me, cannot understand why the terrorists have not attacked our food supply, because it is so easy to do." In the same article, Larry Wein from Stanford University describes the scenario of poisoning a milk tanker with 10 grams of botulinum toxin, and is quoted concluding: "If we didn't realize what was happening, half a million people would drink this milk . . . roughly half of them would die."

Agriculture represents one of America's critical infrastructures. In perusing this text, it will become clear that the events of September 11 have forced an increased focus on protecting the food supply infrastructure in the U.S.

This book (as well as the other titles in Government Institutes's Critical Infrastructure series) was written as a result of September 11. *Food Supply Protection and Homeland Security*, in particular, was fashioned in response to the critical needs of food production managers, food import managers, food infrastructure engineers, design engineers, agricultural managers at any level of food production, students—and for anyone with a general interest in the security of their food supply systems. It is important to note that our food supply system (as is the case with the other twelve critical infrastructures) cannot be made immune to all possible intrusions and attacks; thus, it takes a concerted, well-thought-out effort to incorporate security upgrades in the retrofitting of existing systems and careful security planning for all new food manufacturing and processing sites. These upgrades or design features need to address issues of monitoring, response, critical infrastructure redundancy, and recovery to minimize risk to individual facilities and the infrastructure as a whole.

Food Supply Protection and Homeland Security presents commonsense methodologies in a straightforward manner. This text is accessible to those who have no experience with agriculture and homeland security. If you work through the text systematically, you will gain an understanding of the challenge of domestic preparedness—that is, an immediate need for a heightened state of awareness of the present threat facing the agricultural sector as a potential terrorist target. Moreover, you will gain knowledge of security principles and measures that can be implemented—not only adding a critical component to your professional knowledge but also gaining the tools needed to combat terrorism in our homeland.

REFERENCE

BBC, at news.bbc.co.uk/1/hi/world/Americas /527022.stm, (accessed July 7, 2007).

Prologue

PERSONAL DIARY ENTRY OF MARTHA (LUCI) CHI FOX: JULY 13, 2007

The door opened on the long corridor of the opium den; to the right of the entrance is the window where I purchase the drug. I always pay the same price, 70 centimes for a small five gram container; for several hundred, I can get enough to stay high for a week, at least 10 pipes. However, just the mind-expanding amount did me well for our planning sessions. Besides, with lungs clouded with pleasure I simply function better. In the corridor, past the entranceway, I always pass into that same horrible odor of corruption; it strikes my throat. The corridor turns, turns again, and opens on several small dark rooms, which become veritable labyrinths lighted by lamps that give off a sick yellow light. The walls, caked with old, flaking layered paint, glued in place with dirt, are indented with long enclosures. In each enclosure a man is usually spread out like a cadaver. No one ever moves whenever I pass. Not even a glance. They are always glued to a small pipe whose watery gurgle alone breaks the silence. The others are terribly immobile, with slow gestures, legs strung out, arms in the air, limbs, more like jackstraws, inanimate or dead; the faces are characterized by overly white teeth, the pupils with a black glaze, enlarged, fixed on who knows what; the eyelids do not move; and always on the pasty cheeks, the vague, mysterious smile of the enraptured or departed.

I have no friends, but to those who need to know me and who are my fellow collaborators, I am called Luci. Never mind where I was when I purchased the drugs and met with my collaborators. Come on, when fashioning together a master plan of total death and destruction, does it really matter where terrorists meet? And that word, terrorist, it is so wrong. When someone wants or desires to simply put things straight, why would these people be called terrorists? There are just some things the understanding of which is beyond me.

Anyway, it is in the back rooms of this particular den of opium delights that we, the "leaders" and I, fashioned our master plan. No, we did not chose airplanes loaded with frantic passengers and full of fuel to crash into buildings. Let's face it, killing 3,000 people is one of those been there and done that things. We are onto bigger and better things.

Nor did we choose to use nukes or chemical or biological bombs or devices. Not that we can't get them; if one has enough money, one can buy anything—especially from greedy Americans. However, those types of weapons are just too messy and obvious and traceable. We chose to use a better method.

The method we came up with was developed over time: a masterpiece of deception and cunning. One thing about us, and unlike Americans and others, we have patience. We think through our plans; we think inside, outside, and around the box. Then we test our plans; we practice and do rehearsals. We observe and learn. We are patient.

We have observed the Americans' response to their many food supply emergencies. We have watched how ordinary pet food was contaminated with a deadly chemical—melamine in the wheat gluten and rice protein. Honestly, we were rather surprised at how quickly the Americans caught on to the tainted pet food. Observing this has provided us with a blueprint, a track record of the Americans' response and reaction and their subsequent actions. The point is that there were a lot of lessons learned. We observe and learn. We are patient.

About two weeks after the tainted–pet food scenario we observed once again, this time with the scare of contaminated toothpaste. The toothpaste contained diethylene glycol (the same poison that the Panamanian government mistakenly mixed into cold medicine the previous year, killing at least 100 people). The toothpaste has not killed anyone, but once again, it has tested the enemy's response. Again America's quick response surprised us. But that is okay. We observe and learn. We are patient.

Right now we are on hold. We have learned a lot. We know the soft spots. We will be ready to launch our assault. They will never know what hit them. We are so patient.

Note: In the preceding fictional account, the description of the basic opium den is based on Alfred W. McCoy's *The Politics of Heroin* (New York: Harper & Row, 1972).

POSTSCRIPT: THE FINDINGS ON MELAMINE
USDA Release No. 0129.07: Fact Sheet:

Interim Melamine and Analogues Safety/Risk Assessment
May 25, 2007

- Based on currently available data and information, the consumption of pork, chicken and eggs from animals and fish fed animal feed supplemented with pet food scraps that contained melamine and related compounds is very unlikely to pose a human health risk, according to an assessment by federal scientists.

- This conclusion is from an "Interim Melamine and Analogues Safety/Risk Assessment" conducted by FDA in collaboration with scientists from FSIS and in consultation with scientists from a number of other federal agencies. Melamine analogues include cyanuric acid, which is a melamine analogue that was detected in the pet food.
- A safety/risk assessment is a scientifically based methodology used to estimate the risk to human health from exposure to specified compounds. It is based on available data and certain scientific assumptions in the absence of data.
- The safety/risk assessment provides estimates of the human exposure to melamine and related compounds from the consumption of contaminated pork, poultry, eggs and fish and compares this exposure to levels calculated to be safe to consume.
- The interim assessment reflects a more complete understanding of melamine and related compounds, as well as our ability to detect the compounds in pork, poultry and fish.
- Based on a worst-case scenario, if melamine and cyanuric acid were present in equal amounts in all the solid food consumed by an individual every day, the potential exposure is about 250 times lower than the level considered safe. This is a large safety margin.
- Translating this into consumption levels, a person weighing 132 pounds would have to eat more than 800 pounds per day of pork, poultry or other food containing melamine and its compounds to approach a level of consumption that would cause a health concern.
- The interim human safety/risk assessment notes that melamine is not metabolized, and is rapidly excreted. Thus, it is not believed to accumulate in the body of animals.
- The interim assessment uses the conservative assumption that meat testing can detect melamine levels as low as 50 parts per billion in pork or poultry. However, the assessment assumes that melamine is present at 100 parts per billion to also account for the potential presence of the related compound cyanuric acid in addition to melamine.
- The interim safety/risk assessment undergoes public comment through a Federal Register notice, in addition to the review by external scientific experts.
- The assessment was conducted by scientists from the Food and Drug Administration (FDA) in collaboration with scientists in the Food Safety and Inspection Service (FSIS) of the U.S. Department of Agriculture (USDA), and in consultation with scientists in the Centers for Disease Control and Prevention (CDC) of the Department of Health and Human Services (DHHS), the Environmental Protection Agency (EPA), and the Department of Homeland Security (DHS).

(http://www.usda.gov)

The superior man, when resting in safety, does not forget that danger may come. When in a state of security, he does not forget the possibility of ruin. When all is orderly, he does not forget that disorder may come. Thus his person is not endangered, and his states and all their clans are preserved.

—*Confucius*

1

Introduction

In the war on terrorism, the fields and pastures of America's farmland might seem at first to have nothing in common with the towers of the World Trade Center or our busy seaports. In fact, however, they are merely different manifestations of the same high-priority target, the American economy. Even as he celebrated the toppling of the pillars of our economic power in the videotape released shortly after September 11, 2001, Osama bin Laden urged his followers to hit hard the American economy at its heart and core.

—*Senator Susan M. Collins*

CRITICAL INFRASTRUCTURE

For the United States of America, September 11 was a serious wake-up call. It generated several reactions on our part—obviously, protecting ourselves from further attack became (and hopefully still is) priority number one. In light of this important need, the Department of Homeland Security was created. According to Governor Tom Ridge, "You may say Homeland Security is a Y2K problem that doesn't end January 1 of any given year" (Henry, 2002).

Among other things, the new emphasis on homeland security pointed to the need to protect and enhance the security of the nation's critical infrastructure. *Critical infrastructure* can be defined or listed in many ways. Generally, governments use the term to describe material assets that are essential for the functioning of an economy and society. For the purpose of this text, critical infrastructure includes the material assets associated with:

- Agriculture
- Banking and finance
- Chemical and hazardous materials

- Defense industrial base
- Emergency services
- Energy
- Organizations
- Postal and shipping services
- Public health
- Strategies and assessments
- Telecommunications
- Transportation
- Water

Water infrastructure protection was discussed in detail in the first volume of this series, *Water Infrastructure Protection and Homeland Security*. In this volume, *Food Supply Protection and Homeland Security*, even though the target is different, the message and focus remain the same: to point out, to discuss, and to focus on the threat to our food supply. In addition, this text describes the study, design, and implementation of precautionary measures aimed at reducing the risk to our food supply from both homegrown and/or foreign terrorism.

In this text we are concerned with agricultural (food supply) infrastructure. *Agricultural infrastructure* may be defined as the physical production and distribution systems critical to supporting national security and economic well-being, including all activities essential to food, feed, and fiber production, including all techniques for raising and "processing" livestock.

HSPD-7: PROTECTING CRITICAL INFRASTRUCTURE

In December 2003 the Homeland Security Presidential Directive (HSPD-7) "Critical Infrastructure Identification, Prioritization, and Protection" added agriculture to the list of critical infrastructure to be protected. This directive instructs agencies to develop plans to prepare for and counter the terrorist threat. HSPD-7 mentions the following industries: agriculture and food; banking and finance, transportation (air, sea, and land, including mass transmit, rail, and pipelines); energy (electricity, oil, and gas); telecommunications; public health; emergency services; drinking water; and water treatment (wastewater treatment is implied).

THE ONGOING THREAT

Governor Tom Ridge, a U.S. political figure who served as a member of the U.S. House of Representatives (1983–1995), governor of Pennsylvania (1995–2001), assistant to the president for homeland security (2001–2003), and the first U.S. secretary of Homeland Security (2003–2005), got it right: homeland security is an ongoing problem that must be dealt with 24/7. Simply, there is no magic on-off switch that can be used to turn off the threat of terrorism to the United States or elsewhere.

The threat to our security is not only on-going but is also universal, including potential and real threats from within—from our own citizens. Consider the American Timothy McVeigh, for example, who blew up the government building in Oklahoma City in 1995 killing almost 200 people, including several children. McVeigh, who bombed the building in revenge for the FBI's Waco, Texas, raid, thought the army (he was a former decorated U.S. Army veteran) had implanted a microchip in him to track his movements, according to reports.

It is interesting to note that McVeigh, who was no doubt suffering from some type of severe disturbance, acted primarily alone. Actually, McVeigh is the exception that proves the rule—most terrorist acts on America are planned by a group beforehand. Still, this is not always the case. And, as a point of fact and principle and personal point of view, this author feels that terrorism in the United States is more likely to be perpetrated by homegrown versus foreign terrorists—but the point is we must be ready for both. For example, consider the scenario that follows. While it's not an actual event, note that incidents like this have occurred and could happen again at any time.

Crazy Sally

After making sure the coast was clear, Sally turned the heat exchanger valve wheel carefully, like the dial on a safe full of money. Earlier she had attached a jerry-rigged hose to the heat exchanger drain and placed the other end in the peanut butter batch. Now she was adding the contaminated water to the batch as she continued to look all around, making sure no one was watching. Sally was careful but she had to hurry, the on-coming shift would soon take over the production line and the batch of contaminated peanut butter.

As dayshift production line supervisor of Creamy Gold Peanut Butter Company she knew exactly what she was doing, though it was wrong, unethical, and absolutely criminal. She was adding water to the peanut butter batch, creating a wetter than necessary slurry. Adding too much water at this stage in the peanut butter manufacturing process creates the perfect environment for *Salmonella*. Salmonella are a family of bacteria that can cause diarrhea, fever, and stomach pain; the infection usually lasts five to seven days. This particular strain of bacteria also causes nasty urinary infections. Occasionally, but rarely, it causes death, usually of the elderly or those with faulty immune systems. "Just collateral damage," Sally told herself. "Survival of the fittest, another tool to help me eliminate a society of misfits, commies, decrepit old hangers-on."

Sally, known as Crazy Sally to those who worked for and with her, was a 40-year-old with no friends, not even a pet. She had worked at Creamy Gold for 22 years, having begun her employment the same day she graduated high school. A no-nonsense worker, Sally had climbed the promotion ladder in record time from line worker to foreperson, to line manager, and finally to her shift supervisor position.

Sally's climb to the position of shift supervisor had been spectacular, to say the least. For years the lower ranks of the company were lined with the wrecked careers of those she'd back-stabbed on her way. Actually, when their doom befell them, most didn't know what had hit them. Once she reached the top, she ruled her shift with an iron fist. Absolutely no doubt could possibly exist in any employee's mind about who was in charge. She received great pleasure in dominating and controlling other people. At Creamy Gold, Sally was in her element.

Over the years, the 22 women who worked for her quickly learned that it was either Sally's way or the highway. You did not mess with Sally; instead, you brownnosed to attain a level of individual safety and security that all employees need.

However, Sally had a problem with the nightshift. In particular she had a problem with Thelma, who had become a thorn in Sally's side. Over the years Sally had learned how to get rid of those she didn't like on her shift. She simply fired them. However, getting rid of workers from the other shift had presented a problem to her. That is, it was a problem up until a few years ago when Sally figured out how to get rid of those from the shift she did not supervise.

Two years ago, when Sally decided to mitigate her problem with the night shift of that time period, she figured out how to tap the contaminated water in the heat exchanger and add it to a fresh batch of peanut butter. This fresh batch was the night shift's responsibility to process, test, package, and ship. Sally knew that eventually people would get sick from the contaminated peanut butter and that the regulators would show up to investigate. Of course this is exactly what happened: hundreds became ill from the tainted peanut butter; the batch numbers were identified; the source was identified; the night shift crew was investigated and was fired for gross incompetence on the job. Thus, the current night shift crew with Thelma in charge came about because of the massive firings two years ago.

Based on her success in getting the last crew and supervisor fired, Sally planned to do the same thing this time around. As it turned out, Sally's plan worked to perfection. Several people ingested the tainted peanut butter; several consumers because very ill; the bad batch was identified; the source was identified; the regulators investigated; and the owners of Creamy Gold Peanut Butter fired the entire night shift. Ironically, they asked Sally to help with the interviewing process for picking a new night shift.

Crazy Sally: The Message

The incident just described points to one of the main purposes of this text: to emphasize the importance of recognizing that not only is terrorism real but it can also be domestic or homegrown. Since September 11, the nation's attention has been focused on possible threats from Islamic terrorists and/or foreigners who simply do not like Americans and who will go to great lengths to destroy our way of life. But the Crazy Sallys of the world, the homegrown terrorists, have been steadily plotting and carrying out attacks in unrelated incidents across the U.S. Consider the following cases.

Case 1: Nicotine Poisoning after Ingestion of Contaminated Ground Beef

When reading or hearing about someone being poisoned by nicotine, the first thought that might present itself to us is that that someone smoked too many of those nicotine-filled cigarettes. Or we might jump to the conclusion that the victim chewed on a bit too much chewing tobacco and maybe swallowed a huge mouthful of the juicy mess and hence the nicotine poisoning. Either of these poisoning episodes would be bad enough if they were the actual causal factors involved in the poisoning. But what if the nicotine poisoning was no accident; what if, instead, it was the result of domestic terrorism—perpetrated by a homegrown terrorist? Well, that is exactly what happened in Michigan in 2003.

According to the Centers for Disease Control and Prevention's *Morbidity and Mortality Weekly Report* (CDC MMWR, 2003), on January 3, 2003, the Michigan Department of Agriculture's (MDA) Food and Dairy Division and the U.S. Department of Agriculture (USDA) were notified by a supermarket of a planned recall of approximately 1,700 pounds of ground beef because of customer complaints of illness after eating the product. On January 10, the supermarket notified MDA that their laboratory had determined that the contaminant in the ground beef returned by customers with reported illness was nicotine.

The recall was prompted by complaints from four families comprising 18 persons who became ill immediately after eating product sold on December 31 or January 1. Reported symptoms including burning of the mouth, nausea, vomiting, and dizziness. One person was reported to have been in the emergency department (ED) being treated for atrial fibrillation. The recalled product had been ground in the store using ground beef purchased from an out-of-state processor inspected by the USDA's Food Safety and Inspection Service (FSIS). MDA made routine notifications about the recall to local and state health departments. The product recall was issued on January 3 for beef with a sell-by date of January 1 and January 2; a press release followed on January 8, which expanded the recall to beef with a sell-by date of January 3. After the initial recall notices, approximately 36 persons reported to the supermarket that they or their families had experienced illness after eating the product, and approximately 120 persons returned recalled product.

Company officials submitted samples of ground beef provided by the ill families to a private laboratory, where product testing for foodborne pathogens was negative. Additional testing for chemical contamination was conduced at a large regional medical center. On January 10, company officials notified MDA and USDA that nicotine had been presumptively identified in the ground beef samples tested by the second laboratory, which reported an assay result 1 week later of approximately 300 mg/kg nicotine in the submitted samples. The high nicotine concentrations found in the tested meat products prompted concerns of intentional contamination with a pesticide, which sometimes contain nicotine as an additive. USDA and the Federal Bureau of Investigation (FBI) joined the investigation because interstate commerce could have been involved and intentional contamination was suspected. Because a legal investigation was initiated, federal authorities required that information be released to the public only as necessary to avoid compromising any future criminal case. On January 17, the supermarket issued another press release and recall notice, stating the implicated product contained an unspecified, nonbacterial contaminant that could not be made safe by cooking.

Contamination of the product was believed to have occurred at a single store rather than the meat processing plant. The product was distributed directly from the plant to many other stores, including other stores in the supermarket chain; neither the processing plant nor any other store in the supermarket chain received complaints of illness. No nicotine-containing pesticides were reportedly used or sold in the store where the recalled product was sold.

On January 23, the local health department alerted hospital EDs and selected medical practices serving the area where the store was located. On January 24, after receiving confirmatory test results, the company issued another press release naming nicotine as the contaminant. This announcement was published and broadcast by local media.

The local health department conducted an epidemiologic investigation, including interviews of persons reporting illness, to assess the consistency of the clinical presentation and to establish a case definition. A case was defined as one or more symptoms (i.e., burning sensation to lips, mouth or throat, dizziness, nausea, vomiting, abdominal pain, diarrhea, sweating, blurred vision, headache, body numbness, unusual fatigue or anxiety, insomnia, tachypnea or dyspnea, and tachycardia or tachyarrythmias) in persons who ate ground beef product purchased from the supermarket on either December 31, 2002, or January 1, 2003, with symptom onset occurring within two hours of eating the product.

A total of 148 interviews were conducted with persons who reported they had experienced illness after eating the product and of family members and friends who also might have eaten the contaminated meat. Of those interviewed, 92 persons had illness consistent with the case definition. Patients had a median age of 31 years (range: 1–76 years), and 46 (50 percent) were female; 65 percent of the patients lived in the town where the implicated store was located. The majority of illness occurred during the time that the contaminated produce was sold. Cases were identified as late as 49 days after the last date of potential sale, indicating that some persons froze and then ate the contaminated product after the first recall was issued. Of the 92 patients, four (3 percent) sought medical treatment, including two who reported to their personal physicians with complaints of vomiting and stomach pains and two who were evaluated in EDs. The two who were treated in the EDs included a man aged 39 years with atrial fibrillation and a woman aged 31 years who had nausea, vomiting, and complaint of rectal bleeding. Information is being collected on an additional 16 persons to assess whether their illnesses are consistent with the case definition, including a pregnant woman aged 24 years who was hospitalized for one day with episodic vomiting.

On February 12, a grand jury returned an indictment for arrest of a person accused of poisoning 200 pounds of meat at the supermarket with an insecticide called Black Leaf 40, which has a main ingredient of nicotine. The person was an employee of the supermarket at the time of the contamination. This case helps illustrate how simple it is for one person to intentionally contaminate the food supply and have a major impact.

Case 2: Tainted Salad

In 1984, members of an Oregon cult headed by Bhagwan Shree Rajneesh used cultivated salmonella bacteria to contaminate restaurant salad bars in the hopes of affecting the outcome of a local election. Fortunately there were no fatalities in the incident, but there were approximately 751 cases of individuals becoming ill, and 45 individuals needed to be hospitalized. While this incident was detected by public health officials, it took the FBI an entire year to link the outbreak to the cult (GAO, 2003).

MEDICAL NOTE

Acute nicotine toxicity is associated with overstimulation of nicotinic receptors. Burning in the throat with nausea and vomiting occurs quickly after ingestion.

Case 3: Shigella Donuts

In October 1996, a former laboratory employee pled guilty to contaminating a tray of doughnuts and muffins with the foodborne pathogen *Shigella dysenteriae* Type 2. The employee used an unoccupied supervisor's computer to send out an e-mail inviting 45 other laboratory workers to enjoy pastries in the employee break room. Twelve of the 45 employees ate some amount of a pastry and eventually contracted a severe gastrointestinal illness. Four of those employees required hospitalization, but there were no fatalities. The origin of the pathogen was the laboratory itself, and lax security made it possible for this intentional contamination to occur (GAO, 2003).

Table 1.1 lists other cases of of agro- or bioterrorism in the 1900s.

Obviously, none of the homegrown, intentional, food adulteration incidents over the past few years match the devastation of September 11 or even the 1995 bombing of the Oklahoma City federal building—which killed 168 and remains the deadliest act of terrorism against the nation—by Timothy McVeigh, a U.S. citizen. Nonetheless, homegrown terrorists have had ambitious plans. The people and groups include white supremacists—supremacism is rooted in ethnocentrism ("my group is the center of everything") and a desire for hegemony (dominance of one group over other groups). Of course, their mantra contains varying degrees of racism and xenophobia (fear and hatred of foreigners or strangers)—often associated with ethnic cleansing (the Hitler or Darfur Syndrome) and racial separation. Basically, white supremacy has projected discrimination and prejudice against blacks and other nonwhite groups. It should be pointed out, however, that many white supremacists consider certain types of whites, such as homosexuals, atheists, and non-Protestants, to be less human or inferior based

Table 1.1.   Confirmed Cases of Agriculture/Bioterrorism in the 1900s

Year	Incident	Alleged Perpetrators
1997	Hemorrhagic virus spread among wild rabbit population in New Zealand	New Zealand farmers
1996	Food poisoning using Shigella in a Dallas, Texas, hospital	Hospital lab employee
1995	Food poisoning of an estranged husband using ricin in Johnson County, Kansas	Kansas physician
1984	Food poisoning of public salad bars	Rajneeshee Cult
1970	Food poisoning of four college roommates using parasite-contaminated food	College roommate
1964	Food poisoning in Japan using salmonella and dysentery	Japanese physician
1952	African milk bush used to kill 33 head of livestock in Kenya	Mau Mau insurgents
1939	Food poisoning in Japan using pastries contaminated with salmonella	Japanese physician
1936	Food poisoning in Japan using cakes contaminated with salmonella	Japanese physician
1916	Food poisoning in New York City using arsenic to kill wife's parents	New York dentist

Source: Adaptation from Carus, 2002; Chalk, 2004.

on nonracial grounds. In regard to group-haters, many white supremacists consider Jews to be the gravest threat to the "American" way of life.

Our attention has been heavily focused on foreign terrorism since September 11. However, the lesson to be learned is that, like cancer, homegrown terrorism is insidious and poses a constant, serious threat to all of us. The following cases are among the general terrorism incidents since September 11:

- In 2004, the FBI arrested Demetrius "Van" Crocker, 39, a McKenzie, Tennessee, farmhand with an 85 IQ for attempting to acquire chemical weapons and explosives to blow up a government building.
- In 2003, William Krar, 63, of Noonday, Texas, was arrested for possessing a weapon of mass destruction (a sodium-cyanide bomb capable of killing thousands), nine machine guns, seven sticks of explosives, and more than 100,000 rounds of ammunition.
- In 2003, three Utah domestic terrorists started a fire that caused $1.5 million in damages at a West Jordan lumber company.
- In 2003, a group was charged with conspiring to commit terrorism against an enterprise that uses animals for research.
- In 2003, Rajib Mitra, 26, a domestic terrorist, was arrested for blocking police radio signals and later broadcasting sex sounds over police radios.

It is clear that we need to add terrorism to the long list of emergency situations. In regard to the terrorists being foreigners or of the homegrown variety, does it really matter? A terrorist is a terrorist, regardless of nationality. The point is we need to realize that long gone are those days when being safe meant being careful. Today we must consider and dodge terrorist attacks from Molotov cocktails as well as from armor-piercing bullets—and any other weaponry terrorists can get their hands on. But there is more to worry us. We must also worry about biologics, chemicals, and poisons of one form or another added to our food and/or water supplies.

IS TERRORISM IN THE BARNYARD REALLY POSSIBLE?

According to Breeze (2004), the impact of an act of terrorism on American agriculture can be summed up in four graphic word pictures—terror, money, mass slaughter, and funeral pyres. Put into another context, Breeze's words illustrate the consequences of an attack on our livestock industry through the intentional introduction of a foreign animal disease such as foot-and-mouth disease (FMD). One agricultural economist estimates that a nationwide outbreak of FMD would result in immediate stoppage of our beef industry, which would cost between $750,000 and $1 million per minute for each operating business hour. The result would be too overwhelming for the livestock industry to absorb and would stagger the U.S. economy (Knowles et al., 2005).

Many terrorism experts and economists would have no problem with this summary. However, there are always those who pay it no mind, or do not understand the issues. Others feel that agriculture is a low priority terrorism target—all of this is based on a certain mindset. For example, in my risk assessment and safety classes at Old Dominion University for both grad and undergraduate students, class discussion is often focused on terrorism against the country's critical infrastructure. In regard to the infrastructure discussion, we focus on the thirteen areas listed earlier. It is true that some authors list a greater and some a lesser number of specific critical infrastructures in their writings, but the exact number of infrastructures listed is unimportant.

Eventually the students get around to a discussion of food security. This area of focus is usually saved for last because many students feel that food is less important than water, nuclear power, transportation, telecommunications (especially cell phones and the new Apple iPhone, and so forth), and the others. This may seem strange to the casual reader (and to anyone else for that matter) because we all know that without food there is no life. In questioning the students, I found that they understood the importance and significance of food. That was not the problem. The problem was the pecking order. The students, most of them, simply felt that any attack on food was a very low priority for any terrorist. "Why would terrorists waste their time attacking our food? It seems so implausible," they always say.

An attack on America's food supply implausible? I remember not too long ago when many of us felt that airplanes full of passengers and fuel deliberately flown into skyscrapers, another important building, and a Pennsylvania farm field was science fiction at best, maybe a plot for another one of those Stephen King horror books (another best seller for sure). Indeed, it is a gruesome story line for a horror flick but also certainly not implausible in the real world setting. In regard to attacking American agriculture, that is no problem—American agriculture is a soft target. Surprisingly, it is also a not-too-often thought about target.

To illustrate a hierarchy or ranking of potential terrorist attacks on our infrastructures, consider table 1.2. The table presents a compilation of three separate nonscientific surveys conducted by this author at Old Dominion University (ODU) during the period January–March 2005. A total of 112 environmental health undergraduate/graduate students responded to the surveys. Each survey included the following direction: "Rank the 13 critical infrastructures in order, 1 thru 13, as the terrorists' most likely (1) to attack to least likely to attack (13) preference."

As shown in table 1.2, we might be betting far more than the farm when it comes to our lack of recognition of the need to protect our agriculture infrastructure. Frankly, the results of these nonscientific surveys surprised me. I was not surprised that the students, in this information age, picked telecommunications as the probable number one target of terrorists, but the fact that agriculture and food production ranked last on the

Table 1.2.   Student's Ranking of Critical Infrastructure Most/Least Likely to Be Attacked

Critical Infrastructure	Total Student Votes
Agriculture	3
Banking and Finance	6
Chemical and Hazardous Materials	10
Defense Industrial Bases	5
Emergency Services	5
Energy	10
Organizations	7
Postal and Shipping	7
Public Health	6
Strategies and Assessments	4
Telecommunications	30
Transportation	9
Water	10
Total	112

perceived terrorists' target list was a surprise. With agriculture accounting for 13 percent of U.S. gross national product and with one eighth of all American jobs connected to agriculture, either directly or indirectly (Horn, 1999), I was surprised the students overlooked or downplayed its importance. In addition, it seemed to me that the strength and value of the U.S. food and agricultural system would alone make it an attractive target of terrorism. However, for me the results of the surveys help answer why it is that America's food supply is among the most vulnerable and least protected of all potential targets of terrorists. Simply, when not feeling the pangs of hunger, for many, food is a low priority.

In questioning the respondents about the ranking selections in table 1.2, one of the main problems my students told me they had with a terrorist attack against our food supply was visualizing the potential impact of such an attack on human health. That is, it was/is difficult to estimate the impact on human health that an attack on our food supply would have. Basically, individual understanding required a "leap of faith." To help remove this difficulty, to facilitate the "leap," I simply lectured these students on the World Health Organization's (WHO) take on this issue. Like WHO (2002) and others, Ryan et al. point out that "the potential impact on human health of deliberate sabotage of food can be estimated by extrapolation from the many documented examples of unintentional outbreaks of foodborne disease. The largest, best-documented incidents include an outbreak of *S. typhimurium* infection in 1985, affecting 170,000 people, caused by contamination of pasteurized milk from a dairy plant in the United States" (Ryan et al., 1987).

Initially, when I referred my students to the organization WHO, many of them thought I was referring to the classic rock band. Obviously, the topic of our discussion then and now is much too serious to be confused with rock and roll; thus, traditional regulatory institutions that have some name recognition are often used to make the point. This is usually the case when I refer to reports by the Congressional Budget Office (CBO) and others.

In December 2004, CBO published a report titled *Homeland Security and the Private Sector*. This five-chapter account examines the role of the private sector in responding to the threat of terrorism in the United States since September 11. In keeping with CBO's mandate to provide objective, impartial analysis, the report makes no recommendations—just the facts. In keeping with our intent here, it is chapter 5 of the report, "Food and Agriculture," that is of interest to us and is reproduced in part here:

"FOOD AND AGRICULTURE" [REPRINTED FROM CBO, 2004]

Reports of terrorist groups' interests, as well as the history of events involving food contamination and the use of biological agents, support concerns about the prospect of terrorist attacks on the food and agriculture industry. The industry would be vulnerable to attack because of the large numbers of food items and the many points of access. However, any of those vulnerabilities are already addressed through extensive regulation put in place before September 11 in response to the nation's continuing concerns about food safety. That regulation and the organization of the nation's public health system would help limit the losses from any attacks on food supplies involving a range of known agents. The greatest concern would be threats that could escape or exceed the nation's current detection capabilities or for which an effective response would require an increased level of coordination among agencies and different levels of government.

Vulnerabilities from Contamination, Loss of Food Sources, and Use of Agricultural Resources as Weapons

The use of natural agents in attacks on agriculture or directly on people is commonly described as bioterrorism. That term would include biological attacks—such as with Bacillus anthracis (anthrax) and smallpox—that might not involve farms and food but would require some of the same protective measures and emergency responses. The security of drugs and drinking water supplies is a particularly important, related concern [see volume 1 of this series, *Water Infrastructure Protection and Homeland Security*]. And although the main focus of attention in the event of a biological attack would be on the immediate safety of the food supply much of the value of industry's output is in areas such as forest products, fibers, and other products that are not related to food—and those nonfood resources could be threatened as well.

Types of Attacks

The food and agriculture industry is vulnerable to four types of assaults:

- Contamination of food with natural biological agents, such as Clostridium botulism toxin (botulism) and Escherichia coli bacteria (E. coli);

- Contamination of food with man-made contaminants, such as poisonous minerals or chemicals and foreign objects;
- Attacks to disrupt food supplies, including the use of fires, floods, or biological agents such as foot-and-mouth disease or insects; and
- Use of agricultural resources as weapons for attacks on other targets, such as wildfires that spread to residential areas, nitrate fertilizer for use in explosives, pesticides for poisoning, crop dusters to spread toxins, or radioactive materials used in food irradiation.

The Food and Drug Administration (FDA) [FDA, 2003] has identified several specific hazards to the safety of food supplies. Among the biological hazards, the deadly pathogens anthrax and botulism are considered the greatest dangers. Next are salmonella, strains of E. coli, and ricin. Among the man-made contaminants that present a threat, FDA has noted concerns about heavy metals (such as lead and mercury), pesticides, dioxins, and other substances that could be introduced into the food supply.

Potential Weaknesses in Defenses

The vulnerability to extensive losses would be relatively small if a disease or contaminant maliciously introduced into the food supply was one with which the industry had experience. The government tests for the most common diseases and requires that outbreaks of many diseases (whether in plants and animals or in the human population) be reported. As a result, it is likely that an attack would be detected early, traced to its source, treated, and contained.

Losses could be significantly higher if the attacks involve substances that can enter the supply chain at a point before or after which their origins cannot be traced, substances that are not tested for, and pathogens or contaminants with which government inspectors or health professionals have little experience. Tests may not be available to detect certain agents within foods, and people's exposure to such substances may not be recognized or reported to appropriate state or national organizations to discern a pattern of assault or initiate a response. Further, detection of and response to new modes of attack may require an increased level of coordination among different federal agencies and between different levels of government.

For example, the Department of Agriculture (USDA) tests many meat products for E. coli and salmonella, but it does not routinely test food supplies for contamination from anthrax or ricin. Records are kept on animals, poultry, and eggs that enable USDA to trace the source of contaminants back through much of the supply chain. But after meats are delivered to meat processing centers, for example, there is no way to distinguish what herds (or animals from specific regions or countries) went into what batches of meat products for subsequent delivery to stores. The Food and Drug Administration also requires random testing of many food products (in processing and packing facilities and in transit) for certain contaminants. However, for food products, FDA currently requires only that lot numbers (for tracking purposes) be placed on infant formula and low-acid canned food.

Terrorists' Intent and Past Incidents

Terrorist groups reportedly have shown interest in exploiting weaknesses in the nation's food and agriculture industry, although little information on that threat is publicly available. The terrorist group al Qaeda is known to have considered using crop duster aircraft, apparently with the intent of distributing toxins or pathogens over crops and populated areas. Members of a related group were arrested in London for trying to manufacture the deadly poison ricin—a product of castor beans.

The number of publicly documented crimes intended to harm people or disrupt suppliers is small. However, may of those assaults confirm the potential for serious health and economic consequences. For example, incidents of food sabotage are more commonly perpetrated by disgruntled employees and affect only a few people. But the consequences can be more widespread than the direct numbers harmed, as illustrated in the 1982 case of cyanide-tainted Tylenol capsules. The immediate effect was seven deaths, but the resulting publicity caused a near-total collapse in national demand for that product and led to at least five imitation attacks in subsequent years, all involving fatalities. [Note 3 of this report reads: "Those acts were the poisonings of Lipton Cup-A-Soup in 1986, Excedrin in 1986, Tylenol again in 1986, Sudafed in 1993, and Goody's Headache Powder in 1992."]

Potential Losses from Threats to Health or Consumers' Aversion to Contaminated Products

The immediate consequences of a terrorist attack on food and agriculture may be illness or the loss of life, depending on the nature of the attack and how quickly it is detected. With the important exception of several foodborne outbreaks affecting many thousands, the numbers of people seriously harmed by individual incidents (whether by accident or intent) have been small, at least in part because of current regulations and the success of the nation's public health system in containing outbreak and limiting losses. As a result, the costs of a terrorist attack may be related more to business losses than human losses. Much of the economic cost would result from the increased costs of replacing lost supplies. That cost might be small for the nation but could differ among regional economies.

Losses from Accidental Contaminations

Past incidents involving accidental contaminations of the food supply indicate the potential health consequences of an attack and underscore the importance of current food

"FACTS ABOUT RICIN" [REPRINTED FROM CDC, 2006]

What ricin is

- Ricin is a poison that can be made from the waste left over from processing castor beans.

- It can be in the form of a powder, a mist, or a pellet, or it can be dissolved in water or weak acid.

- It is a stable substance. For example, it is not affected much by extreme conditions such as very hot or very cold temperatures.

Where ricin is found and how it is used

- Castor beans are processed throughout the world to make castor oil. Ricin is part of the waste "mash" produced when castor oil is made.

- Ricin has some potential medical uses, such as bone marrow transplants and cancer treatment (to kill cancer cells).

How you could be exposed to ricin

- It would take a deliberate act to make ricin and use it to poison people. Accidental exposure to ricin is highly unlikely.

- People can breathe in ricin mist or powder and be poisoned.

- Ricin can also get into water or food and then be swallowed.

- Pellets of ricin, or ricin dissolved in a liquid, can be injected into people's bodies.

- Depending on the route of exposure (such as injection or inhalation), as little as 500 micrograms of ricin could be enough to kill an adult. A 500-microgram dose of ricin would be about the size of the head of a pin. A greater amount would likely be needed to kill people if the ricin were swallowed.

- In 1978, Georgi Markov, a Bulgarian writer and journalist who was living in London, died after he was attacked by a man with an umbrella. The umbrella had been rigged to inject a poison ricin pellet under Markov's skin.

(*continues*)

"FACTS ABOUT RICIN" [REPRINTED FROM CDC, 2006] (*continued*)

- Some reports have indicated that ricin may have been used in the Iran-Iraq war during the 1980s and that quantities of ricin were found in al Qaeda caves in Afghanistan.
- Ricin poisoning is not contagious. It cannot be spread from person to person through casual contact.

How ricin works

- Ricin works by getting inside the cells of a person's body and preventing the cells from making the proteins they need. Without the proteins, cells die. Eventually this is harmful to the whole body, and death may occur.
- Effects of ricin poisoning depend on whether ricin was inhaled, ingested, or injected.

Signs and symptoms of ricin exposure

- The major symptoms of ricin poisoning depend on the route of exposure and the dose received, though many organs may be affected in severe cases.
- Initial symptoms of ricin poisoning by inhalation may occur within eight hours of exposure. Following ingestion of ricin, initial symptoms typically occur in less than six hours.
- Inhalation: Within a few hours of inhaling significant amounts of ricin, the likely symptoms would be respiratory distress (difficulty breathing), fever, cough, nausea, and tightness in the chest. Heavy sweating may follow as well as fluid building up in the lungs (pulmonary edema). This would make breathing even more difficult, and the skin might turn blue. Excess fluid in the lungs would be diagnosed by X-ray or by listening to the chest with a stethoscope. Finally, low blood pressure and respiratory failure may occur, leading to death. In cases of known exposure to ricin, people having respiratory symptoms that started within 12 hours of inhaling ricin should seek medical care.
- Ingestion: If someone swallows a significant amount of ricin, he or she would develop vomiting and diarrhea that may become bloody. Severe

dehydration may be the result, followed by low blood pressure. Other signs or symptoms may include hallucinations, seizures, and blood in the urine. Within several days, the person's liver, spleen, and kidneys might stop working, and the person could die.

- Skin and eye exposure: ricin in the powder or mist form can cause redness and pain of the skin and the eyes.

- Death from ricin poisoning could take place within 36 to 72 hours of exposure, depending on the route of exposure (inhalation, ingestion, or injection) and the dose received. If death has not occurred in three to five days, the victim usually recovers.

- Showing these signs and symptoms does not necessarily mean that a person has been exposed to ricin.

How ricin poisoning is treated

Because no antidote exists for ricin, the most important factor is avoiding ricin exposure in the first place. If exposure cannot be avoided, the most important factor is then getting the ricin off of or out of the body as quickly as possible. Ricin poisoning is treated by giving victims supportive medical care to minimize the effects of the poisoning. The types of supportive medical care would depend on several factors, such as the route by which victims were poisoned (that is, whether poisoning was by inhalation, ingestion, or skin or eye exposure). Care could include such measures as helping victims breathe, giving them intravenous fluids (fluids given through a needle inserted into a vein), giving them medications to treat conditions such as seizure and low blood pressure, flushing their stomachs with activated charcoal (if the ricin has been very recently ingested), or washing out their eyes with water if their eyes are irritated.

How you can know whether you have been exposed to ricin

- If we suspect that people have inhaled ricin, a potential clue would be that a large number of people who had been close to each other suddenly developed fever, cough, and excess fluid in their lungs. These symptoms could be followed by severe breathing problems and possibly death.

- No widely available, reliable test exists to confirm that a person has been exposed to ricin.

SALMONELLA ENTERITIDIS IN ICE CREAM

In 1994, approximately 224,000 people were sickened by ice cream contaminated with *Salmonella enteritidis*. The source of the contamination appeared to be pasteurized pre-mix that had been contaminated during transport in tanker trailers that carried non-pasteurized eggs. There were 150 confirmed cases of salmonellosis associated with the outbreak in Minnesota. However, ice cream processed during the contamination period was distributed to 48 states. To calculate the total number of illnesses associated with the outbreak, researchers calculated an attack rate of 6.6 percent. This attack rate was extrapolated to the population that consumed the ice cream, giving a total number sickened of 224,000.

Salmonellosis most commonly causes gastrointestinal symptoms. Almost 91 percent of cases are mild and cause one to three days of illness with symptoms including diarrhea, abdominal cramps, and fever. Moderate cases, defined as cases that require a trip to a physician, account for 8 percent of the cases. These cases typically have duration of two to12 days. Severe cases require hospitalization and last 11 to 21 days. In addition to causing gastroenteritis, salmonellosis also can cause reactive arthritis in a small percentage of cases. Reactive arthritis may be short or long form and is characterized by joint pain. Just over 1 percent of cases develop short-term reactive arthritis and 2 percent of cases develop chronic, reactive arthritis. (FR, 2003)

safety regulations and public health institutions. Researchers at the Centers for Disease Control and Prevention estimate that 76 million illnesses, 325,000 hospitalizations, and 5,000 deaths occur every year because of contaminated food. Specific incidents point to how widespread a contamination can become if not detected quickly. About 170,000 people were sickened by salmonella typhimurium in milk from a U.S. dairy plant, and 224,000 people were sickened by salmonella enteritidis linked to ice cream.

Economic costs associated with those threats to health and safety can be significant. For example, USDA estimates that the annual cost to the nation—in terms of medical costs, productivity losses, and costs of premature deaths—from five major foodborne pathogens totals $6.9 billion [see table 1.3].

Table 1.3. Summary of Five Foodborne Outbreaks

Pathogen	Location and Year	Vehicle	Confirmed or Reported Cases	Total Illness Cost
Salmonella enteritidis	Minnesota, 1994	Ice cream	150 cases; 30 hospitalizations	$3 to 5 billion
Shigella sonnei	Michigan, 1988	Tofu salad	3,175 cases	$45 to 75 million
Outbreaks resulting from deliberate contamination				
Salmonella typhimurium	Dulles, Oregon, 1984	Salad bars	751 cases; 45 hospitalizations	$10 to 18 million
Shigella dysenteriae type 2	Texas, 1996	Muffins and doughnuts	12 cases; 4 hospitalizations	$83,000
Outbreaks resulting from imported foods				
Cyclospora cayaetanensis	United States and Canada, 1996	Raspberries	1,465 cases identified, fewer than 20 hospitalizations	$3,941,000

Source: FR, 2003.

Why Economic Consequences Might Be Small

Retail sales by food and beverage stores (including groceries) were more than $505 billion in 2003, and agricultural exports were valued at more than $59 billion. However, those types of aggregate measures of the value of annual sales or output are likely to overstate the potential economic cost to the nation of disrupting the industry. It is difficult to imagine how all food supplies could be affected or even how the total supply of any basic food source could be affected for a significant amount of time. Replacement supplies (from storage or from unaffected regions) and very close substitutes (from the perspective of consumer welfare) are readily available for virtually every type of food product. People could draw on current inventories of the targeted item (in home and stores), stop consuming any particular food item altogether, stay away from food from a particular agricultural region, or not frequent a given grocery chain or fast-food outlet. For the nation as a whole, the sales lost by products or establishments that were directly affected by an attack would be made up in increased sales elsewhere.

The cost to the national economy would, for the most part, be the increase in the cost of supplying those replacements or substitutes (and the loss in consumer satisfaction). For a number of reasons, even that residual cost should be small. First, the food and agriculture industry is well adapted to the prospect of disruptions from weather and occasional health incidents. For example, in anticipation of periodic crop losses, the most vulnerable crops are grown in multiple regions, and individual farmers diversify their plants and purchase crop insurance. Similarly, food distributors and grocers already have experience with identifying and recalling contaminated lots. Second, government programs are in place to ensure food safety (and limit the health consequences of an attack) and to sustain the income of some agricultural producers (and, indirectly, the businesses and regions that depend on them). As a result, the economic effects of a terrorist incident might well fall within the realm of industry experience and current public plans for detection and response.

Cases in Which Economic and Societal Costs Would Be Highest

Circumstances could exist, however, in which the cost of replacement would be high or the cost to society would be greater than the immediate loss associated with any replacement or substitution for lost supplies. For example, replacement costs could be greater than otherwise if there was a high market concentration in the targeted food or agricultural industry. Where only one or a few businesses account for a large share of sales, the opportunities for drawing on inventories or switching to other suppliers may be limited. Also, in some cases of contamination, the costs of replacing lost supplies may entail more than simply ramping up production. For some diseases, there may be few options to eliminate the risk of further contamination other than burning facilities, plants, and livestock.

The cost to society would be greater than the direct losses associated with replacement and substitution if there were noneconomic losses to consider. For example, if the attack resulted in a major forest fire, costs could include the loss of recreational benefits, erosion from damaged watersheds, and loss of wildlife—values that can be difficult to express in dollar terms. And attacks involving pesticides or other toxins could cause environmental damage.

Regardless of the economic cost to the nation, the potential loss for the particular producers or regional economies could be significant. For example, in seven states, farm employment accounts for more that 5 percent of the total state work force. The nature of many agricultural commodities is that they are produced in discrete growing seasons: once the current supply is lost, the domestic market has to wait through a new cycle.

Other Long-Term Effects on Businesses

Broad consumer concerns about the safety of food supplies can have other adverse economic effects. Any public demonstration of vulnerability to attack can lead to costly, long-term (if not permanent) changes in product handling and consumer demand. The Tylenol case, for instance, led to requirements for tamper-resistant packaging. The situation with mad cow disease, although not deriving from terrorism, has led to new costs, too—from having to discard certain animal parts, restrict the contents of animal feed, and inspect slaughtered animals. Based on the costs to beef producers in Japan for inspecting slaughtered animals, that requirement alone could entail $1.2 billion in expenses for the much larger U.S. beef industry if applied here. (Japan spends

$40.9 million a year inspecting only about 1.3 million slaughtered cattle. The United States slaughters about 37 million cattle annually.)

CONGRESSIONAL RESEARCH SERVICE (CRS): THE AGROTERRORISM THREAT

On August 13, 2004, Jim Monke, an analyst in agricultural policy for the Congressional Research Service (CRS), part of the Library of Congress, reported CRS's view on *Agroterrorism: Threats and Preparedness* to Congress. CRS's overview of the threat and discussions of the importance of agriculture in the U.S. and the economic implications of an agroterrorism incident are reproduced in part below. It is important to point out that the report addresses the use of biological weapons against agriculture, rather than the threat of terrorists using agricultural inputs for other purposes. It also focuses more on agricultural production than food processing and distribution.

Agroterrorism is a subset of the more general issues of terrorism and bioterrorism. People more generally associate bioterrorism with outbreaks of human illness (such as from anthrax or small pox), rather than disease first affecting animals or plants. Agriculture has several characteristics that pose unique problems for managing the threat:

- Agricultural production is geographically disbursed in unsecured environments (e.g., open fields and pastures throughout the countryside). While some livestock are housed in secure facilities, agriculture in general requires large expanses of land that are difficult to secure [using security devices such as alarms, etc.] from intruders.
- Livestock are frequently concentrated in confined locations (e.g., feedlots with thousands of cattle in open-air pens, farms with tens of thousands of pigs, or barns with hundreds of thousand of poultry). [Such feedlots are known as Concentrated Animal Feeding Operations (CAFOs).] Concentration in slaughter, processing, and distribution also makes large scale contamination more likely.
- Live animals, grain, and processed food products are routinely transported and commingled in the production and processing system. These factors circumvent natural barriers that could slow pathogenic dissemination.
- The presence (or rumor) of certain pests or diseases in a country can quickly stop all exports of a commodity and can take months or years to resume.
- The past success of keeping many diseases out of the U.S. means that many veterinarians and scientists lack direct experience with foreign diseases. This may delay recognition of symptoms in case of an outbreak.
- The number of lethal and contagious biological agents is greater for plants and animals than for humans. Most of these diseases are environmentally resilient, endemic in foreign countries, and not harmful to humans—making it easier for terrorists to acquire, handle, and deploy the pathogens.

Thus, the general susceptibility of the agriculture and food industry to bioterrorism is difficult to address in a systematic way due to the highly dispersed yet concentrated nature of the industry and the inherent biology of growing plants and raising animals.

The results of an agroterrorist attack may include major economic crises in the agricultural and food industries, loss of confidence in government, and possibly human casualties. Humans could be at risk in terms of food safety or public health, especially if the chosen disease is transmissible to humans (zoonotic). But an agroterrorist attack need not cause human casualties for it to be effective or to cause large scale economic consequences.

The production agriculture sector would suffer economically in terms of plant and animal health, and the supply of food and fiber may be reduced, especially in certain regions. The demand for certain types of food may decline based on which products are targeted in the attack (e.g., dairy, beef, pork, poultry, grains, fruit, or vegetables), while demand for other types of food may rise due to food substitutions.

An agroterrorism event would cause economic losses to individuals, businesses, and governments through costs to contain and eradicate the disease and to dispose of contaminated products. Economic losses would accumulate throughout the farm-to-table continuum as the supply chain is disrupted, especially if domestic markets for food become unstable or if trade sanctions are imposed by other countries on U.S. exports. The economic impact can spread to farmers, input suppliers, food processors, transportation, retailers, and food service providers.

Public opinion may be particularly sensitive to a deliberate outbreak of disease affecting the food supply. Public confidence in government could be eroded if authorities appear unable to prevent such an attack or to protect the population's food supply. As the United States evolved away from an agrarian society during the 20th century, food and the fear of inadequate food supplies moved further from the minds of most U.S. residents. However, because food remains an important part of everyone's daily routine and survival, significant threats to the currently held notion of food security in the U.S. could cause a reordering of people's priorities.

Because an agroterrorist attack may not necessarily cause human casualties, be immediately detected, or have the "shock factor" of an attack against the more visible public infrastructure of human populations, agriculture may not be a terrorist's first choice of targets. Nonetheless, some types of agroterrorism could be relatively easily achieved and have significant economic impacts. Thus, the possibilities are treated seriously, especially in the post–September 11 world. . . .

Importance of Agriculture in the United States

Agriculture and the food industry are very important to the social, economic, and, arguably, the political stability of the U.S. Although farming employees less than 2 percent of the country's workforce, 16 percent of the workforce is involved in the food and fiber sector, ranging from farmers and input suppliers to processors, shippers, grocers, and restaurateurs. In 2002, the food and fiber sector contributed $1.2 trillion, 11 percent to the gross domestic product (GDP), even though the farm sector itself contributed less than 1 percent [USDA, 2004]. Gross farm sales exceeded $200 billion, and are relatively concentrated through the Midwest, parts of the East Coast, and California. Production is split nearly evenly between crops and livestock. . . .

Economic Consequences

Economic losses from an agroterrorist incident could be large and widespread.

- First, losses would include the value of lost production, the cost of destroying diseased or potentially diseased products, and the cost of containment (vaccines, drugs, diagnostics, pesticides, and veterinary services).
- Second, export markets would be lost as importing countries place restrictions on U.S. products to prevent possibilities of the disease spreading.
- Third, multiplier effects would ripple through the economy due to decreased sales by agriculturally dependent businesses (farm input suppliers, food manufacturing, transportation, retail grocery, and food service) and tourism.
- Fourth, the government could bear significant costs, including eradication and containment costs, and compensation to producers for destroyed animals.

Depending on the erosion of consumer confidence and export sales, market prices of the affected commodities may drop. This would affect producers whose herds or crops were not directly infected, making the event national in scale even if the disease itself were contained to a small region.

On the other hand, demand for food products that are not contaminated may become stronger, and market price could rise for those products. Such goods may include substitutes for the food that was the target of the attack (e.g., chicken instead of beef),

MAD COW DISEASE IN THE UNITED STATES

Before the discovery of BSE in a Washington state dairy cow (December 23, 2003), the U.S., second among beef-exporting countries, shipped about 19 percent of the world beef market, with export valued a $3.9 billion. Australia was first with market share of almost 20 percent, and Brazil third with 18 percent. By 2004, USDA had forecast that Brazil would surpass both Australia and the U.S. to become first and the U.S. would drop to third.

FOOT AND MOUTH DISEASE

A National Defense University study estimates that a limited outbreak of foot and mouth disease (FMD) on just 10 farms could have a $2 billion financial impact (Parker, 2002).

or product that can be certified not to come from regions affected by the attack (e.g., beef from another region of the country, or imported beef). When Canada announced the discovery of mad cow disease (BSE, or bovine spongiform encephalopathy) in May 2003, farm-level prices of beef in Canada dropped by nearly half, while beef prices in the United States remained very strong at record or near record levels. When a cow with BSE was discovered in the United States in December 2003, U.S. beef prices fell, but less dramatically than in Canada.

Consumer confidence in government may also be tested depending on the scale of the eradication effort and means of destroying animals or crops. The need to slaughter perhaps hundreds of thousands of cattle (or tens of millions of poultry) could generate public criticism if depopulation methods are considered inhumane or the destruction of carcasses is questioned environmentally. Dealing with these concerns can add to the cost for both government and industry.

Depending on the disease and means of transmission, the potential for economic damage depends on a number of factors such as the disease agent, location of the attack, rate of transmission, geographical dispersion, how long it remains undetected, availability of countermeasures or quarantines, and incident response plans. Potential costs are difficult to estimate and can vary widely based on compounding assumptions.

FARM-TO-FORK FOOD PRODUCTION AND AGROTERRORISM

The products of agribusiness are mobile; they have to be. We all know that agricultural products are produced at the farm, obviously. But how many people do you actually know who go to the farm to buy their food? Well, wait a minute, it is true that a few of us go to the farm to do our own strawberry picking—some would say (including the author) that no strawberry tastes as good as the one personally picked—they just hang on those plants like jewels from a chain, so plump and sweet, filled with so much more flavor that anything you can buy in the store. Have you been there? Some call it heaven on Earth.

Knowles et al. (2005) point out that the agriculture industry is highly efficient, particularly in the movement of cattle: "Livestock production has evolved into a non-stop operation requiring constant uninterrupted movement of live animals, feed supplies, and finished product. Agromovement may represent the greatest terrorism vulnerability to the industry. Preventing, planning for, and responding to an agroterrorism event require an understanding of this complex cycle of movement."

"Agromovement is defined as the continuous cycle of movement required in farm-to-fork food production, including all aspects of animal transportation, among them the movement of finished products destined for distribution and consumption throughout the world" (Lane, 2002). Like the beef industry, the swine, poultry, and fish industries rely on a cycle of movement. Likewise, a specific process of movement in grain production directly affects livestock production. This movement varies region to region, based on the particular feed requirements for livestock. The continued effective movement of pre- and postharvest products is critical in meeting food product demand.

The beef processors, commonly known as "packers," generally drive the pace of the industry. These large facilities are typically spread over hundreds of acres, and, in the simplest terms, bring live animals in one end of their facilities and ship finished product from the other end. A typical "large" packer (slaughter capabilities of 1,000 head per day or more) will process animals at a rate of 300 to 350 head per hour. Animals are brought to the packer from feeder facilities typically within 150 miles in semitractor trailers, each carrying between 40 and 45 head of cattle. The schedule for processing is generally 16 hours per day, five to six days per week, depending on a number of production factors including demand and market value of the animals.

Throughout the slaughtering process, nearly all parts of the animal carcass are retained, as each has some value as a by-product. This process leads to shipment of by-products like tallow, which is used in the production of facial creams and related products. Hides are transported in shipping containers to tanneries for processing into leather products, while other by-products are shipped by rail. Common beef products, such as hamburger and steaks, are generally shipped by truck. For example, a large packer typically produces 500,000 pounds of hamburger every day, enough to fill more than ten semitractor trailers (Knowles et al., 2005).

Concentrated Animal Feeding Operations (CAFO), or feedyards, are the primary supplier to the packers. These facilities vary in size and may house from 100 head to as many as 100,000 or more, depending on licensing. On average, most house tens of thousands. Annually, feedyards have a turnover rate equal to two to three times their licensed capacity (Spellman and Whiting, 2007). Located within proximity of the packers, these facilities are in the business of "fattening" cattle for slaughter. Fattening the cattle requires 30 pounds per day for each animal in order to reach a target weight of 1200 pounds in 150 days (Spellman and Whiting, 2007; Knowles et al., 2005). Feed product is regularly shipped to the feedyards via truck, and seasonal spikes in volume occur, especially during corn harvest. For example, a typical facility housing 50,000 head requires nearly 300,000 tons of feed products annually. The manure by-product is collected and shipped out by truck, typically for land application. Replacement animals arrive by truck from regions across the United States and Mexico, while "fat cattle" leave for slaughter.

Auctions can be described as the hub of the industry. Typically, these facilities market cattle for producers who take profit. Feedyard operators will buy "feeder cattle" that are normally 700 to 800 pounds. Second, auctions will sell "stocker cattle," which are best described as being weaned off the cow at about 400 pounds, but not yet at the width of feeder cattle. These animals may be bought by producers, including farmers, ranchers, and feedyards, and placed on pasture. Lastly, the auctions will sell heifers, cows, or cow/calf "pairs" for any number of reasons including profit, weather, and age.

Disease Management

Transportation represents a great concern in disease management (Knowles et al., 2005). Live animals are transported for many reasons on a daily basis. Although most are hauled by the producer or by local contract carriers, there is substantial movement from state to sate by other carriers (e.g., regional transport companies). Problems result from tracing trucks that haul livestock. However, cattle moved by local producers are more easily traced than those transported by regional companies.

Another transportation problem is that highly contagious foot-and-mouth disease (FMD) may be spread in vehicles that contain animal waste materials (Knowles et al., 2005). Because contract haulers may move animals from one state to another in "dirty" trucks, the opportunity to spread disease is increased. Further, a disease may be moved via a truck or another vehicle that has entered an infected facility.

Agromovement and Law Enforcement

In addition to challenges in disease management, agromovement-related disease creates problems for law enforcement. In a suspected terrorist event, a truck would be an integral part of the crime scene, requiring law enforcement to process it as evidence. What makes this scenario even worse is that incubation periods of highly contagious disease may take days to even a week or more. Accounting for a particular truck's movement for that period may be difficult or perhaps impossible.

The beef industry is just now beginning to adopt biosecurity measures that may give some protection from a terrorist event. Any interruption in the cycle of movement will be economically devastating, especially locally, where thousands are employed at processing and feeder facilities. The businesses and industries that rely on these employees will be equally affected.

REFERENCES

Breeze, R. 2004. Agroterrorism: Betting far more than the farm. *Biosecurity and Bioterrorism: Biodefense Strategy, Practice and Science* 2(4): 1–14.

Carus, S. 2002. *Bioterrorism and Biocrimes: The Illicit Use of Biological Agents since 1900.* Washington, DC: Center of Counterproliferation Research, National Defense University.

CBO. 2004. *Homeland Security and the Private Sector.* Washington, DC: Congressional Budget Office.

CDC MMWR. 2003. Nicotine poisoning after ingestion of contaminated ground beer—Michigan, 2003. *Morbidity and Mortality Weekly Report* 52(18): 413–416.

CDC. 2006. *Facts about Ricin*, at www.bt.cdc.gov/agent/ricin/facts.asp(accessed June 27, 2007).

Chalk, P. 2004. *Hitting America's Soft Underbelly: The Threat of Deliberate Biological Attacks against the U.S. Agriculture and Food Industry.* Santa Monica, CA: RAND.

Collins, S. M. 2003. *Agroterrorism: The Threat to America's Breadbasket.* Washington, DC: U.S. Senate Committee on Governmental Affairs.

CRS. 2003. *Mad Cow Disease and U.S. Beef Trade.* CRS Report for Congress, at http://www.ers.usda.gov/features/fse/index.htm (accessed July 4, 2007).

FDA. 2003. *Risk Assessment for Food Terrorism and Other Food Safety Concerns*, at www.fsan.fda.gov/~dms/rabtact.html (accessed June 27, 2007).

FR. 2003. Notice of proposed rulemaking. *Federal Register* 68(90):25187.

GAO. Government Accountability Office. 2003. *Bioterrorism: A Threat to Agriculture and the Food Supply*, at www.gao.gov.htex/do4259.html (accessed June 10, 2007).

Henry, K. 2002. New face of security. *Gov. Security* (April): 30–37.

Horn, F. P. 1999. Statement made before the United States Senate Emerging Threats and Capabilities Subcommittee of the Armed Services Committee, at www.Senate.gov/~armed_servies/statement/1999/991027fh.pdf (accessed June 27, 2007).

Knowles, T., J. Lane, G. Bayens, N. Speer, J. Jaax, D. Carter, and A. Bannister. 2005. *Defining Law Enforcement's Role in Protecting American Agriculture from Agroterrorism.* Washington, DC: U.S. Department of Justice, at www.ncjrs.gov/pdffiles1/nij/grants (accessed July 7, 2007).

Lane, J. 2002. Sworn Testimony, Congressional Field Hearing, House Committee on Government Reform, Abilene, KS.

McCoy, A. W. 1972. *The Politics of Heroin in Southeast Asia.* New York: Harper and Row.

Monke, J. 2004. *Agroterrorism: Threats and Preparedness.* Washington, DC: Report to Congress.

Parker, H. S. 2002. *Agricultural Bioterrorism: A Federal Strategy to Meet the Threat.* McNair Paper 65. Nation Defense University, at http://www.ndu.edu/inss/McNair/mcnair65/McN_65.

Ryan, C. A., M. K. Nickels, N. T. Hargrett-Bean, et al. 1987. Massive outbreak of antimicrobial-resistant salmonellosis traced to pasteurized milk. *J Am Med Assoc* 258:3269–3274.

Spellman, F. R., and N. E. Whiting. 2007. *Environmental Management of Concentrated Animal Feeding Operations (CAFO)*. Boca Raton, FL: CRC Press.

USDA. 2004. Economic Research Service. *Agricultural Outlook*, tables at www.ers.usda.gov/publications/Agoutlook/AOTables.

USDA. 2007. *Fact Sheet: Interim Melamine and Analogues Safety/Risk Assessment*. Washington, DC: United States Department of Agriculture.

WHO. 2002. Food Safety Issues: Terrorist Threats to Food. World Health Organization, at www.who.int/fsf (accessed June 26, 2007).

What Are Terrorism and Agroterrorism?

Since September 11th, we have necessarily sharpened our focus on unconventional methods of future attacks, including the potential for Agroterrorism. Most people do not equate terrorist attacks with Agroterrorism. But the threat is real and the impact could be devastating.

—*John E. Lewis (2005)*

TERRORISM

If we were to ask 100 different individuals to define terrorism we might well receive 100 different definitions. Consider the following: In 2001 and again in 2003, pre- and post–September 11, after reading Crazy Sally's peanut butter contamination incident (see chapter 1), 100 randomly selected Old Dominion University Environmental Health juniors and seniors ("Generation Why" students ranging in age from 20 to 46 years old) were asked to read about Sally's peanut butter contamination incident and reply to a nonscientific survey questionnaire. The two questions and the students' responses to this unscientific survey are listed in table 2.1.

USA TODAY TERRORISM NOTICE: JUNE 29, 2007

Car Packed with Explosives Defused in London

Table 2.1.   In your opinion,

Question (1): Sally was

Students' Responses Descriptors*	Number of Responses	
	Pre-9/11 (2001)	Post-9/11 (2003)
Crazy	20	2
A disgruntled employee	8	2
Insane	32	4
Misguided	1	0
A cold-blooded murderer	3	5
A misfit	1	0
Deranged	6	4
A lunatic	5	6
A bully	21	20
A terrorist	3	57
Not sure	0	0
Totals	100	100

Question (2): Sally's actions are best described as

Students' Response Descriptors*	Number of Responses	
	Pre-9/11 (2001)	Post-9/11 (2003)
Madness	45	5
Frustration	9	2
Desperation	4	0
Disfunctional thinking	2	0
Legitimate concern	1	0
Threatening	6	1
Terrorism	5	79
Workplace violence	20	0
Not sure	8	13
Totals	100	100

* Student response descriptors were provided to the students by the instructor.

From the Old Dominion University survey it is clear that the students' perceptions of Sally's actions in the peanut butter processing incident shifted dramatically from before to after September 11. For example, before September 11, students most often described Sally as "crazy" and "insane"; however, after September 11, students were more likely to describe her as a "terrorist." Likewise, "madness" and "workplace violence" ranked high in the "before" students' descriptions of Sally's actions, while the "after" students overwhelmingly described her actions as "terrorism."

It is interesting to note that even though the 2001 respondents were reporting prior to both September 11 and the September/October 2001 anthrax attacks, they were reporting after such events as the World Trade Center attack of 1993 and Timothy McVeigh's 1995 mass murder of the occupants of the government building in Oklahoma City, Oklahoma. This may explain why for the year 2001 students were somewhat reluctant to describe Sally's actions as terrorism and/or to label her as a terrorist.

After studying this apparent anomaly (in the author's view) for several years, it seems obvious that terrorism, like environmental pollution, is a personal judgement call. Consider, for example, two neighbors living next door to a foul-smelling wastewater treatment plant. One of the neighbors works full-time at the treatment plant, while the other neighbor works elsewhere. Each morning when the neighbor who does not work at the treatment plant steps outside to go to work, she holds her nose against the horrendous odor emanating from the plant site. There is absolutely no doubt in her mind that she lives next door to a pollution source. Every time the other neighbor, the full-time employee of the wastewater treatment plant, steps outside to go to the plant to work his shift, he smells the same odor. However, when the plant employee smells the odor, he does not smell pollution; instead, he detects the sweet smell of money in the bank and job security. Again, terrorism, like pollution, may be a judgment call.

Terrorism by Any Other Name Is . . .

From the preceding discussion, we might want to sum up terrorism as being relative, a personal judgement. But is it really relative? Is it a personal judgement? What is terrorism?

Take your choice. Seemingly, there is an endless list of definitions. Let's review a few of these definitions.

Terrorism and the Red Queen Principle

In my lecture "The Ongoing Fight against Terrorism," I relate (later followed by student input/comments) the following analogy to my Old Dominion University environmental health students. This analogy is loosely based on the "Red Queen Principle" put forward by van Valen (1973), who pointed out that coevolution between predators (terrorists) and prey (us) can lead to situations in which neither antagonist improves its fitness, since both populations continually adapt to each other.

C. M. Lively (2007) points out:

The phrase "Red Queen Hypothesis" comes from Chapter 2 in *Through the Looking Glass* (Carroll 1872). In Alice's dream about the looking glass house, she first finds that things appear left-to-right, as if shown in a mirror. She then finds that chess pieces are alive. She will later encounter several of these pieces (most notably the Red Queen), after she leaves the looking glass house to see the garden.

Alice decides that it would be easier to see the garden if she first climbs the hill, to which there appears to be a very straight path. However, as she follows the path, she finds that it leads her back to the house. When she tries to speed up, she not only returns to the house, she crashes into it. Hence, forward movement takes Alice back to her starting point (Red Queen dynamics), and rapid movement causes abrupt stops (extinction).

Eventually, Alice finds herself in a patch of very vocal and opinionated flowers; the rose is especially vocal. The flowers tell Alice that someone like her (the Red Queen) often passes through, and Alice decides to seek her. When Alice spots the Red Queen, she begins moving toward her. But, the Red Queen quickly disappears from sight. Alice decides to follow the advice of the rose, and go the other way ("I should advise you to walk the other way"). Immediately she comes face-to-face with the Red Queen (see Lythgoe and Read 1998).

The Red Queen then leads Alice directly to the top of the hill. . . . At the top of the hill, the Red Queen begins to run, faster and faster. Alice runs after the Red Queen, but is further perplexed to find that neither one seems to be moving. When they stop running, they are in exactly the same place. Alice remarks on this, to which the Red Queen responds: "Now, here, you see, it takes all the running you can do to keep in the same place."

And this is my point—so it may be with terrorism. The terrorists and we change our tactics to stay in the same place; both are simply running in place. Cessation of change may result in extinction—hopefully in the terrorists' extinction and not in our own.

It is interesting to note (based on the author's personal experience) that when it comes to maintaining an organization's antiterrorism awareness, attitude, and profile, a paradox becomes evident within a few weeks or months after an initial terrorism event (e.g., September 11). The paradox is:

In the fight against terrorism

Some people make things happen;

Some people think they make things happen;

Some people watch things happen;

Some people wonder what happened;

Some people don't know anything happened at all.

Standard Dictionary and Other Definitions of Terrorism

After reviewing several dictionaries, you will find that a fairly standard definition of *terrorism* is the "unlawful use or threatened use of force or violence by a person or an organized group against people or property with the intention of intimidating or coercing societies or governments, often for ideological or political reasons."

America's *National Strategy for Homeland Security* defines terrorism as "Any premeditated, unlawful act dangerous to human life or public welfare that is intended to intimidate or coerce civilian populations or governments" (NSHS, 2006).

The U.S. State Department defines terrorism as "Premeditated, politically motivated violence perpetrated against noncombatant targets by subnational groups or clandestine agents" (USC, 2005).

The FBI defines terrorism as "The unlawful use of force or violence against persons or property to intimidate or coerce a government, the civilian population, or any segment thereof, in furtherance of political or social objectives" (FBI, 2006).

The FBI divides terrorism into two categories: domestic (homegrown), involving groups operating in and targeting the U.S. without foreign direction; and international, involving groups that operate across international borders and/or have foreign connections.

At this point the obvious question is, do you now know what terrorism is? That is, can you definitively define it? If not, you are not alone. Maybe we need to look at other sources—views from some real experts on terrorism.

The following is Osama bin Ladin's view on terrorism: "Wherever we look, we find the U.S. as the leader of terrorism and crime in the world. The U.S. does not consider it a terrorist act to throw atomic bombs at nations thousands of miles away [Japan during World War II], when those bombs would hit more than just military targets. Those bombs rather were thrown at entire nations, including women, children, and elderly people" (Bergen, 2002).

The following is another view (court testimony) on terrorism from Ramzi Ahmed Yousef, who helped organize the first terrorist attack on the World Trade Center:

You keep talking also about collective punishment and killing innocent people to force governments to change their policies; you call this terrorism when someone would kill innocent people or civilians in order to force the government to change its policies. Well, then you were the first one who invented this terrorism.

You were the first one who killed innocent people, and you are the first one who introduced this type of terrorism to the history of mankind when you dropped an atomic bomb which killed tens of thousands of women and children in Japan and when you killed over a hundred thousand people, most of them civilians, in Tokyo with fire bombings. You killed them by burning them to death. And you killed civilians in Vietnam with chemicals as with the so-called Orange agent. You killed civilians and innocent people, not soldiers, innocent people every single war you went. You went to wars more than any other country in this century, and then you have the nerve to talk about killing innocent people.

And now you have invented new ways to kill innocent people. You have so-called economic embargo which kills nobody other than children and elderly people, and which other than Iraq you have been placing the economic embargo on Cuba and other countries for over 35 years . . . .

The Government in its summations and opening statement said that I was a terrorist. Yes, I am a terrorist and I am proud of it. And I support terrorism so long as it was against the United States Government and Israel, because you are more than terrorists; you are the one who invented terrorism and use it every day. You are butchers, liars and hypocrites. (*New York Times*, 1998)

The following is an old cliché on a terrorist: "One man's terrorist is another man's freedom fighter."

Again, from the preceding points of view, it can be seen that defining terrorism or the terrorist is not straightforward and never easy. Even the standard dictionary definition leaves us with the vagaries and ambiguities of other words typically associated with terrorism, as in the definitions of *unlawful* and *public welfare* (Sauter and Carafano, 2005).

At this point, the reader may wonder, "Why should we care; that is, what difference does it make what the definition of terrorist or terrorism is?" Definitions are important because in order to prepare for the terrorism contingency, domestic or international, we must have some feel, as with any other problem, for what it is we are dealing with. We are fighting a war of ideas. We must attempt to understand both sides of the argument, even though the terrorist's side makes no sense to most Americans or other freedom-loving occupants of the globe.

While it is difficult to pinpoint an exact definition of terrorism, we certainly have little difficulty in identifying it when we see it, when we feel it, or when we suffer from it. Consider, for example, the earlier account of Sally's actions and the tainted peanut butter. Put yourself in the place of those consumers who purchased and later consumed the tainted peanut butter. In particular, put yourself in the place of one of those immune-weakened elderly citizens who sat down to enjoy a peanut butter sandwich and who instead ended up violently ill and later dead. This poor soul could not have known that an American terrorist had caused an act of terrorism on U.S. soil that killed her. No, she did not know that. However, there is one thing she knew for certain; she knew that crushing feeling of terror as she struggled to breathe and to live. Thus, by any other name, *terrorism* is best summed up as an absolute feeling of Terror—nothing judgmental about that—just terror with a capital *T*.

AGROTERRORISM

Deep in America's heartland—where our country's vast agricultural system sustains not only the nutritional requirements of nearly 300 million people, but contributes over US $50 billion each year to America's export-economy—there is a new, lingering worry on our security experts' minds. This new, dark fear is of a deliberate terror attack of America's food supply.

—*Barry S. Zellen (2004)*

Agroterrorism (as with any other term, there are numerous definitions available from various sources) can be defined as terrorist attacks aimed at reducing the food supply by destroying crops using biological pests and diseases or chemicals that defoliate vegetation. Peter Chalk (2003) defines agroterrorism as "the deliberate introduction of a disease agent, either against livestock or into the food chain, to undermine socio-economic stability and/or generate fear." Jim Monke (2004) defines agroterrorism as "the deliberate introduction of an animal or plant disease with the goal of generating fear, causing economic losses, and/or undermining stability."

VOCABULARY OF HATE

After September 11, several authors published, and the media transmitted, seemingly endless accounts of various hate groups operating throughout the globe. Overnight Americans became aware of various theories, philosophies, and terminology very few had ever heard of or thought about. This trend is ongoing.

Various pundits on the "new" genre of terrorism, have stated that for Americans to understand why foreign terrorists behead innocent people (or anyone else, for that matter) on television or blow up hospitals full of the sick or wounded or schoolhouses full of children, they must get inside the mind of a terrorist.

The average American might ask: "Get inside the mind of a terrorist? How the hell do you get inside the mind of madmen?"

This is where we make our first mistake, thinking the terrorists act in the manner they do because they are mad, nonrational, disturbed, or psychotic. In the case of Timothy McVeigh, we might be able to characterize him and his actions in this manner. Yet, McVeigh is the exception that proves the rule—terrorist attacks, by real terrorists, are primarily planned beforehand by a group. It is important to remember that McVeigh acted primarily alone.

The terrorists that crashed airplanes into the Twin Towers, Pentagon, and that farm field in Pennsylvania were all of the same mindset; they worked as a group. Likewise, the terrorists that attack Baghdad every day work as a group. Terrorists that did all the damage in Bali and Spain and elsewhere acted as a group. Thus, though we would like to classify all the terrorists as we classify Timothy McVeigh, we can't do that. One madman working alone is something we can reasonably assume. However, thinking that hundreds or thousands of like minded madmen all work in groups is a stretch. The cold blooded manner in which terrorists go about their business suggests that they are not crazy, insane, or mad, but instead extremely harsh and calculating. If we dismiss them as madmen, we underestimate their intelligence. When we do that, we lose. No, we cannot underestimate the enemy—the terrorists. They are smart, cold-blooded, and calculating. In order to protect our critical agricultural infrastructure, we must be smarter and expect the unexpected—we must be proactive and not just reactive in implementing our countermeasures. You might think that the old, time-worn notion that when dealing with terrorists we must think outside the box is germane to this discussion. I would argue that this is not the case. Instead, when dealing with terrorists and terrorism we must think inside the box—the cranial box. Simply, we must be smarter than the enemy, although this is easier said than done. If you love freedom, the fact that it must be done is not arguable or an option.

THE LANGUAGE OF TERRORISM

Anyone who is going to work at improving the security of America's critical infrastructure must be well versed in the goals and techniques used by the terrorists. Moreover, we cannot implement effective countermeasures unless we know our vulnerabilities. Along with this, we must also understand the terrorists. We must not only understand what they are capable of doing, but also have some feel for their language or vocabulary, which will help us to understand where they are coming from and where they might be headed, so to speak.

As with any other technical presentation, understanding the information presented is difficult unless a common vocabulary is established. Voltaire said it best: "If you wish to converse with me, please define your terms." It is difficult enough to understand terrorists and terrorism; thus, we must be familiar with terms they use and that are used to describe them, their techniques, and their actions. In addition, selected terms and definitions specific to agroterrorism have been included.

DEFINITION OF TERMS

Abu Sayyaf—Meaning "bearer of the sword," it is the smaller of the two Islamist groups whose goal is to establish an Iranian-style Islamic state in Mindanao in the Southern Philippines. In 1991, the group split from the Maro National Liberation Front. With ties to numerous Islamic fundamentalist groups, they finance their operations through kidnapping for ransom, extortion, piracy, and other criminal acts. It is also thought that they receive funding from al Qaeda. It is estimated that there are between 200 and 500 Abu Sayyaf terrorists, mostly recruited from high schools and colleges.

Acid bombs—Crude bomb made by combining muriatic acid with aluminum strips in a two-liter soda bottle.

Aerosol—A fine mist or spray, which contains minute particles.

Aflatoxin—Toxin created by bacteria that grow on stored foods, especially on rice, peanuts, and cotton seeds.

Afghanistan—At the time of September 11, 2001, Afghanistan was governed by the Taliban and Osama bin Laden called it home. Amid U.S. air strikes, which began on October 7, 2001, the U.S. sent in more than $300 million in humanitarian aid. In

December 2001, Afghanistan reopened their embassy for the first time in more than 20 years.

Agency—A division of government with a specific function, or a nongovernmental organization (e.g., private contractor, business, etc.) that offers a particular kind of assistance. In the incident command system, agencies are defined as jurisdictional (having statutory responsibility for incident mitigation) or assisting and/or cooperating (providing resources and/or assistance).

Agromovement—is the continuous cycle of movement required in farm-to-fork food production, including all aspects of animal transportation and the transportation of finished products destined for distribution or export through throughout the world (Lane, 2002).

Agroterrorism—see definitions offered earlier in this text chapter.

Airborne—Carried by or through the air.

Air marshal—A federal marshal whose purpose is to ride commercial flights dressed in plain clothes and armed to prevent hijackings. Israel's use of air marshals on El Al is credited as the reason Israel has had a single hijacking in 31 years. The U.S. started using air marshals after September 11. Despite President Bush's urging there are not enough air marshals to go around, so many flights do not have them.

al-Gama'a al-Islamiyya (The Islamic Group, IG)—Islamic group which emerged spontaneously during the 1970s in Egyptian jails and later in Egyptian universities. After President Sadat released most of the Islamic prisoners in 1971, groups of militants organized themselves in groups and cells, and al-Gama'a al-Islamiyya was one of them.

al Jazeera—Satellite television station based in Qatar and broadcast throughout the Middle East, al Jazeera has often been called the CNN of the Arab world.

Alpha radiation—The least penetrating type of nuclear radiation. Not considered dangerous unless particles enter the body.

al Qaeda—"The Base." An international terrorist group founded in approximately 1989 and dedicated to opposing non-Islamic governments with force and violence. One of the principal goals of al Qaeda was to drive the U.S armed forces out of the Saudi Arabian peninsula and Somalia by violence. Currently wanted for several terrorist attacks, including those on the U.S. embassy in Kenya and Tanzania as well as the first and second World Trade Center bombings, and the attack on the Pentagon.

al Tahwid—Palestinian group based in London which professes a desire to destroy both Israel and the Jewish people throughout Europe. Eleven al Tahwid were arrested in Germany allegedly as they were about to begin attacking that country.

American Airlines Flight 11—Boeing 767 carrying 81 passengers, 9 flight attendants, and 2 pilots, which was highjacked and crashed into the north tower of the World Trade Center at 8:45 a.m. Eastern Time on September 11, 2001. Flight 11 was en route to Los Angeles from Boston.

American Airlines Flight 77—Boeing 757 carrying 58 passengers, 4 flight attendants, and 2 pilots, which was highjacked and crashed into the Pentagon at 9:40 a.m. Eastern Time on September 11, 2001. Flight was en route to Los Angeles from Dulles International Airport in Virginia.

Ammonium nitrate–fuel oil—A powerful explosive made by mixing fertilizer and fuel oil. The type of bomb used in the first World Trade Center attack as well as [the] Oklahoma City bombing.

Analyte—A chemical substance being analyzed, usually described in terms of its molecular composition, taxonomic nomenclature, or other characteristic.

ANFO—Ammonium nitrate–fuel oil (see above).

Animal and Plant Health Inspection Service (APHIS)—A division within the U.S. Department of Agriculture, it is responsible for protecting and promoting U.S. agricultural health, administering the Animal Welfare Act, and carrying out wildlife damage management activities. One of APHIS's primary objectives is to provide the U.S. with safe and affordable food.

Anthrax—Often fatal infectious disease contracted from animals. Anthrax spores have such a long survival period; the incubation period is short; disability is severe, making anthrax a bioweapon of choice of several nations.

Antidote—A remedy to counteract the effects of poison.

Antigen—A substance which stimulates an immune response by the body. The immune system recognizes such substances as foreign and produces antibodies to fight them.

Antitoxin—An antibody which neutralizes a biological toxin.

Armed Islamic Group (GIA)—Algerian Islamic extremist group which aims to overthrow the secular regime in Algeria and replace it with an Islamic state. The GIA began its violent activities in early 1992 after Algiers voided the victory of the largest Islamic party, Islamic Salvation Front (FIS), in the December 1991 elections.

Asymmetric threat—The use of crude or low-tech methods to attack a superior or more high-tech enemy.

Axis of Evil—Iran, Iraq, and North Korea as mentioned by President G. W. Bush during his State of the Union speech in 2002 as nations which were a threat to U.S security due to harboring terrorism.

Baath Party—The official political party in Iraq until the U.S. debaathified Iraq in May 2003 after an invasion which lasted a little over a month. Saddam Hussein, the former ruler of the Baath party, was targeted by American-led coalition forces and fled. Baath party members have been officially banned from participating in any new government in Iraq.

Beltway Sniper—For nearly a month in October 2002, the Washington DC, Maryland, and Virginia area was the hunting grounds for 41-year old John Allen Muhammad and 17-year old Lee Boyd Malvo. Dubbed "the Beltway Sniper" by the media, they shot people at seemingly random places such as schools, restaurants, and gas stations.

bin Laden, Osama (also spelled "Usama")—A native of Saudi Arabia, was born the 17th of 24 sons of Saudi Arabian builder Mohammed bin Oud bin Laden, a Yemeni immigrant. Early in his career, he helped the mujahedeen fight the Soviet Union by recruiting Arabs and building facilities. His hatred of the U.S. is apparently because he views that nation as having desecrated holy ground in Saudi Arabia with their presence during the first Gulf War. Expelled from Saudi Arabia in 1991 and from Sudan in 1996, he operated terrorist training camps in Afghanistan. His global network al Qaeda is credited with the attacks on the U.S. on September 11, 2001, the attack on the USS Cole in 2000, and a number of other terrorist attacks.

Biochemical warfare—Collective term for use of both chemical warfare and biological warfare weapons.

Biochemterrorism—Terrorism using as weapons biological or chemical agents.

Biological ammunition—Ammunition designed specifically to release a biological agent used as the warhead for biological weapons. Biological ammunition may take many forms, such as a missile warhead or bomb.

Biological attack—The deliberate release of germs or other biological substances that cause illness.

Biological Weapons Convention (BWC)—Officially known as the "Convention on the Prohibition of Development, Production, and Stockpiling of Bacteriological

(Biological) and Toxin Weapons and Destruction." The BWC works toward general and complete disarmament, including the prohibition and elimination of all types of weapons of mass destruction.

Biosafety Level 1—Safety standards suitable for work involving well-characterized biological agents not known to consistently cause disease in healthy adult humans, and of minimal potential hazard to lab personnel and the environment. Work is generally conducted on open bench tops using standard microbiological practices.

Biosafety Level 2—Safety standards suitable for work involving biological agents of moderate potential hazard to personnel and the environment. Lab personnel should have specific training in handling pathogenic agents and be directed by competent scientists. Access to the lab should be limited when work is being conducted, extreme precautions should be taken with contaminated sharp items, and certain procedures should be conducted in biological safety cabinets or other physical containment equipment if there is a risk of creating infectious aerosols or splashes.

Biosafety Level 3—Safety standards suitable for work done with indigenous or exotic biological agents that may cause serious or potentially lethal disease as a result of exposure by inhalation. Lab personnel must have specific training in handling pathogenic and potentially lethal agents and be supervised by competent scientists who are experienced in working with these agents. All procedures involving the manipulation of infectious material are conducted within biological safety cabinets or other physical containment devices, or by personnel wearing appropriate personal protective clothing and equipment. The lab must have special engineering and design features.

Biosafety Level 4—Safety standards suitable for work with the most infectious biological agents. Access to the two Biosafety Level 4 labs in the U.S. is highly restricted.

Bioterrorism—The use of biological agents (such as bacteria and viruses) in a terrorist operation. The most likely biological toxins terrorists might adopt are anthrax, salmonella, E. coli, hoof-and-mouth disease, the plague, smallpox, botulism, and tularemia.

Bioterrorism Act—The Public Health Security and Bioterrorism Preparedness and Response Act of 2002.

Biowarfare—The use of biological agents to cause harm to targeted people either directly, by bringing the people into contact with the agents, or indirectly, by infecting other animals and plants, which would in turn cause harm to the people.

Blister agents—Agents which cause pain and incapacitation instead of death and might be used to injure many people at once, thereby overloading medical facilities and causing fear in the population. Mustard gas is the best known blister agent.

Blood agents—Agents based on cyanide compounds. More likely to be used for assassination than for terrorism.

Botulism—The botulinum toxin is exceedingly lethal and quite simple to produce. It takes just a small amount of the toxin to destroy the central nervous system. Botulism may be contracted by the ingestion of contaminated food or through breaks or cuts in the skin. Food supply contamination or aerosol dissemination of the botulinum toxin are the two ways most likely to be used by terrorists.

Bush Doctrine—The policy that holds responsible nations which harbor or support terrorist organizations and says that such countries are considered hostile to the U.S. From President Bush's speech: "A country that harbors terrorists will either deliver the terrorist or share in their fate. . . . People have to choose sides. They are either with the terrorists, or they're with us."

Camp X-Ray—The Guantanamo Bay, Cuba, which houses al Qaeda and Taliban prisoners.

Carrier—Person or animal that is potentially a source of infection by carrying on infectious agent without visible symptoms of the disease.

Causative agent—The pathogen, chemical, or other substance that is the cause of disease or death in an individual.

Cell—The smallest unit within a guerrilla or terrorist group. A cell generally consists of two to five people dedicated to a terrorist cause. The formation of cells is born of the concept that an apparent "leaderless resistance" makes it hard for counterterrorists to penetrate.

Chain of custody—The tracking and documentation of physical control of evidence.

Chemical agent—Toxic substances intended to be used for operations to debilitate, immobilize, or kill military or civilian personnel.

Chemical ammunition—Munitions, commonly a missile, bomb, rocket, or artillery shell, designed to deliver chemical agents.

Chemical attack—The intentional release of toxic liquid, gas or solid in order to poison the environment or people.

Chemical warfare—The use of toxic chemicals as weapons, not including herbicide used to defoliate battlegrounds or riot control agents such as gas or mace.

Chemical weapons—Weapons that produce effects on living targets via toxic chemical properties. Examples would be sarin, VX nerve gas, or mustard gas.

Chemterrorism—The use of chemical agents in a terrorist operation. Well-known chemical agents include sarin and VX nerve gas.

Choking agent—Compounds that injure primarily in the respiratory tract (i.e., nose, throat, and lungs). In extreme cases membranes swell up, lungs become filled with liquid, and death results from lack of oxygen.

Cipro—Bayer's antibiotic which combats inhalation anthrax.

Confirmed—In the context of the threat evaluation process, a water contamination incident is definitive evidence that the water has been contaminated.

Counterterrorism—Measures used to prevent, preempt, or retaliate against terrorist attacks.

Credible—In the context of the threat evaluation process, a water contamination threat is characterized as 'credible' if information collected during the threat evaluation process corroborates information from the threat warning.

Crime triangle—Includes the offender, victim/commodity, and location of a criminal act, including an act of terrorism. Intelligence analysis begins at the most basic level and involves collecting information about the crime triangle (Carter, 2004).

Criminal intelligence—A combination of credible information which has been evaluated and from which conclusions can be drawn, as defined by the International Association of Chiefs of Police; it is the collection and analysis of information to produce an intelligence end product designed to inform law enforcement decision-making at both the tactical and strategic levels, as defined by the Global Intelligence Working Group; and it is "raw" information that is unevaluated and "finished" intelligence that has had some degree of analysis, both of which focus on those who would do harm in the form of terrorist acts or other crimes as defined by the FBI's Office of Intelligence (Carter, 2004).

Cutaneous—Related to or entering through the skin.

Cutaneous anthrax—Contracted via broken skin. The infection spreads through the bloodstream causing cyanosis, shock, sweating, and finally death.

Cyanide agents—Used by Iraq in the Iran war against the Kurds in the 1980s, and also by the Nazis in the gas chambers of concentration camps, cyanide agents are colorless liquids which are inhaled in gaseous form, while liquid cyanide and cyanide salts are absorbed by the skin. Symptoms are headache, palpitations, dizziness, and respiratory problems followed later by vomiting, convulsions, respiratory failure and unconsciousness and eventually by death.

Cyberterrorism—Attacks on computer networks or systems, generally by hackers working with or for terrorist groups. Some forms of cyberterrorism include denial of service attacks, inserting viruses or stealing data.

Dirty bomb—A makeshift nuclear device which is created from radioactive nuclear waste material. While not a nuclear blast, an explosion of a dirty bomb causes localized radioactive contamination as the nuclear waste material is carried into the atmosphere where it is dispersed by the wind.

Ebola—Ebola hemorrhagic fever (Ebola EF) is a severe, often-fatal disease in non-human primates such as monkeys, chimpanzees, gorillas and in humans. Ebola has appeared sporadically since 1976 when it was first recognized.

eBomb (or e-bomb)—Electromagnetic bomb which produces a brief pulse of energy which affects electronic circuitry. At low levels, the pulse temporarily disables electronics systems, including computers, radios, and transportation systems. High levels completely destroy circuitry, causing mass disruption of infrastructure while sparing life and property.

Ecoterrorism—Sabotage intended to hinder activities that are considered damaging to the environment.

Euroterrorism—Associated with left-wing terrorism of the 1960s, 1970s, and 1980s involving the Red Brigade, Red Army Faction, and November 17th Group, among other groups which targeted American interests in Europe and NATO. Other groups include Orange Volunteers, Red Hand Defenders, Continuity IRA, Loyalist Volunteer Force, Ulster Defense Association, and First of October Anti-Fascist Resistance Group.

Fallout—The descent to the Earth's surface of particles contaminated with radioactive material from a radioactive cloud. The term can also be applied to the contaminated particulate matter itself.

Fatah—"Conquest by means of jihad." Political organization created in the 1960s and led by Yasser Arafat. With both a military and intelligence wing, it has carried out terrorist attacks on Israel since 1965. It joined the PLO in 1968. Since September 11, 2001, the Fatah was blamed for attempting to smuggle 50 tons of weapons into Israel.

Fatwa—A legal ruling regarding Islamic Law.

Fedayeen Saddam—Iraq's paramilitary organization said to be an equivalent to the Nazi's SS. The militia is loyal to Saddam Hussein and is responsible for using brutality on civilians who are not loyal to the policies of Saddam. They do not dress in uniform.

Filtrate—In ultrafiltration, the water that passes through the membrane and which contains particles smaller than the molecular weight cutoff of the membrane.

Fomites—Inanimate objects that carry infectious agents from one animal to another such as needles, contaminated clothing, boots or shoes, vehicles, or farm equipment, and contaminated food and water supplies (Spickler and Roth, 2004).

Foot-and-Mouth Disease (FMD)—A highly infectious viral disease that affects cloven-hoofed animals including cattle, swine, deer, goats, and sheep. Spread in aerosols and on fomites such a manure-contaminated tires, boots, and clothing, FMD causes vesicles on the tongue and hoof lesions on cloven-hoofed animals. The erosions are painful to the animal and cause lameness, a refusal to eat, and weight loss (Spickler and Roth, 2004).

Foreign Animal Disease (FAD)—A transmissible livestock disease believed to be absent from the United States and its territories. Many animal diseases which are considered foreign were present in the U.S at one time, but they have been eradicated. Foreign animal disease may be referred to as *exotic animal disease* (Spickler and Roth, 2004).

Frustration-Aggression Hypothesis—A hypothesis that every frustration leads to some form of aggression and every aggressive act results from some prior frustration. As defined by Gurr (1968): "The Necessary precondition for violent civil conflict is relative deprivation, defined as actors' perception of discrepancy between their value expectations and their environments' apparent value capabilities. This deprivation may be individual or collective."

Fundamentalism—Conservative religious authoritarianism. Fundamentalism is not specific to Islam; it exists in all faiths. Characteristics include literal interpretation of scriptures and a strict adherence to traditional doctrines and practices.

Geneva Protocol 1925—The first treaty to prohibit the use of biological weapons. The 1925 Geneva Protocol for the Prohibition of the Use in War of Asphyxiating, Poisonous or Other Gases and Bacteriological Methods of Warfare.

Germ warfare—The use of biological agents to cause harm to targeted people either directly, by bringing the people into contact with the agents, or indirectly, by infecting other animals and plants, which would in turn cause harm to the people.

Glanders—An infectious bacterial disease known to cause inflammation in horses, donkeys, mules, goats, dogs and cats. Human infection has not been seen since

1945, but because so few organisms are required to cause disease, it is considered a potential agent for biological warfare.

Grab sample—A single sample collected at a particular time and place that represents the composition of the water, air, or soil only at that time and location.

Ground zero—From 1946 until September 11, 2001, ground zero was the point directly above, below, or at which a nuclear explosion occurs or the center or origin of rapid, intense, or violent activity or change. After September 11, 2001, the term, when used with initial capital letters, refers to the ground at the epicenter of the World Trade Center attacks.

Guerrilla warfare—The term was invented to describe the tactics Spain used to resist Napoleon, though the tactic itself has been around much longer. Literally, it means "little war." Guerilla warfare features cells and utilizes no front line. The oldest form of asymmetric warfare, guerilla warfare is based on sabotage and ambush with the objective of destabilizing the government through lengthy and low-intensity confrontation.

Hamas—A radical Islamic organization which operates primarily in the West Bank and Gaza Strip whose goal is to establish an Islamic Palestinian state in place of Israel. On the one hand, Hamas operates overtly in their capacity as social services deliverers, but its activists have also conducted many attacks, including suicide bombings, against Israeli civilians and military targets.

Hazard assessment—The process of evaluating available information about a site to identify potential hazards that might pose a risk to the site characterization team. The hazard assessment results in assigning one of four levels to risk: lower hazard, radiological hazard, high chemical hazard, or high biological hazard.

Hemorrhagic fevers—In general, the term *viral hemorrhagic fever* is used to describe a severe multisystem syndrome wherein the overall vascular system is damaged, and the body becomes unable to regulate itself. These symptoms are often accompanied by hemorrhage; however, the bleeding itself is not usually life threatening. Some types of hemorrhagic fever viruses can cause relatively mild illnesses.

Hizbollah (Hezbollah)—"The Party of God." One of many terrorist organizations which seek the destruction of Israel and of the U.S. They have taken credit for numerous bombings against civilians, and have declared that civilian targets are warranted. Hezbollah claims it sees no legitimacy for the existence of Israel, and that their conflict becomes one of legitimacy that is based on religious ideals.

Homeland Security Office—Agency organized after September 11, 2001, with former Pennsylvania Governor Tom Ridge heading it up. The Office of Homeland Security is at the top of approximately 40 federal agencies charged with protecting the U.S. against terrorism.

Homicide bombings—The White House coined the term to replace the old "suicide bombings."

Incident—A confirmed occurrence that requires response actions to prevent or minimize loss of life or damage to property and/or natural resources. A drinking water contamination incident occurs when the presence of a harmful contaminant has been confirmed.

Inhalation anthrax—Contracted by inhaling anthrax spores. This results in pneumonia, sometimes meningitis, and finally death.

Intifada (intifadah)—(alternatively Intifadah, from Arabic "shaking off") The two intifadas are similar in that both were originally characterized by civil disobedience by the Palestinians which escalated into the use of terror. In 1987, following the killing of several Arabs in the Gaza Strip, the first intifada began and went on until 1993. The second intifada began in September 2000, following Ariel Sharon's visit to the Temple Mount.

Islam—"Submit." The faith practiced by followers of Muhammad. Islam claims more than a billion believers worldwide.

Jihad—"Struggle." The definition is a subject of vast debate. There are two definitions generally accepted. The first is a struggle against oppression, whether political or religious. The second is the struggle within oneself, or a spiritual struggle.

Kneecapping—This common punishment used by Northern Ireland's IRA involves breaking or sooting the kneecaps of those accused of collaborating with the British.

Koran—The holy book of Islam, considered by Muslims to contain the revelations of God to Mohammed. Also called Qu'ran.

Laboratory Response Network (LRN)—A network of labs developed by the CDC, APHL, and FBI for the express purpose of dealing with bioterrorism threats, including pathogens and some biotoxins.

Lassa fever—An acute, often fatal, viral disease characterized by high fever, ulcers of the mucous membranes, headaches, and disturbances of the gastrointestinal system.

LD50—A dose of a substance which kills 50 percent of those infected.

Mindset—A noun defined by *American Heritage Dictionary* as: "1. A fixed mental attitude or disposition that predetermines a person's response to and interpretation of situations; 2. and inclination or a habit." *Merriam Webster's Collegiate Dictionary* (10th ed.) defines it as "1. A mental attitude or inclination; 2. a fixed state of mind." The term dates from 1926 but apparently is not included in dictionaries of psychology.

Molotov cocktail—a crude incendiary bomb made of a bottle filled with flammable liquid and fitted with a rag wick.

Monkeypox—The Russian bioweapon program worked with this virus, which is in the same family as smallpox. In June 2003, a spate of human monkeypox cases was reported in the U.S. Midwest. This was the first time that monkeypox was seen in North America, and it was the first time that monkeypox was transferred from animal to human. There was some speculation that it was a bioattack.

Mullah—A Muslim, usually holding an official post, who is trained in traditional religious doctrine and law.

Muslim (also Moslem)—Followers of the teachings of Mohammed, or Islam.

Mustard gas—Blistering agents which cause severe damage to the eyes, internal organs, and respiratory system. Produced for the first time in 1822, mustard gas was not used until World War I. Victims suffered the effects of mustard gas 30 to 40 years after exposure.

Narcoterrorism—The view of many counterterrorist experts that there exists an alliance between drug traffickers and political terrorists.

National Animal Identification System (NAIS)—A national program intended to identify all animals from birth to slaughter/death. In April 2004, the USDA announced the framework for implementing NAIS, a system that, when fully operation, will be capable of tracing a sick animal or animals back to the most likely source of infection.

National Pharmaceutical Stockpile—A stock of vaccines and antidotes which are stored at Centers for Disease Control in Atlanta, to be used against biological warfare.

Nerve agent—The Nazis used the first nerve agents: insecticides developed into chemical weapons. Some of the better known nerve agents include VX, sarin, soman, and tabun. These agents are useful because only a small quantity is necessary to inflict a substantial damage. Nerve agents can be inhaled or can absorb through intact skin.

Nuclear blast—An explosion of any nuclear material which is accompanied by a pressure wave, intense light and heat, and widespread radioactive fallout which can contaminate the air, water and ground surface for miles around.

Opportunity Contaminant—Contaminants that might be readily available in a particular area, even through they may not be highly toxic or infectious or easily dispersed and stable in treated drinking water.

Pathogen—Any agent which can cause disease.

Pig swill—A mixture of liquid and waste food, table scraps, or garbage fed to animals, normally pigs. On a large scale, pig swill comes from restaurants and schools. Farmers who use pig swill as animal feed are required to heat the swill in excess of 100 degrees centigrade to kill potential pathogens. Pig swill (untreated food waste from a restaurant) was the source of the outbreak of foot-and-mouth disease in the United Kingdom in February 2001 (Spickler and Roth, 2004).

Plague—The pneumonic plague, which is more likely to be used in connection with terrorism, is naturally carried by rodents and fleas but can be aerosolized and sprayed from crop dusters. A 1970 World Health Organization assessment asserted that, in a worst case scenario, a dissemination of 50 kg in an aerosol over a city of 5 million could result in 150,000 cases of pneumonic plague, 80,000–100,000 of which would require hospitalization, and 36,000 of which would be expected to die.

Political terrorism—Terrorist acts directed at governments and their agents and motivated by political goals (i.e., national liberation).

Possible—In the context of the threat evaluation process, a water contamination threat is characterized as "possible" if the circumstances of the threat warning appear to have provided an opportunity for contamination.

Potassium iodide—FDA-approved nonprescription drug for use as a blocking agent to prevent the thyroid gland from absorbing radioactive iodine.

Presumptive results—Results of chemical and/or biological field testing that need to be confirmed by further lab analysis. Typically used in reference to the analysis of pathogens.

Psychopath—A mentally ill or unstable person, especially one having a psychopathic personality (q.v.), according to *Webster's*.

Psychopathology—The study of psychological and behavioral dysfunction occurring in mental disorder or in social disorganization, according to *Webster's*.

Psychopathy—A mental disorder, especially an extreme mental disorder marked usually by egocentric and antisocial activity, according to *Webster's*.

Psychotic—Of, relating to, or affected with psychosis, which is a fundamental mental derangement (as schizophrenia) characterized by defective or lost contact with reality, according to *Webster's*.

Rapid field testing—Analysis of water during site characterization using rapid field water testing technology in an attempt to tentatively identify contaminants or unusual water quality.

Retentate—In ultrafiltration, the retentate is the solution that contains the particles that do not pass through the membrane filter. The retentate is also called the *concentrate*.

Ricin—A stable toxin easily made from the mash that remains after processed castor beans. At one time, it was used as an oral laxative, castor oil; castor oil causes diarrhea, nausea, vomiting, abdominal cramps, internal bleeding, liver and kidney failure, and circulatory failure. There is no antidote.

Salmonella—An infection caused by a gram-negative bacillus, a germ of the Salmonella genus. Infection with this bacteria may involve only the intestinal tract or may be spread from the intestines to the bloodstream and then to other sites in the body. Symptoms of salmonella enteritis include diarrhea, nausea, fever, abdominal pain, and fever. Dehydration resulting from the diarrhea can cause death, and the disease could cause meningitis or septicemia. The incubation period is between 8 and 48 hours, while the acute part of the illness can hang on for 1 to 2 weeks.

Sarin—Colorless, odorless gas. With a lethal dose of .5 mg (a pinprick-sized droplet), it is 26 times more deadly than cyanide gas. Because the vapor is heavier than air, it hovers close to the ground. Sarin degrades quickly in humid weather, but sarin's life expectancy increases as temperature gets higher, regardless of how humid it is.

Sentinel Laboratory—An LRN lab that reports unusual results that might indicate a possible outbreak, and refers specimens that may contain select biological agents to reference labs within the LRN.

Site characterization—The process of collecting information from an investigation site in order to support the evaluation of a drinking water contamination threat. Site characterization activities include the site investigation, field safety screening, rapid field testing of the water, and sample collection.

Sleeper cell—A small cell which keeps itself undetected until such time as they can "awaken" and cause havoc.

Smallpox—The first biological weapon, used during the 18th century, smallpox killed 300 million people in the 19th century. There is no specific treatment for smallpox disease, and the only prevention is vaccination. This currently poses a problem, since the vaccine was discontinued in 1970 and the WHO declared small-pox eradicated. Incubation is 7 to 17 days, during which the carrier is not contagious. 30 percent of people exposed are infected, and it has a 30 percent mortality rate.

Sociopath—Basically synonymous with psychopath (q.v.). Sociopathic symptoms in the adult sociopath include an inability to tolerate delay or frustration, a lack of guilt feelings, a relative lack of anxiety, a lack of compassion for others, a hypersensitivity to personal ills, and a lack of responsibility. Many authors prefer the term *sociopath* because this type of person had defective socialization and a deficient childhood.

Sociopathic—Of, relating to, or characterized by asocial or antisocial behavior or a psychopathic (q.v.) personality, according to *Webster's*.

Spore—An asexual, usually single-celled reproductive body of plants such as fungi, mosses or ferns; a microorganism, as a bacterium, in a resting or dormant state.

Terrorist group—A group which practices or has significant elements which are involved in terrorism.

Threat—An indication that a harmful incident, such as contamination of the drinking water supply, may have occurred. The threat may be direct, such as a verbal or written threat, or circumstantial, such as a security breach or unusual water quality.

Toxin—Poisonous substance produced by living organisms capable of causing disease when introduced into the body tissues.

Transponder—A device on an airliner that sends out signals allowing air traffic controllers to track the airplane. Transponders were disabled in some of the planes highjacked September 11, 2001.

Transportation Security Administration (TSA)—A new agency created by the Patriot Act of 2001 for the purpose of overseeing technology and security in American airports.

Tularemia—Tularemia is an infectious disease caused by a hardy bacterium Francisella tularensis, found in animals, particularly rabbits, hares, and rodents. Symptoms depend upon how the person was exposed to tularemia but can include difficulty breathing, chest pain, bloody sputum, swollen and painful lymph glands, ulcers on the mouth or skin, swollen and painful eyes, and sore throat. Symptoms usually appear from three to five days after exposures but sometimes will take up to two weeks. Tularemia is not spread from person to person, so people who have it need not be isolated.

Ultrafiltration—A filtration process for water that uses membranes to preferentially separate very small particles that are larger than the membrane's molecular weight cut-off, typically greater than 10,000 Daltons. (A Dalton is a unit of mass, defined as 1/12 the mass of a carbon-12 nucleus. It's also called the atomic mass unit, abbreviated as either "amu" or "u").

Vector—An organism that carries germs from one host to another.

Vesicle—A blister filled with fluid.

Weapons of mass destruction (WMD)—According to the National Defense Authorization Act: Any weapon or device that is intended, or has the capability, to cause death or serious bodily injury to a significant number of people through the release, dissemination, or impact of (a) toxic or poisonous chemicals or their precursors, (b) a disease organism, or (c) radiation or radioactivity.

Xenophobia—Irrational fear of strangers or those who are different from oneself.

Zyklon b—A form of hydrogen cyanide. Symptoms of inhalation include increased respiratory rate, restlessness, headache, and giddiness followed later by convulsions, vomiting, respiratory failure and unconsciousness. Used in the Nazi gas chambers in WWII.

REFERENCES

Bell, G. 1982. *The Masterpiece of Nature: The Evolution and Genetics of Sexuality*. Berkeley: University of California Press.

Bergen, P. L. 2002. *Holy War, Inc: Inside the Secret World of Osama bin Ladin*. New York: Touchstone Press, pp. 21–22.

Carroll, L. 1872. *Through the Looking Glass and What Alice Found There*. London: Macmillan.

Carter, D. 2004. *Law Enforcement Intelligence: A Guide for State, Local, and Tribal Law Enforcement Agencies*. Washington, DC: Office of Community Oriented Policing Services, U.S. Department of Justice.

Chalk, P. 2003. *Agroterrorism: What Is the Threat and What Can Be Done about It?* Santa Monica, CA: National Defense Research Institute.

11 September, 2001. 2006. *Glossary of Terrorism Terms*. Last updated August 14, 2006, at www.11-sept.org/Glossary.

Gurr, T. R. 1968. Psychological factors in civil violence. *World Politics* 20(32) January: 245–278.

Lane, J. 2002. Sworn Testimony, Congressional Field Hearing, House Committee on Government Reform, Abilene, KS.

Lewis, J. E. 2005. Congressional Testimony before Senate Committee on Agriculture, Nutrition, and Forestry. Washington, DC: FBI.

Lively, C. M. 2007. *Red Queen Hypothesis*, at www.Indiana.edu (accessed June 30, 2007).

Lythgoe, K. A., and A. F. Read. 1998. Catching the Red Queen? The advice of the rose. *Trends Ecol. Evol.* 13:473–474.

Monke, J. 2004. *Agroterrorism: Threats and Preparedness.* Washington, DC: Congressional Research Service. The Library of Congress.

NSHS, 2006. *National Strategy for Homeland Security*, at www.whitehouse/homeland (accessed May 13, 2006).

New York Times. 1998. Excerpt from court testimony. Page B4.

Old Dominion University (2001; 2003). *Violence in the Workplace: Security Concerns.* From a series of lectures presented by Frank R. Spellman to environmental health students. Norfolk, VA.

Payne, Carroll. 2007. Understanding terrorism—Definition of terrorism. *World Conflict Quarterly*, at www.globalterrorism101.com (accessed June 10, 2007).

Sauter, M. A., and J. J. Carafano. 2005. *Homeland Security: A Complete Guide to Understanding, Preventing, and Surviving Terrorism.* New York: McGraw-Hill.

Spellman, F. R. 1997. *A Guide to Compliance for Process Safety Management/Risk Management Planning (PSM/RMP).* Lancaster, PA: Technomic Publishing Company.

Spickler, A., and J. Roth. 2004. *Emerging and Exotic Diseases of Animals*, 2nd ed. Ames: Iowa State University, College of Veterinary Medicine.

The Virginian-Pilot. 2007. *First, Pet Food. Then Toy Trains. Then Toothpaste. Now Seafood.* Norfolk, VA: From Wire Reports.

USAToday. 2007. *Car Packed with Explosives Defused in London*, at www.USAToday.com (accessed June 29, 2007).

USC. 2005. *Annual Country Reports on Terrorism.* U.S. Code, Title 22, Chapter 38, Section 2656f.

Van Valen, L. 1973. A new evolutionary law. *Evol. Theory*1:1–30.

Zellen, B. S. 2004. Preventing Armageddon II: Confronting the specter of agriterror. *Strategic Insights* 3(12).

USDA and Homeland Security

A major agroterrorist attack would have substantial economic repercussions, especially when allied industries and services—suppliers, transporters, distributors, and restaurant chains—are taken into account.The fiscal downstream effect of a deliberate act of sabotage would be multidimensional, reverberating through other sectors of the economy and ultimately impacting the consumer

—*RAND, 2003*

U.S. DEPARTMENT OF AGRICULTURE (USDA)

Agriculture is generally defined as all activities essential to food/feed/fiber production, including all techniques for raising and "processing" livestock. In light of this, consider USDA's description of itself:

FSIS NEWS RELEASE, FEBRUARY 3, 2007

Indiana Firm Recalls Canned Chicken Noodle Soup Due to Undeclared Allergens

ABOUT USDA

Mission Statement

We provide leadership on food, agriculture, natural resources, and related issues based on sound public policy, the best available science, and efficient management.

Vision

We want to be recognized as a dynamic organization that is able to efficiently provide the integrated program delivery needed to lead a rapidly evolving food and agriculture system.

Strategic Plan Framework

USDA has created a strategic plan to implement its vision. The framework of this plan depends on these key activities: expanding markets for agricultural products and support international economic development; further developing alternative markets for agricultural products and activities; providing financing needed to help expand job opportunities and improve housing, utilities, and infrastructure in rural America; enhancing food safety by taking steps to reduce the prevalence of foodborne hazards from farm to table; improving nutrition and health by providing food assistance and nutrition education and promotion; and managing and protecting America's public and private lands working cooperatively with other levels of government and the private sector. (USDA, 2004a)

FSIS NEWS RELEASE, FEBRUARY 18, 2007

South Carolina Firm Recalls Chicken Breast Strips for Possible *Listeria* Contamination

USDA AGENCIES AND OFFICES

Within the USDA there are several separate agencies and offices. These are listed and described on the USDA Web site (www.usda.gov), and the list is reproduced below. It is important to note that these agencies and offices within the USDA work in synergy to contribute to the efforts of homeland security and keeping America's food supply safe (USDA, 2006).

USDA Agencies

- **Agricultural Marketing Service (AMS):** Facilitates the strategic marketing of agricultural products in domestic and international markets while ensuring fair practices and promoting a competitive and efficient marketplace. AMS constantly works to develop new marketing services to increase customer satisfaction.
- **Agricultural Research Service (ARS):** Is USDA's principal in-house research agency. ARS leads America towards a better future through agricultural research and information.
- **Animal and Plant Health Inspection Service (APHIS):** Provides leadership in ensuring the health and care of animals and plants. The agency improves agricultural productivity and competitiveness and contributes to the national economy and the public health.
- **Center for Nutrition Policy and Promotion (CNPP):** Works to improve the health and well-being of Americans by developing and promoting dietary guidance that links scientific research to the nutrition needs of consumers.
- **Cooperative State Research, Education and Extension Service (CREES):** In partnership with land-grant universities, and other public and private organizations, CREES provides the focus to advance a global system of extramural research, extension, and higher education in the food and agricultural sciences.
- **Economic Research Service (ERS):** Is USDA's principal social science research agency. Each year, ERS communicates research results and socioeconomic indicators via briefings, analyses for policymakers and their staffs, market analysis updates, and major reports.
- **Farm Service Agency (FSA):** Implements agricultural policy, administers credit and loan programs, and manages conservation, commodity, disaster and farm marketing programs through a national network of offices.
- **Food and Nutrition Service (FNS):** Increases food security and reduces hunger in partnership with cooperating organizations by providing children and low-income people access to food, a healthy diet, and nutrition education in a manner that supports American agriculture and inspires public confidence.
- **Food Safety and Inspection Service (FSIS):** Enhances public health and well-being by protecting the public from foodborne illness and ensuring that the nation's meat, poultry and egg products are safe, wholesome, and correctly packaged.
- **Foreign Agricultural Service (FAS):** Works to improve foreign market access for U.S. products. This USDA agency operates programs designed to build new markets and improve the competitive position of U.S. agriculture in the global marketplace.

- **Forest Service (FS):** Sustains the health, diversity and productivity of the nation's forests and grasslands to meet the needs of present and future generations.
- **Grain Inspection, Packers and Stockyards Administration (GIPSA):** Facilitates the marketing of livestock, poultry, meat, cereals, oilseeds, and related agricultural products. It also promotes fair and competitive trading practices for the overall benefit of consumers and American agriculture. GIPSA ensures open and competitive markets for livestock, poultry, and meat by investigating and monitoring industry trade practices.
- **National Agricultural Library (NAL):** Ensures and enhances access to agricultural information for a better quality of life.
- **National Agricultural Statistics Service (NASS):** Serves the basic agricultural and rural data needs of the country by providing objective, important and accurate statistical information and services to farmers, ranchers, agribusinesses and public officials. This data is vital to monitoring the ever-changing agricultural sector and carrying out farm policy.
- **Natural Resources Conservation Service (NRCS):** Provides leadership in a partnership effort to help people conserve, maintain and improve our natural resources and environment.
- **Risk Management Agency (RMA):** Helps to ensure that farmers have the financial tools necessary to manage their agricultural risks. RMA provides coverage through the Federal Crop Insurance Corporation, which promotes national welfare by improving the economic stability of agriculture.
- **Rural Development (RD):** Helps rural areas to develop and grow by offering federal assistance that improves quality of life. RD targets communities in need and then empowers them with financial and technical resources.

USDA Offices

- **Departmental Administration (DA):** Provides central administrative management support to Department officials and coordinates administrative programs and services.
- **National Appeals Division (NAD):** Conducts impartial administrative appeal hearings of adverse program decisions made by USDA and reviews of determinations issued by NAD hearing officers when requested by a party to the appeal.
- **Office of the Assistant Secretary for Civil rights (OASCR) or ASCR:** Facilitates the fair and equitable treatment of USDA customers and employees, while ensuring the delivery and enforcement of civil rights programs and activities. ASCR ensures compliance with applicable laws, regulations, and policies for USDA customers and employees regardless of race, color, national origin, gender, religion, age, disability, sexual orientation, martial or familial status, political beliefs, parental status, protected genetic information, or because all or part of an individual's income is derived from any public assistance program.
- **Office of Budget and Program Analysis (OBPA):** Provides centralized coordination and direction for the Department's budget, legislative and regulatory functions. It also provides analysis and evaluation to support the implementation of critical policies. OBPA administers the Department's budgetary functions and develops and presents budget-related matters to Congress, the news media, and the public.

- **Office of the Chief Economist (OCE):** Advises the Secretary on the economic situation in agricultural markets and the economic implications of policies and programs affecting American agriculture and rural communities. OCE serves as the focal point for economic intelligence and analysis related to agricultural markets and for risk assessment and cost-benefit analysis related to Department regulations affecting food and agriculture.

- **Office of the Chief Financial Officer (OCFO):** Shapes an environment for USDA officials eliciting the high-quality financial performance needed to make and implement effective policy, management, stewardship, and program decisions.

- **Office of the Chief Information Officer (OCIO):** Has the primary responsibility for the supervision and coordination of the design, acquisition, maintenance, use, and disposal of information technology by USDA agencies. OCIO strategically acquires and uses information technology resources to improve the quality, timeliness and cost-effectiveness of USDA services.

- **Office of Communications (OC):** Is USDA's central source of public information. The office provides centralized information services using the latest, most effective and efficient technology and standards for communication. It also provides the leadership, coordination, expertise, and counsel needed to develop the strategies, products, and services that are used to describe USDA initiatives, programs, and functions to the public.

- **Office of Congressional Relation (OCR):** Serves as the USDA's liaison with Congress. OCR works closely with members and staffs of various House and Senate committees to communicate the USDA's legislative agenda and budget proposals.

- **Office of the Executive Secretariat (OES):** Ensures that all Department officials are included in the correspondence drafting and policy-making process through a managed clearance and control system. Keeping policy officials informed of executive documents enhances the Secretary's ability to review sound and thought-out policy recommendations before making final decisions.

- **Office of the Inspector General (OIG):** Investigates allegations of crime against the Department's program, and promotes the economy and efficiency of its operations.

- **Office of the General Counsel (OGC):** Is an independent legal agency that provides legal advice and services to the Secretary of Agriculture and to all other officials and agencies of the Department with respect to all USDA programs and activities.

FSIS NEWS RELEASE, JANUARY 3, 2007

Louisiana Firm Recalls Head Cheese Products for Possible Listeria Contamination

USDA HOMELAND SECURITY EFFORTS [REPRINTED FROM USDA, 2004B]

Shortly after the events of September 11, 2001, USDA formed a Homeland Security Council within the Department to develop a Department-wide plan and coordinate efforts among all USDA agencies and offices. Efforts have focused on three key areas: food supply and agricultural production, USDA facilities, and USDA staff and emergency preparedness. In addition, USDA has worked closely with the rest of the Administration and Congress during the creation of the new Department of Homeland Security (DHS). Highlights include:

Protecting U.S. Borders from Invasive Pests and Diseases

USDA continues to enhance prevention efforts to keep foreign agricultural pests and diseases from entering the United States. Eighteen new veterinarians have been added to the agricultural quarantine inspection staff at borders and ports of entry to ensure strong preparedness programs are in place to protect U.S. agriculture, and 20 new food import surveillance officers have been added to ports of entry. Approximately 2,600 members of the border inspection force have been transferred to DHS. In close consultation with DHS, USDA will continue to train inspectors and set policy for plants, animals and commodities entering the U.S.

In March 2004, DHS, Bureau of Customs and Border Protection (CBF), Border Patrol (BP) announced the 2004 Arizona Border Control initiative to achieve operational control of the Arizona border and to support the DHS priority mission of anti-terrorism, detection, arrest and deterrence of all cross-border illicit trafficking. The initiative calls for more cooperation between DHS, the Department of Interior and USDA Forest Service in allowing more access to border public lands. Forest Service resource managers are working within environmental laws to enhance the BP's effectiveness without disturbing the environment. Forest Service Law Enforcement personnel are assisting BP in deterring illegal activities on National Forest System lands.

FSIS NEWS RELEASE, JANUARY 25, 2007

California Firm Recalls Pasta Salad with Chicken for Possible *Listeria* Contamination

The Department continues to maintain Forest Service Law Enforcement personnel along the hundreds of miles of contiguous National Forest System lands on the nation's northern and southern borders.

Protecting the Health of Farm Animals, Crops and Natural Resources

USDA has amended its regulations under the Agricultural Bioterrorism Protection Act of 2002 (Public Law 107-168) to allow provisional registration certificates to be issued pending completion of security risk assessments for individuals and entities possessing select agents or toxins. This provisional measure, which gives additional time for the U.S. Attorney General to complete security risk assessments, was needed to ensure that research, diagnostic, and educational programs were not disrupted. Provisional certificates of registration were issued to 75 entities, although 17 were exempt from regulations and 18 were withdrawn.

USDA has created a National Surveillance Unit within its Animal and Plant Health Inspection Service's Veterinary Services program. The unit will provide a focal point for the collection, processing and delivery of surveillance information that is needed in order to make risk analyses and take action. The unit will design surveillance strategies and coordinate and integrate surveillance activities, working collaboratively with other APHIS programs, state counterparts and stakeholders. This integrated approach will provide data and information necessary to guide actions to protect the health and enhance the marketability of the nation's livestock and poultry.

In an effort to develop a more comprehensive approach to animal health surveillance, USDA appointed a national surveillance system coordinator. The coordinator will work with the national surveillance effort and will also implement the enhancements recommended by the National Association of State Departments of Agriculture's Animal Health Safeguarding program.

The Department has worked with land-grant universities and state veterinary diagnostic laboratories around the country to create plant and animal health laboratory networks that have increased our capability to respond in an emergency.

USDA developed guidance documents to help remind farmers and ranchers of steps they can take to secure their operations. Information was posted on the USDA Web site and distributed through the USDA Extension system to reach every county and parish in the nation. USDA upgraded security efforts at USDA state and county offices, including a Web-based tracking system for disaster reporting, maintaining databases of fertilizer, food, feed, and seed listings, and coordinating with state and county Emergency Boards to assist during an emergency.

USDA held its 100th Foreign Animal Disease course in September 2003 for federal and state veterinarians from all 50 states to help states better prepare for accidental and intentional introductions of foreign animal diseases. USDA continues to

FSIS NEWS RELEASE, JANUARY 29, 2007

Arkansas Firm Recalls Ground Beef Products for Possible E. coli 0157:H7
Contamination

conduct emergency preparedness satellite seminars to share vital information for
federal and state veterinary officials and emergency planners, military representatives and academia on emergency preparedness. USDA has provided $43 million to
states, universities and tribal lands to increase homeland security prevention, detection and response efforts.

USDA developed the National Animal Health Reserve Corps to mobilize close to
300 private veterinarians from around the United States to assist locally during an
emergency.

In March 2004, USDA released a compact disc, "Food Security: The Threat to American Livestock," developed in conjunction with Auburn University, which addresses
emergency preparedness and brings homeland security issues to the forefront for private veterinary practitioners and other agricultural first responders as they conduct
their daily activities. It offers comprehensive information on infectious disease threats
to livestock, animal disease awareness briefings, standard veterinary medical information for diagnosing such diseases and emergency information gathering and reporting
mechanisms. Additionally, this new information resource outlines routine biosecurity
measures for on-site farm visits, recommends emergency response plans and suggests
disease-monitoring methods.

The Department has upgraded its Cooperative Extension Disaster Education Network systems and Web site with homeland security information.

USDA is spending $25 million to develop rapid tests for agents that pose the most
serious threats to our agricultural system. Some examples are foot-and-mouth disease,
rinderpest (cattle plague), and soybean and wheat rust.

Assuring a Safe Food Supply

USDA enhanced security at all food safety laboratories and expanded their capability and capacity to test for nontraditional microbial, chemical, and radiological
threat agents.

USDA established an Office of Food Security and Emergency Preparedness to serve as the lead coordinator in the development of the infrastructure and capacity to prevent, prepare for, and respond to an intentional attack on the U.S. food supply.

USDA prepared and distributed food security guidance documents to meat, poultry and egg products processors, transporters, distributors, and consumers.

USDA issued instructions to its field and laboratory personnel specifying actions that are to be taken when DHS raises the homeland security advisory system threat level to orange or red.

USDA coordinated with other government food agencies to develop prevention, detection and response procedures to protect the nation's food supply. USDA completed vulnerability assessments for domestic and imported meat, poultry and egg products. Results from these assessments are being used to develop strategies and countermeasures to reduce or eliminate the potential risks at vulnerable points along the farm-to-table continuum.

USDA hired new import surveillance liaison inspectors, who are stationed around the nation at import houses and ports of entry to enhance surveillance of imported products.

USDA developed a food security plan and has conducted training for employees, veterinarians, and inspectors on threat prevention and preparedness activities.

USDA food safety labs have a lead role in the formation of a network that integrates the Nation's laboratory infrastructure and sure capacity at the local, state, and federal levels.

USDA implemented the National Consumer Complaint Monitoring System, a surveillance and sentinel system that monitors and tracks food-related consumer complains 24/7 and serves as a real-time, early warning system of a potential attack on the food supply.

USDA conducted and participated in numerous drills and exercises at the federal and state level to hone response procedures.

FSIS NEWS RELEASE, FEBRUARY 28, 2007

South Carolina Firm Expands Recall of Chicken Breast Strips for Possible Listeria Contamination

FSIS NEWS RELEASE, MARCH 2, 2007

Washington Firm Recalls Ground Beef for Possible *E. coli* 0157: H7 Contamination

Protecting Research and Laboratory Facilities

USDA is spending $88 million for security assessments, background investigations, physical security upgrades and additional security personnel at research and laboratory facilities. Security assessments have been completed. Based on these findings, USDA is implementing security countermeasures. Furthermore, all USDA laboratories with select agents and toxins are in compliance with the requirements of the Agricultural Bioterrorism Protection Act of 2002.

All positions at USDA laboratories, federal or non-federal, are being examined to establish their public trust level and to identify the appropriate level of background investigation required. USDA has also developed policies and procedures for non-citizens working in USDA facilities, including name traces, background investigations, and a centralized tracking system. USDA also supports efforts to increase security at the university laboratories that it funds.

Emergency Preparedness and Response

A Department-wide National Interagency Incident Management System (NIIMS), based on the successful system utilized by USDA's Forest Service, is being implemented. This system includes incident command and control systems, coordination systems, training and qualification systems and publication management systems.

On February 28, 2003, President Bush signed Homeland Security Presidential Directive 5, which established a single, comprehensive approach to domestic incident management to be managed by the Secretary of the U.S. Department of Homeland Security (DHS). On March 1, 2004, DHS Secretary Tom Ridge announced the National Incident Management System (NIMS), the nation's first standardized management plan with a unified structure for federal, state, and local lines of government for incident response. USDA's NIMS uses the same systems within USDA for incident management as those standardized for the nation under NIMS.

USDA developed additional security procedures for use when the threat of terrorist attacks, as determined by the Homeland Security Advisory System, increases. This approach was integrated with the administration-wide Liberty Shield initiative.

USDA created APHIS Emergency Coordinator positions throughout the United States. These officers work closely with state animal health and emergency management officials to ensure the efficiency of each state's system for rapid detection of foreign animal diseases, and assist the sites with all aspects of emergency preparedness.

APHIS oversaw the distribution of $7.7 million in Emergency Management and Foreign Animal Disease (FAD) Surveillance funds. These funds were disbursed to states and Native American tribal nations to help enhance their emergency preparedness, surveillance programs, and laboratory networks.

USDA's APHIS Emergency Operations Center (AEOC), a world-class facility used to coordinate and support emergency response in APHIS, was completed. The AEOC, which enhances APHIS's ability to provide leadership during national emergencies, was used as a focal point during the Exotic Newcastle Disease (END) outbreak, the monkey pox outbreak and the confirmation of bovine spongiform encephalopathy (BSE) in Canada.

Case 1: Exotic Newcastle Disease (END) Outbreak

USDA's Animal and Plant Health Inspection Service posted the following in *Animal Disease Alert* February 2003:

Exotic Newcastle Disease (END) is a contagious and fatal viral disease affecting all species of birds. END is so virulent that many birds die without having developed any clinical signs. END can infect and cause death even in vaccinated poultry. Mortality is up to 90 percent of exposed birds. The U.S. Department of Agriculture's (USDA) Animal and Plant Health Inspection Service (APHIS) is the federal agency that takes the lead in excluding END from the Untied States and responding to any END outbreaks that do occur.

Clinical Signs

END affects the respiratory, nervous, and digestive systems. The incubation period for the disease ranges from 2 to 15 days. An infected bird may exhibit the following signs:

- Respiratory: sneezing, gasping for air, nasal discharge, coughing
- Digestive: greenish, watery diarrhea
- Nervous: depression, muscular tumors, drooping wings, twisting of head and neck, circling, complete paralysis
- Reduction in or complete loss of egg production
- Swelling of the tissues around the eyes and in the neck
- Sudden death

Introduction and Spread of END

END is spread primarily through direct contact between healthy birds and the bodily discharges of infected birds. The disease is transmitted through infected birds' droppings and secretions from the nose, mouth, and eyes.

END can also be spread easily by mechanical means. Virus-bearing material can be picked up on shoes and clothing and carried from an infected flock to a healthy one. The disease is often spread by vaccination and debeaking crews, manure haulers, rendering-truck drivers, feed-delivery personnel, poultry buyers, egg service people, and poultry-farm owners and employees.

END can survive for several weeks in a warm and humid environment on birds' feathers, manure, and other materials. It can survive for very long periods in frozen material. However, the virus is destroyed rapidly by dehydration and by the ultraviolet rays in sunlight.

Biosecurity Measures on the Farm

The only way to eradicate END from commercial poultry is by destroying all infected flocks and imposing strict quarantine and in-depth surveillance programs. Poultry producers should strengthen biosecurity practices to prevent the introduction of END into their flocks. Biosecurity is also important to protect backyard and hobby flocks. The following are tips on proper biosecurity practices:

- Permit only essential workers and vehicles on the premises.
- Provide clean clothing and disinfection facilities for employees.
- Clean and disinfect vehicles (including tires and undercarriages) entering and leaving the premises.
- Avoid visiting other poultry operations.
- Maintain an "all-in, all-out" philosophy of lock management with a single-age flock.
- Protect flocks from wild birds that may try to nest in poultry houses or feed with domesticated birds.
- Control movements associated with the disposal and handling of bird carcasses, litter, and manure.
- Take diseased birds to a diagnostic laboratory for examination.

Biosecurity Measures for Backyard-Poultry Enthusiasts and Pet-Bird Owners

END is also a threat to the caged-bird industry and poultry hobbyists. Birds illegally smuggled into the United States are not quarantined and tested by USDA and therefore may carry the END virus. Owners of pet birds should

- Request certification from suppliers that birds are legally imported or are of U.S. stock, are healthy prior to shipment, and will be transported in new or thoroughly disinfected containers.
- Maintain records of all sales and shipments of flocks.
- Isolate all newly purchased birds for at least 30 days.

- Implement stringent biosecurity practices to prevent the introduction of END to pets and backyard flocks.

What Happens in an Outbreak

In the event of an END outbreak, if you live on or near an affected premises, you may see individuals dressed in white suits, plastic boots, eye goggles, masks, and other special clothing before they enter your yard. These are federal or state animal health officials trained in disease control techniques. Animal health officials take great precautions not to spread END from one location to another.

Animal health officials who have *not* been in affected yards will canvas the area and place quarantines on the premises of neighbors who own birds. If they have not had exposure to infected birds, these birds will be monitored periodically for signs of disease until the quarantine can be lifted. If they have been exposed to the disease, they may need to be humanely depopulated in order to prevent further spread.

Once a premises is identified as END possible, federal and state personnel will humanely depopulate infected and exposed birds. The carcasses of the birds will be removed from the premises in a manner that prevents the spread of infection. Cleaning and disinfection of the area will then be conducted as quickly and thoroughly as possible.

In addition, to preventing END from being introduced into U.S. poultry flocks, APHIS requires that all imported birds (poultry, pet birds, birds exhibited at zoos, and ratites [i.e., flightless birds, such as kiwi, emu, ostrich, and rhea]) be tested and quarantined for diseases before entering the country.

Case 2: Monkeypox

On June 12, 2003, CDC published the following fact sheet about Monkeypox:

What Is Monkeypox?

Monkeypox is a rare viral disease that occurs mostly in central and western Africa. It is called 'Monkeypox' because it was first found in 1958 in laboratory monkeys. Blood tests of animals in Africa later found that other types of animals probably had monkeypox. Scientists also recovered the virus that causes monkeypox from an African squirrel. These types of squirrels might be the common host for the disease. Rats, mice, and rabbits can get monkeypox, too. Monkeypox was reported in humans for the first time in 1970.

Is There Monkeypox in the United States?

In early June 2003, monkey pox was reported among several people in the United States. Most of these people got sick after contact with pet prairie dogs that were sick with monkeypox. This was the first time that there has been an outbreak of monkeypox in the United States.

What Causes Monkeypox?

The disease is caused by *Monkeypox virus*. It belongs to a group of viruses that includes the smallpox virus (variola), the virus used in the smallpox vaccine (vaccinia), and the cowpox virus.

What Are the Signs and Symptoms of Monkeypox?

In humans, the signs and symptoms of monkeypox are like those of smallpox, but usually they are milder. Another difference is that monkeypox causes the lymph nodes to swell.

About 12 days after people are infected with the virus, they will get a fever, headache, muscle aches, and backache; their lymph nodes will swell; and they will feel tired. One to three days (or longer) after the fever starts, they will get a rash. This rash develops into raised bumps filled with fluid and often starts on the face and spreads, but it can start on other parts of the body too. The bumps go through several stages before they get crusty, scab over, and fall off. The illness usually lasts for two to four weeks.

Can You Die from Monkeypox?

In Africa, monkeypox has killed between 1 percent and 10 percent of people who get it. However, this risk would probably be lower in the United States, where nutrition and access to medical care are better.

How Do You Catch Monkeypox?

People can get monkeypox from an animal with monkeypox if they are bitten or if they touch the animal's blood, body fluids, or its rash. The disease also can spread from person to person through large respiratory droplets during long periods of face-to-face contact or by touching body fluids of a sick person or objects such as bedding or clothing contaminated with the virus.

How Do You Treat Monkeypox?

There is no specific treatment for monkeypox. In Africa, people who got the smallpox vaccine in the past had lower risk of monkeypox. CDC has sent out guidelines explaining when smallpox vaccine should be used to protect against monkeypox. For example, people taking care of someone infected with monkeypox should think about getting vaccinated.

Case 3: Bovine Spongiform Encephalopathy (BSE)

In 2004 the FDA published the following report:

Questions and Answers on Bovine Spongiform Encephalopathy

What Is BSE?

BSE (bovine spongiform encephalopathy) is a progressive neurological disorder of cattle; its symptoms are similar to a disease of sheep, called scrapie (a fatal, degenerative disease affecting the central nervous system of sheep and goats). BSE has been called "mad cow disease." BSE and scrapie both result from infection with a very unusual infectious agent. As of January 2004, more than 180,000 cases of BSE were confirmed in Great Britain in more than 35,000 herds of cattle. The epidemic peaked in January 1993 at almost 1,000 new cases per week. Although the origin of the disease is uncertain it may have resulted from the feeding of scrapie-containing meat and bone meal (MBM) to cattle or from feeding cattle MBM derived from a cow or other animal that developed the disease due to a spontaneous mutation (http://www.bseinquirey.gov.uk/). There is strong evidence and general agreement that the outbreak was amplified by feeding meat-and-bone meal prepared from cattle to young calves.

What Causes BSE?

The nature of the infectious agent that causes BSE and scrapie is unknown. Currently, the most accepted theory is that the agent is a modified form of a normal cell protein known as a prion. A prion is not a bacterium, parasite, or virus, and thus treatments usually used for treating or preventing bacterial infections (e.g., antibiotics) or viral infections are not effective against prions.

Where Is the BSE Agent Found in Cattle?

In cattle naturally infected with BSE, the BSE agent has been found in brain tissue, in the spinal cord, and in the retina of the eye. Additional experimental studies suggest that the BSE agent may also be present in the small intestine, tonsil, bone marrow, and dorsal root ganglia (lying along the vertebral column).

Which Countries Have Reported BSE?

The vast majority of cases of BSE (more than 97 percent as of 2003) have been reported from the United Kingdom during an epidemic. However, endemic cases have also been reported in other European countries including: the Republic of Ireland, Switzerland, France, Liechtenstein, Luxembourg, Netherlands, Portugal and Denmark. The numbers of reported cases by country are available on the Web site of the Office International des Epizooties (www.oie.int/). These numbers should be interpreted with caution, however, because the intensity and methods of surveillance probably vary over time and by country. In 2003 one case was reported in Canada and one in the United States (in a cow born in Canada).

How Was BSE spread?

It is thought that BSE was spread via meat-and-bone meal fed to cattle. The practice of using this material as a source of protein in cattle feed has been common for several decades. In the late 1970s there was a change in the production (rendering) process used to make this meat and bone meal. One hypothesis has been that this change permitted the infectious agent of scrapie (a transmissible spongiform encephalopathy, or TSE, of sheep) to survive the rendering process, and get transmitted to other animals, such as cows, that are fed meat-and-bone meal nutritional supplements. An inquiry by the British government has however concluded that scrapie-infected MBM was not the source of BSE, nor was the change in the rendering practices responsible for survival of the BSE agent. Rather, this inquiry has stated that BSE may have originated spontaneously as result of a genetic mutation and was amplified by the feeding of contaminated MBM to cattle. . . .

What Measures Has the U.S. Government Taken to Ensure That People Are Not Exposed to the BSE Agent in Foods?

The USDA is responsible for the health of U.S. livestock. To prevent BSE from entering the country, the USDA Animal and Plant Health Inspection Service (APHIS) has, since

1989, prohibited the importation of live ruminants from countries where BSE is known to exist in native cattle. On December 12, 1997, APHIS stopped the importation of live ruminants and most ruminant products, including meat, meat-and-bone meal, offals, glands, etc., from all of Europe. FDA is responsible for animal feeds in the U.S. In August 1997, FDA prohibited the use of most mammalian protein in the manufacture of animal feeds given to ruminants. Following the discovery of one cow with BSE in the U.S., the USDA and FDA have announced additional measures to enhance protections against the spread of BSE in U.S. cattle and to minimize human exposure to bovine materials that may contain the BSE agent. USDA has issued an interim final rule (Federal Register January 12, 2004 Vol. 69, Number 7) removing downer animals and specified risk materials and tissues from the human food chain; requiring additional process controls for establishments using advance meat recovery (AMR); holding meat from cattle that have been targeted for BSE surveillance testing until the test has confirmed negative; and prohibiting the air injection stunning of cattle http://www.aphis.usda.gov/lpa/isses/bse/bse.html).

In January 2004, FDA proposed additional safeguards including: excluding brain, spinal cord, gut and eyes of older animals from human food and from rendered material in animal feeds, eliminating poultry litter, cow blood and processed plate waste as feed ingredients for cattle, labeling requirements for pet food, and additional control measures to prevent cross contamination of feed and feed ingredients at food mills. In addition, since 1990, the USDA has led an interagency surveillance program for evidence of BSE in the U.S. USDA has tested 20,000 animals annually for each of the last two years, and approximately 75 percent of these were downers at slaughter (http://www.aphis.usda.gov /lpa/issues/be/se-surveillance.html).

A BSE risk assessment performed by Harvard University's Center for Risk Analysis at the School of Public Health concluded that even if BSE were to occur in the U.S. the measures already taken would largely prevent its spread to animals or humans, and the disease would gradually disappear over a number of years (2001, www.aphis.usda.gov/lpa /issues/bse/bse-riskassmt.html).

How Is the BSE Agent Detected?

The presence of the BSE agent in tissues is generally determined by injecting animals, usually mice, with samples, then observing the mice to see if they die and have characteristic brain tissue changes. Mouse inoculation studies take a long time (up to 700 days) to detect the agent, and a negative result (that is, lack of brain tissue changes in the injected mice) may only mean that there was too little of the infectious agent to cause symptoms, not that the material was completely free of the infectious agent. It is also possible to detect the presence of the abnormal prion protein in tissues (such as brain) using special staining procedures although these methods do not allow an accurate assessment of infectivity of the infected material.

Does BSE or a Similar Disease Occur in Humans?

BSE belongs to a group of progressive degenerative neurological disease known as transmissible spongiform encephalopathies (TSEs). TSE diseases are always fatal. The TSE dis-

FSIS NEWS RELEASE, MARCH 27, 2007

Missouri Firm Recalls Bacon due to Insufficient Cooling

eases include scrapie, which affects sheep and goats; transmissible mink encephalopathy; feline (cat) spongiform encephalopathy; and chronic wasting disease of deer and elk. There are six TSE diseases that affect people: kuru, classical Creutzfeldt-Jacob disease (CJD) and variant Creutzfeldt-Jakob disease (vCJD), Gerstmann-Sträussler-Scheinker syndrome, fatal familial insomnia, and sporadic fatal insomnia. The human diseases are very rare; for example, classical CJD has been well studied and occurs sporadically worldwide at a rate of about one case per one million people each year. (FDA, 2004)

OTHER EFFORTS

The USDA (2004b) report continues:

Protecting Other Infrastructure

USDA Forest Service Law Enforcement continues to conduct security assessments of research facilities and air tanker bases nationwide.

USDA's Forest Service continues to enhance efforts to protect National Forest System lands and facilities, including dams, reservoirs, pipelines, water treatment plants, power lines and energy production facilities on government property.

Securing Information Technology

USDA reviewed and conducted tests of all USDA network systems to assess threat levels. The security status of key IT personnel was upgraded. The training and planning sessions were also upgraded to strengthen the Department's continuity of operations plans.

The Department enhanced the monitoring and surveillance of its telecommunications network and assisted with offsite facilities enhancement to prepare for emergencies.

Continuity of Operations

Full and complete continuity of operations policies and plans are developed for all USDA agencies and offices. Alternate work places have been upgraded and improved to avoid disruption in the work of USDA. USDA's National Interagency Incident Management System (NIIMS) is being expanded Department wide and training in NIIMS is being extended to include more employees.

FSIS NEWS RELEASE, APRIL 13, 2007

Minnesota Firm Recalls Sausage Products That May Contain *Staphylococcus aureus* Enterotoxin

Audits and Investigations

USDA launched an aggressive initiative to identify and protect USDA physical and cyber-based assets, prevent USDA assets from being used against the U.S., and preclude USDA programs from being used to finance terrorism.

USDA's Forest Service Law Enforcement continues to participate with Federal Bureau of Investigation Joint Terrorism task forces nationwide on investigations related to domestic terrorism.

Seventeen audit reports have been issued and 27 audits that impact homeland security are currently in the process of being completed. The audits review existing controls, identify potential vulnerabilities and recommend additional measures to protect USDA assets and resources. USDA is also participating in interagency audit efforts at the federal level to ensure that government-wide and cross-agency vulnerabilities are addressed.

USDA has initiated 47 criminal investigations related to counterterrorism and homeland security activities and participates in efforts to target businesses transferring money overseas to terrorists groups.

In fiscal year 2003, USDA's Office of the Inspector General issued seven audit reports relating to homeland security and investigations yielded 17 indictments, 23 convictions, and $2.5 million in monetary results.

APHIS

According to APHIS Services (2007), APHIS, the Animal and Plant Health Inspection Service, is responsible for "protecting and promoting U.S. agricultural health, administering the Animal Welfare Act, and carrying out wildlife damage management activities."

The APHIS mission is an integral part of U.S. Department of Agriculture's (USDA) efforts to provide the nation with safe and affordable food. Without APHIS protecting America's animal and plant resources from agricultural pests and diseases, threats to our food supply and to our nation's economy would be enormous. For example, if Mediterranean fruit fly and Asian longhorned beetle, two major agriculture pests, were left unchecked by APHIS, production and marketing losses of several billions of dollars would occur annually in this country. And, if APHIS was not on the job as the first line of defense, 24 hours a day, 7 days a week, animal diseases like foot-and-mouth disease and bovine spongiform encephalopathy (mad cow disease) could devastate our livestock industry and our food supply. All these plant and animal pests and disease threats could cost billions of dollars in lost domestic and international markets and have a huge impact on U.S. consumers, but APHIS has aggressively and successfully worked to prevent and respond to these situations.

In recent years, the scope of APHIS's protection function has expanded beyond pest and disease management. Because of its technical expertise and leadership in assessing and regulating the risk associated with agricultural imports, APHS has assumed a greater role in the global agricultural arena. Now, the agency must respond to other countries' animal and plant health import requirements and negotiate science-based standards that ensure America's agricultural exports, worth over $50 billion annually, are protected from unjustified trade restrictions.

In response to needs expressed by the American people and Congress, APHIS's protection role also includes wildlife damage management, the welfare of animals, human health and safety, and ecosystems vulnerable to invasive pests and pathogens. In carrying out its diverse protection responsibilities, APHIS makes every effort to address the needs of all those involved in the U.S. agricultural sector.

In November 2003, Dr. Charles Lambert explained the function of both APHIS and FSIS in a presentation, *Agroterrorism: The Threat to America's Breadbasket*, before the Senate Committee on Governmental Affairs. The following descriptions of both APHIS and FSIS in their roles after September 11, 2001, are taken primarily from Dr. Lambert's presentation.

Sharing Information

Events since 9/11 have led APHIS to take steps to increase its network of partners and better share information with cooperators. In any emergency situation, the better prepared with information and training everyone is the more effective the response will be.

USDA knows that there can never be enough people involved in safeguarding activities. APHIS, for example, is proactively training and talking to stakeholder organizations like the National Association of State Departments of Agriculture, the United States Animal Health Association, university systems, and country extension agents about how to effectively safeguard the United States against the potential introduction of a foreign plant or animal pathogen.

To get the information out to those who will see the disease first, APHIS, in 2001, held three two-week long Foreign Animal Disease Awareness training seminars for federal-state veterinarians from all 50 states. These seminars help federal and state animal health

FSIS NEWS RELEASE, APRIL 18, 2007

Wisconsin Firm Recalls Salami Products Due to Undeclared Allergen

managers prepare for both accidental and intentional introductions of foreign animal disease, improve communications, and strengthen cooperative partnerships. In addition, APHIS has been holding Emergency Preparedness Satellite Seminars yearly to share vital information with veterinary practitioners across the country on how to identify and respond to an animal health emergency. More than 1,700 federal and state veterinary officials and emergency planners, military representatives, and veterinary college students and professors have participated in the satellite broadcasts.

Working with federal counterparts is essential. In the event of an agroterror attack on our homeland, the Department of Homeland Security (DHS) and APHIS will work as partners to safeguard America's food and agricultural resources. DHS will lead the team of first responders to contain and manage the threat while APHIS provides crucial scientific and diagnostic expertise. This expertise will be critical in managing a potential disease outbreak as well as assisting intelligence and first-responder agencies to find those responsible for the terrorist attack. In preparation, APHIS has established a liaison at DHS who is responsible for the inclusion of agroterror response information into existing DHS first responder training, as well as beginning the development of specific agroterrorism training for traditional first responders.

APHIS has also entered into interagency agreements with other government agencies such as the Defense Threat Reduction Agency and the U.S. Army Research, Development, and Engineering Command. These agreements are allowing APHIS to benefit from activities such as open source intelligence gathering on potential threats to U.S. agriculture and the evaluation of newly developed rapid diagnostic equipment.

Improving Detection and Surveillance

APHIS continues to improve its capabilities in the area of animal disease detection. For example, APHIS regularly holds foreign animal disease diagnostician training for federal and state veterinary medical officers at the Plum Island Animal Disease center in New York. More than 300 active state and federal officials have received this training and are ready to respond to suspicious animal disease cases.

We know that smuggled agricultural products present a higher risk of introducing exotic pests and diseases into the United States than does international trade. With this in mind, APHIS created the Safeguarding, Interdiction, and Trade Compliance (SITC) team three years ago to address this risk to U.S. agriculture. The team is now working in partnership with the Department of Homeland Security and state and local law enforcement officials to mitigate the risk of smuggled commodities in shipments from foreign companies and passengers.

In addition, APHIS monitors pests and diseases overseas in order to determine the risk or possibility that the disease could impact U.S. agriculture. APHIS has implemented the Offshore Pest Information System, which will monitor and document changes in distribution and outbreak status of specific, designated high risk exotic plant pests and animal diseases, including pathways, in their countries of origin. APHIS currently has 64 Foreign Service Officials stationed in 27 countries on six continents; these officials are working closely with their foreign counterparts to collect this information and provide data to the agency's headquarters. Based on this information, U.S. safeguarding efforts can be focused accordingly.

For example, soybean rust is a disease that could devastate the soybean growers within the United States, and APHIS remains very concerned about the likelihood and effect of an introduction into the United States. Because of this, APHIS is currently conducting a comprehensive pathway risk analysis for soybean rust. The program is collecting information from importers, exports, the soybean industry, scientific experts, and foreign governments in order to better determine the potential pathways for the spread of soybean rust to the United States. Once this analysis is completed, it will be reviewed by APHIS to determine the appropriate next steps to take, including the possible development of new regulations. These efforts will help prepare for natural introductions of the disease as well.

Case 4: Soybean Rust

Soybean rust is an airborne disease and can remain airborne throughout large sections of soybean-growing areas, spreading from south to north on seasonal wind currents and persisting on alternate host plants. The rust spores could over winter on any numb or host plant species in the southeastern United States. Green beans, kidney beans, lima beans, and cowpeas are . . . at risk. The fungi cause lesions on the bottom of leaves in mid to late summer. The yield losses result when the rust lesions cover most of the leaf area, causing premature defoliation. Yield losses associated with soybean rust have generally ranged form 10 to 80 percent if untreated. (USDA, 2007)

Managing an Emergency

One of the most important developments in increasing the effectiveness of our emergency response is the implementation of the National Interagency Incident

FSIS NEWS RELEASE, APRIL 20, 2007

Pennsylvania Firm Recalls Beef Products for Possible *E. coli* O157:H7
Contamination

Management System or NIIMS. The implementation of NIIMS is consistent with
Presidential Homeland Security Directive 5, which directs that the U.S. government
will have a single, comprehensive approach to incident management, including a
National Incident Management System (NIMS). The NIMS, currently under development, will update and make applicable across all disciplines the NIIMS. By providing uniformity in organizational structure and terminology for emergency
responders, NIIMS, and the forthcoming NIMS, will facilitate coordination among
responders from different agencies and jurisdictions. This concept of emergency response coordination has been used widely in the emergency management community, including USDA's Forest Service in responding to fires.

NIIMS/NIMS provide tools that help leadership determine the seriousness of an incident by assessing the potential duration and geographic spread of the situation. It
provides a classification system to guide the commitment of personnel and material
resources. NIIMS/NIMS also allows leaders to adapt the scope of the response efforts
to address incidents that grow in size and complexity.

Select Agents

APHIS is also responsible for the implementation of the Agricultural Bioterrorism
Protection Act of 2002, a subpart of the Public Health Security and Bio-terrorism Preparedness Response Act of 2002. Under the Agricultural Bioterrorism Protection Act,
entities that possess, use, or transfer agents or toxins deemed a severe threat to animal
or plant health or products must notify and register with the secretary of the U.S. Department of Agriculture (USDA). Under the Public Health Security and Bio-terrorism
Preparedness Response Act, entities that posses, used, or transfer toxins or agents
deemed a severe threat to public health must register with the Secretary of the U.S Department of Health and Human Services (HHS).

Agents and toxins that appear on both the HHS and USDA's lists of agents and toxins have been designated "overlap agents," since both USDA and HHS have regulatory

FSIS NEWS RELEASE, APRIL 20, 2007

California Firm Recalls Ground Beef Products for Possible *E. coli* O157:H7 Contamination

authority over them. An entity/facility that needs to register in order to possess, use, or transfer an overlap agent must submit its registration information to either APHIS or the Centers for Disease Control and Prevention (CDC) but is not required to submit the application to both APHIS and CDC (Lambert, 2003).

FSIS

APHIS Services (2007) notes that the events surrounding September 11, 2001, have heightened not only the already vigilant efforts of APHIS, but also those of the USDA's Food Safety and Inspection Service (FSIS). The FSIS regulates and inspects meat and poultry products to ensure that they are safe, wholesome, and accurately labeled. FSIS has made great strides by introducing science-based policies designed to reduce the risks of foodborne illnesses. Food security is vital to our nation's homeland security, and FSIS has assessed its emergency preparedness and response capabilities in light of this reality.

Each day, FSIS has more than 7,600 inspectors and veterinarians in more than 6,000 federal meat, poultry, and egg product plants, and at ports-of-entry, to prevent, detect, and respond to food-related emergencies. With a strong food safety infrastructure already in place, FSIS has been focusing on fortifying existing programs and improving internal and external lines of communication. FSIS has an extensive system in place to properly respond to a food emergency resulting from terrorism, and as part of the homeland security supplement the agency used $1.5 million to hire an additional 20 inspectors for imported meat and poultry.

Office of Food Security and Emergency Preparedness

To date, FSIS has undertaken a number of initiatives to protect meat, poultry, and egg products from the potential of a terrorist attack. Immediately following September 11, FSIS established the Food Bio-security Action Team (F-BAT). The charge of F-BAT was to coordinate all activities related to biosecurity, counterterrorism, and

FSIS NEWS RELEASE, MAY 1, 2007

California Firm Recalls Ready-To-Eat Turkey Products for Possible *Listeria* Contamination

emergency preparedness within FSIS. These activities are coordinated with USDA's Homeland Security Council, other government agencies, and industry. Currently, FSIS's newly created Office of Food Security and Emergency Preparedness (OFSEP) has assumed the responsibilities of F-BAT and serves as the centralized office within FSIS for food security issues.

OFSEP interacts closely with USDA's Homeland Security Council and represents the agency on all food security matters throughout the federal government, as well as in state and local activities. The office's mission is to lead in the development of the agency's infrastructure and to prepare for, prevent, and responded to, deliberate attacks or other threats to the U.S. food supply.

As the lead coordinator and primary point of contact on all food security and emergency preparedness activities within FSIS, OFSEP focuses primarily on:

- Emergency preparedness and response
- Federal/state/industry relations
- Continuity of operations (COOP)
- Scientific expertise in chemical, biological, and radiological terrorism
- Security clearance and safeguarding classified information.

To ensure coordination of these activities involves all program areas of the agency, OFSEP established a new standing advisory group, the Food Security Advisory Team (FSAT), comprised of representatives of the major program areas within FSIS, to provide program-specific technical support.

Coordination with Federal, State, and Local Agencies

FSIS collaborates and coordinates closely with its state partners to ensure an effective prevention and response program. Some of the many state organizations FSIS works with include the Association of Food and Drug Officials (AFDO), the Association of State and Territorial Health Officials (ASTHO), and the National Association of State Departments of Agriculture (NASDA). Most recently, FSIS teamed with FDA in cosponsoring a joint meeting between ASTHO and NASDA, entitled "Homeland Security: Protecting Agriculture, the Food Supply, and Public Health—The Role of the States." The purpose of this meeting was to enhance collaboration between state public health and agriculture agencies and the federal government. Both the secretary of agriculture and the secretary of health and human services were on hand for this joint meeting. APHIS and FSIS receive threat information and written reports form the intelligence community to update the department on terrorist threat reporting relative to food and agriculture. This intelligence allows APHIS and FSIS to prioritize their response based on both perceived vulnerability and what is known of the terrorist threat.

FSIS also works closely with the White House Homeland Security Council, the Department of Homeland Security (DHS), and the USDA Homeland Security staff to coordinate strategies to protect the food supply from an intentional attack. For example, FSIS, FDA, and DHS are working with industry partners to encourage the establishment of a new food information sharing and analysis organization for the food sector. This public/private partnership will aid in the protection of the critical food infrastructure by increasing information sharing about threats, incidents, and vulnerabilities related to food.

Surveillance and Detection Activities

In fiscal year 2003, FSIS undertook many new initiatives, as well as strengthened its existing infrastructure, to enhance its ability to detect any potential intentional threat to the food supply.

FSIS has strengthened its controls to protect the public from the entry of contaminated product from abroad. FSIS continually assesses foreign country inspection systems to ensure that they maintain food safety standards and operations equivalent to the U.S. inspection system. To supplement the activities of its import inspectors, FSIS has added import surveillance liaison inspectors who are on duty at U.S. ports-of-entry. As of March 2003, 20 of these inspectors have been conducting a broader range of surveillance activities than traditional import inspectors. They also work to improve coordination with other agencies that are tasked with ensuring the safety of imported food products.

Also in 2003, FSIS made significant enhancements to its national surveillance system for monitoring and tracking food-related consumer complaints. The Consumer Complaint Monitoring System (CCMS) serves as a real-time early warning system for potential terrorist attacks on the food supply. CCMS uses an electronic database to record, triage, and track food-related consumer complaints. The CCMS has been upgraded to provide 24/7 coverage, and complaints can be entered at FSIS field offices and accessed at headquarters in order to provide a more real-time response.

As part of FSIS's initiative to better prepare its workforce to respond to a potential terrorist attack, employee directives were issued in March to instruct in-plant and laboratory personnel on how to respond when the DHS raises the Homeland Security Advisory System threat level to Orange or Red (see case 5, below). The directives include additional inspection tasks and laboratory testing requirements. They also encourage FSIS personnel to cooperate with establishments by altering plant management to the threat level change and verifying that they are carrying out necessary food security procedures. FSIS is developing additional compounds to the directive that will address computer security, import reinspection, communication, and human health surveillance monitoring.

Case 5: Homeland Security Advisory System

In the U.S., the Homeland Security Advisory System (terror alert level) is a color-coded terrorism threat advisory scale. The different levels trigger specific action by federal agencies and state and local governments, and they affect the level of security at some airports and other public facilities. The five colored-coded threat levels, reflecting the probability of a terrorist attack and its potential gravity, are:

- *Severe* (red): severe risk
- *High* (orange): high risk
- *Elevated* (yellow): significant risk
- *Guarded* (blue): general risk
- *Low* (green): low risk

Strengthening Laboratory Capabilities

In fiscal year 2003, FSIS made important progress on the scientific front. FSIS laboratories expanded their capability to test for nontraditional microbial, chemical, and radiological threat agents and increased their surge capacity. In addition, construction is underway on a Biosecurity Level 3 laboratory that will enable FSIS to conduct analyses on a larger range of potential bioterrorism agents.

Additionally, FSIS is participating with the HHS, EPA, the Department of Energy, and the states to integrate the nation's laboratory infrastructure and surge capacity. Over 60 laboratories representing 27 states and five federal agencies have agreed to participate in the Food Emergency Response Network, or FERN. FERN, which is coordinated by FSIS and FDA, focuses on method validation, research, training, proficiency programs, surveillance, response and surge capacity, and communication. By providing a greater capability to test for biological, chemical, and radiological agents in food,

---

FSIS NEWS RELEASE, MAY 10, 2007

Minnesota Firm Recalls Beef Trim Due to Possible *E. coli* O157:H7 Contamination

---

FERN will provide the nation with a strong scientific infrastructure to better protect the food supply.

FSIS also participates in the Electronic Laboratory Exchange Network, or eLEXNET. This Internet-based system will be the mechanism by which the FERN laboratories report results form all bioterrorism or chemical terrorism related analyses. FSIS also participates in the CDC Laboratory Response Network that provides training and microbiological methods to participants.

FSIS's Information Sharing and Outreach Activities

Just as all parts of the food supply chain work to ensure that meat, poultry, and egg products are safe and wholesome, each part of the food supply chain also plays a role in ensuring that products are secure from intentional contamination. FSIS has made a strong effort to reach out to industry to encourage food security programs. In May 2002, FSIS released voluntary security guidelines for food processors. The guidelines were designed to help plants identify ways to strengthen their security plans.

In August 2003, the agency published guidelines for those that transport and distribute FSIS-regulated products. These voluntary guidelines are designed to help facilities and shippers that process or transport meat, poultry, and egg products strengthen their food safety and security plans. Using these guidelines, FSIS is currently working with food processing plants, transporters, and distributors to encourage reviews of their security procedures.

A new publication entitled *Food Safety and Food Security: What Consumers Need to Know* offers comprehensive and practical information about safe food handling practices, foodborne illness, and ways to keep food safe during an emergency. It also includes information on how to report any suspected instances of food tampering.

When information is shared between all stakeholders committed to providing safe meat, poultry, and egg products to consumers, everyone is better prepared to react when an emergency situation arises.

FSIS NEWS RELEASE, JUNE 21, 2007

Illinois Firm Recalls Beef and Chicken Bases Due to Mislabeling

FSIS Preparedness Efforts

As FSIS works to provide food security information to external groups, the agency is also working to ensure that its own employees are well trained and prepared to handle crisis situations. When the agency's voluntary food security guidelines were released, employees were trained in the application of the guidelines. FSIS has also initiated a comprehensive two-year training and education effort for all agency employees. This food security awareness training focuses on preventing attacks on the food supply and emphasizes the importance of cooperation between federal, state, and local governments and the private sector. Because of this, representatives from other federal agencies, state governments, and local responders have also attended this FSIS training.

FSIS continues to identify vulnerabilities in the food supply chain and dedicate resources to develop ways to minimize food security risks. These efforts will help to ensure that safety and security of the U.S. meat, poultry, and egg products (Lambert, 2003).

The strong working relationships that the federal agencies, states, and industry have are vital to the efforts to safeguard U.S. agriculture. Preserving traditional relationships and building new ones, such as with DHS, will strengthen the efforts. Likewise, USDA remains committed—through biosecurity and emergency preparedness activities—to ensuring the continued good health and value of U.S. agriculture.

Case 6: Foodborne Illness

USDA (2005) points out that foodborne illness often shows up as flu-like symptoms such as nausea, vomiting, diarrhea, or fever. Each organism may cause different symptoms. Age and physical condition place some persons at higher risk than others for any type of bacteria. Very young children, pregnant women, the elderly, and people with compromised immune systems (such as people undergoing cancer treatments, or that have kidney disease, AIDS, diabetes, etc.) are at greatest risk from any harmful bacteria. Some persons may become ill after consuming only a few bacteria; others may remain symptom-free after consuming thousands. Symptoms usually occur between one hour and up to three weeks after eating contaminated food.

REFERENCES

APHIS Services. 2007. *About APHIS*, www. aphis.usda.gov (accessed June 19, 2007).

CDC. 2003. *What You Should Know about Monkeypox*. Washington, DC: Department of Health and Human Services.

FDA. 2004. *Bovine Spongiform Encephalopathy (BSE)*, at http://www.FDA.gov/cber/bse/bseqa.htm (accessed June 16, 2007)

Lambert, C. 2003. *Agroterrorism: The Threat to America's Breadbasket*. Washington, DC: Statement presented to Senate Committee on Governmental Affairs, www.senate.gov/~gov _affairs/index.cfm?Furseaction=Hearings (accessed June 25, 2007).

RAND. 2003. *Agroterrorism: What Is the Threat and What Can Be Done about It?* Santa Monica, CA: RAND Corp.

USDA. 2003. *Exotic Newcastle Disease*. United States Department of Agriculture. Animal Disease Alert.

USDA. 2004a. *About USDA*, at www.USDA.gov.

USDA. 2004b. *USDA Homeland Security Efforts*. Washington, DC: United States Department of Agriculture, at www.usda.gov.

USDA. 2005. *What Consumers Need to Know . . . Foodborne Illness*. www.fsis.usda.gov/OA/ pubs/fac_fbi.htm (accessed June 25, 2007).

USDA. 2006. *Agencies and Offices*. Washington, DC: United States Department of Agriculture, at www.usda.gov.

USDA. 2007. Soybean Rust Information Site, at http://www.usda.gov.soybeanrust/ (accessed June 20, 2007).

The Bioterrorism Act and the FDA

In the domestic market, substandard items and adulterated foods abound. Formaldehyde is used to lengthen the shelf life of rice noodles and tofu in some Asian countries. Borax is commonly used to preserve fish and meats in Indonesia and elsewhere.

—*Margie Mason, 2007*

On June 12, 2002, President George W. Bush signed into law the Public Health Security and Bioterrorism Preparedness and Response Act of 2002 (P.L. 107-188, H.R. 3448), which was intended to bolster the nation's ability to respond effectively to bioterrorist threats and other public health emergencies. The act builds on the programs and authorities established in Title III of the Public Health Service (PHS) Act by the Public Health Threats and Emergencies Act of 2000 (P.L. 106505, title I).

P.L. 107-188 is a five-year authorization bill, which calls for a total of $2.4 billion in funding in FY2002, $2.0 billion in FY2003, and such sums as may be necessary for the remaining years. The act authorizes the secretary of Health and Human Services (HHS) to upgrade and renovate facilities at the Centers for Disease Control and Prevention (CDC), purchase smallpox vaccine, expand the national stockpile of drugs, vaccines, and other emergency medical supplies, and provide grants to state and local governments and hospitals to improve preparedness and planning. The secretaries of HHS and Agriculture are required to register and regulate facilities that handle potentially dangerous biological agents.

Of interest to the reader of this text is the antiterrorism legislation within the Act, which includes provisions to protect the nation's food and drug supply and enhance agricultural security, including new regulatory powers for the Food and Drug Administration (FDA) to block the importation of unsafe foods. These provisions and requirements are in Title III Subtitle A—Protection of Food Supply—of the act.

FDA NOTE

Nearly 20 percent of all imports into the U.S. are food and food products. (FDA, 2003)

21 CFR PART 170.3 FOOD FOR HUMAN CONSUMPTION: DEFINITIONS

For the purposes of this chapter and the material that follows, the following definitions, adapted from 21 CFR Part 170.3 (2004), apply:

General Terms

Secretary—means the secretary of Health and Human Services.

Department—means the department of Health and Human Services.

Commissioner—means the commissioner of Food and Drugs.

Act—means the Federal Food, Drug, and Cosmetic Act.

Food additives—includes all substances not exempted by section 201(s) of the act, the intended use of which results or may reasonably be expected to result, directly or indirectly, either in their becoming a component of food or otherwise affecting the characteristics of food. A material used in the production of containers and packages is subject to the definition if it may reasonably be expected to become a component, or to affect the characteristics, directly or indirectly, or food packed in the container. "Affecting the characteristics of food" does not include such physical effects as protecting contents of packages, preserving shape, and preventing moisture loss. If there is no migration of a packaging component from the package to the food, it does not become a component of the food and thus is not a food additive. A substance that does not become a component of food, but that is used, for example, in preparing an ingredient of the food to give a different flavor, texture, or other characteristic in the food, may be a food additive.

A food contact substance—is any substance that is intended for use as a component of materials used in manufacturing, packing, packaging, transporting, or holding food if such use is not intended to have any technical effect in such food.

Common use in food—means a substantial history of consumption of a substance for food use by a significant number of consumers.

Substance—includes a food or food component consisting of one or more ingredients.

Scientific procedures—include those human, animal, analytical, and other scientific studies, whether published or unpublished, appropriate to establish the safety of a substance.

Nonperishable processed food—means any processed food not subject to rapid decay or deterioration that would render it unfit for consumption. Examples are flour, sugar, cereals, packaged cookies, and crackers. Not included are hermetically sealed foods or manufactured dairy products and other processed foods requiring refrigeration.

Related Food Terms

The following general food categories are established to group specific related foods together for the purpose of establishing tolerances or limitations for the use of direct human food ingredients. . . . :

- Baked goods and baking mixes, including all ready-to-eat and ready-to-bake products, flours, and mixes requiring preparation before serving.
- Beverages, alcoholic, including malt beverages, wines, distilled liquors, and cocktail mix.
- Beverages and beverage bases, nonalcoholic, including only special or spice teas, soft drinks, coffee substitutes, and fruit and vegetable flavored gelatin drinks.
- Breakfast cereals, including ready-to-eat and instant and regular hot cereals.
- Cheeses, including curd and whey cheese, cream, natural, grating, processed, spread, dip, and miscellaneous cheeses.
- Chewing gum, including all forms.
- Coffee and tea, including regular, decaffeinated, and instant types.
- Condiments and relishes, including plain seasoning sauces and spreads, olives, pickles, and relishes, but not spices or herbs.
- Confections and frostings, including candy and flavored frostings, marshmallows, baking chocolate, and brown lump, rock, maple, powdered, and raw sugars.
- Dairy product analogs, including nondairy milk, frozen or liquid creamers, coffee whiteners, toppings, and other nondairy products.
- Egg products, including liquid, frozen, or dried eggs, and egg dishes made therefrom, i.e., egg roll, egg foo young, egg salad, and frozen multicourse egg meals, but not fresh eggs.

- Fats and oils, including margarine, dressings for salads, butter, salad oils, shortenings and cooking oils.
- Fish products, including all prepared main dishes, salads, appetizers, frozen multi-course meals, and spreads containing fish, shellfish, and other aquatic animals, but not fresh fish.
- Fresh eggs, including cooked eggs and egg dishes made only from fresh shell eggs.
- Fresh fish, including only fresh and frozen fish, shellfish, and other aquatic animals.
- Fresh fruits and fruit juices, including only raw fruits, citrus, melons, and berries, and home-prepared "ades" and punches made therefrom.
- Fresh meats, including only fresh or home-frozen beef or veal, pork, lamb or mutton and home-prepared fresh meat-containing dishes, salads, appetizers, or sandwich spreads made therefrom.
- Fresh poultry, including only fresh or home-frozen poultry and game birds and home-prepared fresh poultry-containing dishes, salads, appetizers, or sandwich spreads made therefrom.
- Fresh vegetables, tomatoes, and potatoes, including only fresh and home-prepared vegetables.
- Frozen dairy desserts and mixes, including ice cream, ice milks, sherbets, and other frozen dairy desserts and specialties.
- Fruit and water ices, including all frozen fruit and water ices.
- Gelatins, puddings, and fillings, including flavored gelatin desserts, puddings, custards, parfaits, pie fillings and gelatin base salads.
- Grain products and pastas, including macaroni and noodle products, rice dishes, and frozen multicourse meals, without meat or vegetables.
- Gravies and sauces, including all meat sauces and gravies, and tomato, milk, buttery, and specialty sauces.
- Hard candy and cough drops, including all hard type candies.
- Herbs, seeds, spices, seasonings, blends, extracts, and flavorings, including all natural and artificial spices, blends, and flavors.
- Jams and jellies, commercial, including only commercially processed jams, jellies, fruit butters, preserves, and sweet spreads.
- Jams and jellies, home-prepared, including only home-prepared jams, jellies, fruit butters, preserves, and sweet spreads.
- Meat products, including all meats and meat containing dishes, salads, appetizers, frozen multicourse meat meals, and sandwich ingredients prepared by commercial processing or using commercially processed meats with home preparation.
- Milk, whole and skim, including only whole, low fat, and skim fluid milks.
- Milk products, including flavored milks and milk drinks, dry milks, toppings, snack dips, spreads, weight control milk beverages, and other milk origin products.

- Nuts and nut products, including whole or shelled tree nuts, peanuts, coconut, and nut and peanut spreads.
- Plant protein products, including the National Academy of Sciences/National Research Council "reconstituted vegetable protein" category, and meat, poultry, and fish substitutes, analogs, and extender products made from plant proteins.
- Poultry products, including all poultry and poultry-containing dishes, salads, appetizers, frozen multicourse poultry meals, and sandwich ingredients prepared by commercial processing or using commercially processed poultry with home preparation.
- Processed fruits and fruit juices, including all commercially processed fruits, citrus, berries, and mixtures; salads, juices and juice punches, concentrates, dilutions, "ades," and drink substitutes made therefrom.
- Processed vegetables and vegetable juices, including all commercially processed vegetables, vegetable dishes, frozen multicourse vegetable meals, and vegetable juices and blends.
- Snack foods, including chips, pretzels, and other novelty snacks.
- Soft candy, including candy bars, chocolates, fudge, mints, and other chewy or nougat candies.
- Soups, home-prepared, including meat, fish, poultry, vegetable, and combination home-prepared soups.
- Soups and soup mixes, including commercially prepared meat, fish, poultry, vegetable, and combination soups and soup mixes.
- Sugar, white, granulated, including only white granulated sugar.
- Sugar substitutes, including granulated, liquid, and tablet sugar substitutes.
- Sweet sauces, toppings and syrups, including chocolate, berry, fruit, corn syrup, and maple sweet sauces and toppings.

Functional Effect Terms

The following terms describe the physical or technical functional effects for which direct human-food ingredients may be added to foods. They are adopted from the National Academy of Sciences/National Research Council National survey of food industries, reported to the Food and Drug Administration under the contract title "A Comprehensive Survey of Industry on the Use of Food Chemicals Generally recognized as Safe" (September 1972), which is incorporated by reference. . . .

- Anticaking agents and free-flow agents: Substances added to finely powdered or crystalline food products to prevent caking, lumping, or agglomeration.
- Antimicrobial agents: Substances used to preserve food by preventing growth of microorganisms and subsequent spoilage, including fungi-stats, mold and rope inhibitors, and the effects listed by the National Academy of Sciences/National Research Council under "preservatives."

- Antioxidants: Substances used to preserve food by retarding deterioration, rancidity, or discoloration due to oxidation.
- Colors and coloring adjuncts: Substances used to impart, preserve, or enhance the color or shading of a food, including color stabilizers, color fixatives, color-retention agents, etc.
- Curing and pickling agents: Substances imparting a unique flavor and/or color to a food, usually producing an increase in shelf life stability.
- Dough strengtheners: Substances used to modify starch and gluten, thereby producing more stable dough, including the applicable effects listed by the National Academy of Sciences/National Research Council under "dough conditioner."
- Drying agents: Substances with moisture-absorbing ability, used to maintain an environment of low moisture.
- Emulsifiers and emulsifier salts: Substances which modify surface tension in the component phase of an emulsion to establish a uniform dispersion or emulsion.
- Enzymes: Enzymes used to improve food processing and the quality of the finished food.
- Firming agents: Substances added to precipitate residual pectin, thus strengthening the supporting tissue and preventing its collapse during processing.
- Flavor enhancers: Substances added to supplement, enhance, or modify the original taste and/or aroma of a food, without imparting a characteristic taste or aroma of its own.
- Flavoring agents and adjuvants: Substances added to impart or help impart a taste or aroma in food.
- Flour treating agents: Substances added to milled flour, at the mill, to improve its color and/or baking qualities, including bleaching and maturing agents.
- Formulation aids: Substances used to promote or produce a designed physical state or texture in food, including carriers, binders, fillers, plasticizers, film-formers, and tableting aids, etc.
- Fumigants: Volatile substances used for controlling insects or pests.
- Humectants: Hygroscopic substances incorporated in food to promote retention of moisture, including moisture-retention agents and antidusting agents.
- Leavening agents: Substances used to produce or stimulate production of carbon dioxide in baked goods to impart a light texture, including yeast, yeast foods, and calcium salts listed by the National Academy of Sciences/National Research Council under "dough conditioners."
- Lubricants and release agents: Substances added to food contact surfaces to prevent ingredients and finished products from sticking to them.
- Non-nutritive sweeteners: Substances having less than 2 percent of the caloric value of sucrose per equivalent unit of sweetening capacity.

FDA NOTE

FDA anticipates that the U.S. will receive over eight million food shipments from over 200,000 foreign manufacturers in 2006, a huge volume that continues to grow rapidly. (FDA, 2003)

- Nutrient supplements: Substances that are necessary for the body's nutritional and metabolic processes.
- Nutrient sweeteners: Substances having greater than 2 percent of the caloric value of sucrose per equivalent unit of sweetening capacity.
- Oxidizing and reducing agents: Substances which chemically oxidize or reduce another food ingredient, thereby producing a more stable product, including the applicable effect listed by the National Academy of Sciences/National Research Council under "dough conditioners."
- pH control agents: Substances added to change or maintain active acidity or basicity, including buffers, acids, alkalies, and neutralizing agents.
- Processing aids: Substances used as manufacturing aids to enhance the appeal or utility of a food or food component, including clarifying agents, clouding agents, catalysts, flocculents, filter aids, and crystallization inhibitors, etc.
- Propellants, aerating agents, and gases: Gases used to supply force to expel a product or used to reduce the amount of oxygen in contact with the food in packaging.
- Sequestrants: Substances that combine with polyvalent metal ions to form a soluble metal complex, to improve the quality and stability of products.
- Solvents and vehicles: Substances used to extract or dissolve another substance.
- Stabilizers and thickeners: Substances used to produce viscous solutions or dispersions, to impart body, improve consistency or stabilize emulsions, including suspending and bodying agents, setting agents, jellying agents, and bulking agents, etc.
- Surface-active agents: Substances used to modify surface properties of liquid food components for a variety of effects, other than emulsifiers, but including solubilizing agents, dispersants, detergents, wetting agents, rehydration enhancers, whipping agents, foaming agents, and defoaming agents, etc.
- Surface-finishing agents: Substances used to increase palatability, preserve glass, and inhibit discoloration of foods, including glazes, polishes, waxes, and protective coatings.

- Synergists: Substances used to act or react with another food ingredient to produce a total effect different or greater than the sum of the effects produced by the individual ingredients.
- Texturizers: Substances that affect the appearance or feel of the food.

TITLE III SUBTITLE A—PROTECTION OF FOOD SUPPLY

Subtitle A of Title III of the Bioterrorism Act provides the secretary of Health and Human Services with authority to protect the nation's food supply against the threat of intentional contamination and other food-related emergencies. The FDA is responsible for implementing these provisions. This authority improves our ability to act quickly in responding to a threatened or actual terrorist attack, as well other food-related emergencies. Since this legislation was signed into law, the FDA has been working hard to implement this effectively and efficiently.

Each section (and applicable requirements) of Subtitle A of Title III is listed in the following in bullet format for ease of understanding and use.

Section 301—Food Safety and Security Strategy

- Requires the president's Council on Food Safety to develop a crisis communications and education strategy regarding bioterrorist threats to the food supply
- Expands entities to consult to include secretaries of transportation and treasury
- Addresses threat assessments, technologies and procedures for securing facilities and modes of transportation, response and notification procedures, and risk communications to the public

Section 302—Protection against Adulteration of Food

- Amends 801 to direct secretary to give high priority to increasing imported food inspections with greatest priority for inspections to detect intentional adulteration

SECTION 302 NOTE

FDA received counterterrorism funds that enabled it to hire additional staff, most of whom were hired to address food safety issues, primarily at the border. With these additional employees, FDA has more than doubled the number of ports that have an FDA presence from 40 to 90. FDA has increased by more than six-fold the number of food examinations at the border. (FDA, 2003)

- Requires high priority to improving information management systems for imported foods to improve ability to allocate resources, detect intentional adulteration, and facilitate the importation of food that is in compliance
- Requires improved linkages with other federal, state, and tribal food safety agencies
- Requires research to develop improved rapid testing and sampling methodologies to detect adulteration
- Requires coordination as appropriate on the research
- Requires annual report to Congress describing process made in research

Section 303—Administrative Detention

Detention:

- Authorizes an officer or qualified employee of the FDA to order detention of food if there is credible evidence or information that the food presents threat of serious adverse health consequences or death
- Detention must be approved at district director level or higher, as designated by the secretary
- Detention may not exceed 20 days, unless more time (not to exceed 30 days) is necessary for the secretary to pursue a seizure or injunction
- Detention may require marking or labeling as detained
- Requires removal to secure facility as appropriate
- Establishes process that requires secretary, after an opportunity for informal hearing, to decide appeals in five days: subject to judicial review, process terminates if secretary files for seizure or injunction, and detention order terminates if secretary does not comply with appeal requirements
- Prohibits transfer of an article of food in violation of detention order or removal or alteration of any required mark or label

Temporary Hold:

- Provides for temporary holds at ports of entry
- Requests may be made to treasury to hold food at port of entry for 24 hours when credible evidence or information that an article of food presents a threat of serious

SECTION 303 NOTE

In the 2004 amendment to Section 303, the FDA expedited procedures for detaining an article of food, expedited procedures for detaining perishable foods, and the process for appealing a detention order.

adverse health consequences or death and the officer needs more time to inspect, examine, or investigate

- Requests must be approved by district director level or higher
- Requires removal to secure facility as appropriate
- Requires notification of port-of-entry state

Section 304—Debarment for Repeated or Serious Food Import Violations

- Establishes debarment for persons convicted of a felony related to food importation or for persons who have engaged in a pattern of importing or offering for import adulterated food that presents a threat of serious adverse health consequences or death to humans or animals
- It is a prohibited act to import or offer for import food by, with the assistance of, or at the direction of a debarred person
- Requires that food offered for import by a debarred person be held at the port of entry, at a secure facility as appropriate, and not transferred
- Article may be delivered to a nondebarred person if person establishes article is in compliance

Section 305—Registration of Food Facilities

- Requires registration of domestic and foreign food facilities
- Includes any factory, warehouse, or establishment that manufactures, processes, packs, or holds food
- Exempts farms, restaurants, other retail food establishments, nonprofit food establishments in which food is prepared or served directly to the consumer, and fishing vessels that do not process
- Limits foreign facilities to those whose products are exported to the U.S. without further processing or packaging outside the U.S.
- Owner, operator, or agent in charge shall submit the registration
- Foreign facilities shall provide name of U.S. agent
- Registration is one-time rather than annual
- Registrants to notify FDA of changes in timely manner
- Registration shall include names and addresses of each facility, all trade names and, when necessary, the general food category (as specified in 21 CFR 170.3)
- Secretary to notify registrants of receipt and assign each facility a number
- Requires secretary to maintain up-to-date list
- Specifies list and registration information not subject to disclosure
- Failure to register is a prohibited act
- Requires that an article of food offered for import from an unregistered foreign facility be held at the port of entry until facility is registered
- Secretary may encourage electronic registration

SECTION 305 NOTE

Requires registration of foreign and domestic food facilities that manufacture, process, pack, or hold food for consumption by humans or animals in the United States.

Section 306—Maintenance and Inspection of Records for Foods

- Authorizes the secretary to have access to certain records when there is a reasonable belief that an article of food is adulterated and presents a threat of serious adverse health consequences or death to humans or animals
- Applies to all records relating to the manufacture, processing, packing, distribution, receipt, holding, or importation of food
- Excludes farms and restaurants
- Limits requirement to establish records for traceback to the immediate previous source and the immediate subsequent recipient
- Excludes information such as recipes, financial data, personnel data, research data, and sales data
- Limits recordkeeping requirement to two years
- Secretary to ensure protection from disclosure of sensitive information
- Prohibited act to refuse to permit access to or copying of any required record or to fail to establish or maintain any required record

SECTION 306 NOTE

Section 306 authorizes FDA to have access to certain records when the agency has a reasonable belief that an article of food is adulterated and presents a threat of serious adverse health consequences or death to humans or animals.

SECTION 307 NOTE

This section of the Bioterrorism Act requires the submission to FDA of prior notice of food, including animal feed that is imported or offered for import into the U.S. This advance information enables FDA to more effectively target inspections at the border to ensure the safety of imported foods before they move into the U.S.

Section 307—Prior Notice of Imported Food Shipments

- Requires prior notice of imported food shipments
- Notice to provide the article, manufacturer and shipper, grower (if known), country of origin, country from which it was shipped, and anticipated port of entry
- If notice not provided, article refused admission
- If inadequate notice provided, article held at the port of entry until proper notice is provided; requires secretary to determine whether there is any credible evidence or information indicating that the article presents a threat of serious adverse health consequences or death to humans or animals
- Prohibited act to fail to provide notice
- Requires the secretary, after consultation with treasury, to issue regulations to specify the period of advance notice; may not exceed five days

Section 308—Authority to Mark Articles Refused Admission into U.S.

- Authorizes the secretary to require refused food (other than food required to be destroyed) to be marked "UNITED STATES: REFUSED ENTRY"
- Marking to be done at owner's expense
- Food misbranded if it fails to bear the required label, food presents a threat of serious adverse health consequences or death to humans or animals, or FDA notified the owner that the label is required and that the food presents such a threat

Section 309—Prohibiting against Port Shopping

- Deems food adulterated if a food is offered for import that has been previously refused admission unless the person reoffering the food establishes that the article is in compliance.

SECTION 308 NOTE

This section authorizes the secretary to require the marking of refused food (other than food required to be destroyed). This provision is intended to prevent unsafe foods that have been refused entry into the U.S. from entering U.S. markets via the practice of "port shopping."

Section 310—Notices to States Regarding Imported Food

- Requires notice to states when there is credible evidence or information that a shipment presents a threat of serious adverse health consequences or death to humans or animals
- Notice to be given to state in which the food is held or will be held and the states in which the manufacturer, packer, or distributor of the food is located
- Requests the state to take appropriate action to protect the public health

Section 311—Grants to States for Inspections

- Provides for grants to states, territories, and Indian tribes that undertake examinations, inspections, and investigations, and related activities
- Not limited to goods
- Provides for grants to the states to assist them with the costs of taking appropriate action after receiving notification under Section 310 above

Section 312—Surveillance and Information Grants and Authorities

- Provides for grants to states and Indian tribes to expand participating in networks (such as PulseNet) to enhance federal, state, and local food safety efforts
- May include meeting the costs of establishing and maintaining the food safety surveillance, technical, and laboratory capacity needed for participation

Section 313—Surveillance of Zoonotic Diseases

- Secretaries of DHHS and agriculture to coordinate surveillance of zoonotic diseases

Section 314—Authority to Commission other Federal Officials to Conduct Inspections

- Authorizes the secretary to commission other federal employees to do examinations and inspections

- Not limited to foods
- Requires a memorandum of understanding between both agencies which must address training and reimbursement
- Is restricted to facilities or other locations that are jointly regulated

PATHOGENS

Zoonotic Diseases

CDC (2007) states that diseases transmitted from animals are called zoonotic diseases. Zoonotic diseases can be caused by parasites and can cause various symptoms such as diarrhea, muscle aches, and fevers. Sometimes infected persons experience severe symptoms that can be life-threatening.

Foods can be contaminated if animals such as cows and pigs are infected with parasites such as *Cryptosporidium* and *Trichinella*. People can acquire trichinellosis by ingesting Trichinella-infected, undercooked meat such as bear, boar, or domestic pigs. Cryptosporidiosis can be acquired by people if orchards or water sources near cow pastures become contaminated from infected cows and people consume the fruit without proper washing.

Some dog and cat parasites can infect people. Young animals, such as puppies and kittens, are more likely to be infected with ascarids (commonly called roundworms) and hookworms. Contact with wild animals or places where wild animals have been can expose people to parasites. For example, people can be infected by the raccoon parasite *Baylisascaris* when they handle soil that is contaminated with infected raccoon feces.

A selected (partial) list of zoonotic diseases includes:

- Animal bites
- Anthrax
- Brucellosis
- Cat scratch disease
- E. coli 0157
- Hendra virus

- Hepatitis E. virus
- Listeriosis
- Lyme disease
- Menangle virus
- Rocky Mountain spotted fever
- Tularemia
- Vesicular stomatitis virus
- West Nile virus

POSSIBLE PATHOGENS IN AN AGROTERRORIST ATTACK

In addition to the zoonotic diseases listed in the box above, there are numerous other animal and plant pathogens and pests that can cause significant economic and other problems with our food supply. Though this is the case, according to CRS (2003), of the hundreds of animal and plant pathogens and pests available to an agroterrorist, perhaps fewer than a couple of dozen represent significant economic threats. Determinants of this level of threat are the agent's contagiousness and potential for rapid spread, and its international status as a "reportable" pest or disease (i.e., subject to international quarantine) under rules of the World Organization for Animal Health (also commonly know as the OIE, the Office International des Epizooties).

A widely accepted view among scientists is that livestock herds are much more susceptible to agroterrorism than are crop plants. Much of this has to do with the success of efforts to systematically eliminate animal disease from U.S. herds, which leaves current herds either unvaccinated or relatively unmonitored for such disease by farmers and some local veterinarians. Once infected, livestock can often act as the vector for continuing to transmit the disease, facilitating an outbreak's spread, especially when live animals are transported. Certain animal disease may be more attractive to terrorists because they can be zoonotic, or transmissible to humans.

In contrast, a number of plant pathogens continue to exist in small areas of the U.S. and continue to infect limited areas of plants each year, making

(continues)

PATHOGENS *(continued)*

outbreaks and control efforts more routine. Moreover, plant pathogens are generally more technically difficult to manipulate. Some plant pathogens may require certain environmental conditions of humidity, temperature, or wind to take hold or spread. Other plant diseases may take a longer time than an animal disease to become established or achieve destruction on the scale that a terrorist may desire.

Animal Pathogens

The Agricultural Bioterrorism Protection Act of 2002 created the current, official list of potential animal pathogens. The list is specified in the select agent rules implemented by USDA-APHIS and the Centers for Disease Control and Prevention (CDC) of the Department of Health and Human Services (HHS). The act requires that these lists (table 4.1) be reviewed at least every two years.

The select agent list for animal pathogens draws heavily from the enduring and highly respected OIE lists of high-concern pathogens, Lists A and B. Furthermore, the select agent list is comprised of an APHIS-only list (of concern to animals) and an overlap list of agents selected both by APHIS and CDC (of concern to both animals and humans).

OIE Lists A and B

Prior to the Agricultural Bioterrorism Protection Act, the commonly accepted animal diseases of concern were all of the OIE's "List A" diseases and some of the "List B" diseases. These diseases represent a subset of the select agent list (table 4.1) as described below.

The OIE's List A diseases are transmissible animal diseases that have the potential for very serious and rapid spread, irrespective of national borders. List A diseases have serious socioeconomic or public health consequences and are of major importance in international trade (OIE, 2003).

By March 2007, the OIE replaced Lists A and B with a single list that is more compatible with the Sanitary and Phytosanitary Agreement (SPS) of

Table 4.1.   Livestock Diseases in the Select Agent List

Animal Diseases Caused by Agents/Toxins Listed by APHIS in 9 CFR 121.3(d)	Overlap Diseases and Agents/Toxins Listed by Both APHIS and CDC in 9 CFR 121.3(b)
African horse sickness	Anthrax
African swine fever	Botulinum neurotoxins
Akabane	Botulinum neurotoxin–producing *Clostridium*
Avian influenza	Botulinum neurotoxin–producing *Clostridium*
Bluetongue	Brucellosis of cattle
Bovine spongiform encephalopathy	Brucellosis of sheep
Camel pox	Brucellosis of pigs
Classical swine fever	Glanders
Contagious caprine pleuropneumonia	Melioidiosis
Contagious bovine pleuropneumonia	Botulism
Foot-and-mouth disease (FMD)	*Clostridium perfringens*
Goat pox	(Valley fever)
Heartwater	Q fever
Japanese encephalitis	Eastern equine encephalitis
Lumpy skin disease	Tularemia
Malignant catarrhal fever	Hendra virus
Menangle virus	Nipah virus
Newcastle disease	Rift valley fever
Peste des petits ruminants	Shigatoxin
Rinderpest	Staphylococcal enterotoxins
Sheep pox	T-2 toxin
Swine vesicular disease	Venezuelan equine encephalitis
Vesicular stomatitis	—

Source: 9 CFR 121.3(b) and (d), supplemented with common disease names as appropriate.

the World Trade Organization (WTO). The new list classifies all listed diseases equally, giving each the same degree of importance in international trade. In creating the list, the OIE reviewed its criteria for including a disease, and the disease or epidemiological events that require member countries to file reports (Vallat, 2004).

Select Agents List

The regulations establishing the select agent list for animals (9 CFR 121.3) set forth the requirements for possession, use, and transfer of these biological agents or toxins to ensure safe handling and for security to protect them from use in domestic or international terrorism. APHIS determines

(continues)

PATHOGENS (*continued*)

that the biological agents and toxins on the list have the potential to pose a severe threat to agricultural production or food products. (Note: The 23 animal diseases listed exclusively by APHIS in 9 CFR 1213(d)—the left column of table 4.1—include 15 of the 16 OIE "List A" diseases and 5 of the "List B" diseases.)

Foot-and-mouth disease (FMD) is probably the most frequently mentioned disease when agroterrorism is discussed, due to its ease of use, ability to spread rapidly, and potential for great economic damage. Widespread animal diseases like brucellosis, influenza, or tuberculosis receive relatively less attention than FMD, hog cholera, or Newcastle disease. However, emerging diseases such as Nipah virus, Hendra virus, and the H5NI strain of avian influenza (zoonotic disease that have infected people) can be lethal since vaccines are elusive or have not been developed.

Plant Pathogens

The Agricultural Bioterrorism Protection Act of 2002 (Subtitle B of P.L. 107-18) also instructed APHIS and CDC to create the current official list of potential plant pathogens. The federal government lists biological agents and toxins for plants in 7 CFR 331.3 (table 4.2). The act requires that these lists be reviewed at least every two years, and revised as necessary.

Table 4.2. Plant Diseases in the Select Agent List

Plant Diseases	Causes: Select Agents Listed in 7 CFR 331.3
Citrus greening	*Liberobacter africanus*
Philippine downy mildew (of corn)	*Peronosclerospora philippinensis*
Soybean rust	*Phakopsora pachyrihizi*
Plum pox (of stone fruits)	*Plum pox potyvirus*
Bacterial wilt, brown rot (of potato)	*Ralstonia solanacearum*
Brown stripe downy mildew (of corn)	*Sclerophthora rayssiae*
Potato wart or potato canker	Synchytrium endobioticum
Bacterial leaf streak (of rice)	Xanthomonas oryzae
Citrus variegated chlorosis	
Xylella fastidiosa	

Source: 7 CFR 331.3(a), supplemented with common disease names as appropriate.

Prior to the act, there was not a commonly recognized list of the most dangerous plant pathogens, although several diseases were usually mentioned and are now included in the APHIS select agent list.

Other plant pathogens not included in the select agent list possibly could be used against crops of certain geographic regions. Examples include Karnal bunt and citrus canker, which both currently exist in the U.S. in regions quarantined or under surveillance by USDA. As with other agents, the effectiveness of such an attack to spread such a disease may be dependent on environmental conditions and difficult to achieve.

OIE

The OIE (Office International des Epizooties, or World Organization for Animal Health) is an international organization created in 1924 with 166 member countries. It is a well-respected information clearinghouse for animal disease and health. Member countries report diseases that occur on their territory, and the OIE disseminates the information, allowing other countries to take preventive action. The OIE also analyzes scientific information on animal disease control, provides technical support, and develops normative documents concerning international trade and sanitary rules that are recognized by the World Trade Organization.

FDA FOOD SAFETY AND SECURITY PROGRESS: A 10-POINT PROGRAM

Securing our food supply against terrorist threats is one of our most important public health priorities, especially at a time of heightened alert.

—*Tommy G. Thompson*

The FDA (2003) points out that it is

> responsible for ensuring the safety and security of 80 percent of the U.S. food supply. The FDA's legislative mandate is to protect the public health by ensuring the safety of the production, processing, packaging, storage, and holding of domestic and imported food except those products (meat, poultry, and processed egg products) that are under the jurisdiction of the U.S. Department of Agriculture.

Although food safety and security are different aspects of food protection they are inherently connected. The FDA, at the direction of the Department of Health and Human Services (DHHS), has established a 10-Point Program for ensuring the safety and security of the food supply. Based on activities in the FDA's 10-Point Program, the agency is employing overall strategies to (1) develop increased awareness among federal, state, local, and tribal governments and the private sector by collecting, analyzing, and disseminating information and knowledge (Awareness); (2) develop capacity for identification of a specific threat or attack on the food supply (Prevention); (3) develop effective protection strategies to "shield" the food supply from terrorist threats (Protection); (4) develop capacity for a rapid, coordinated response to a foodborne terrorist attack (Response); and (5) develop capacity for a rapid, coordinated recovery from a foodborne terrorist attach (Recovery).

Within the food security and safety strategies, FDA's program features 10 areas of focus based on the following principles:

- Food Security and safety are integrated goals. By building upon the nation's core food safety/public health systems and expertise, while strengthening expertise and capabilities needed to address the terrorist threat, the FDA is enhancing food security and is improving food safety in the process.
- The food safety and security system is comprehensive, addressing the full range of assessment, prevention, and response needs, throughout the food production and distribution chain. The system must be efficient and in the context of both safety and security, address the most significant threats first whenever possible.
- The food and security system is also built on a solid foundation of a national partnership with other entities involved in food safety and security that fully integrates the assets of state, local and tribal governments, other federal agencies, and the private sector.
- Americans must have confidence that the government is taking all reasonable steps to protect the food supply, and is providing Americans with timely and relevant information about threats and will provide timely and relevant information about an attack if one occurs.

THE 10-POINT PROGRAM (REPRINTED FROM FDA, 2003)

1. Stronger FDA—New Staff

In the wake of September 11, 2001, HHS, working with bipartisan Congressional support and action, obtained funding for the FDA. FDA moved expeditiously and quickly to establish this additional investigative and scientific team by rapidly hiring and training 655 additional field personnel. Of the 655, 97 percent are allocated to food-safety field activities: 300 support the conduct of consumer safety investigations at U.S. ports of entry, 100 support laboratory analyses on imported products, 33 are for criminal investigations of import activities, and the remaining personnel support domestic efforts. . . .

U.S. borders are flooded with FDA-regulated imports from all over the world, and the continuous threat of terrorism requires FDA to remain vigilant in its effort to retain a competent, trained workforce if we are to maintain a high level of readiness. With FDA's limited resources to meet the challenge of assuring the food safety and security for more than six million entries per year, FDA must strategically develop hiring, targeting resources and succession planning to be prepared in the event of a terrorist attack.

FDA not only mobilized new staff but redirected, trained current investigators and scientists to integrate and strengthen its food safety and security mission and ensured that the agency has the necessary scientific and logistical expertise to respond to an event that could threaten the safety and security of the food supply. FDA has hired or retrained scientific experts in biological, chemical and radiological agent research, detection methodology, preventive technologies and acquired substantial knowledge of these agents to help support domestic and import activities. FDA's Office of Regulatory Affairs (ORA) has developed a succession plan to ensure that the agency will continue to have highly trained and competent scientists, investigators, analysts, and managers to accomplish the agency's overall mission of consumer protection. FDA realizes that recruitment and retention of its highly skilled and sometimes very specialized workforce requires thoughtful planning so that it can be ready to effectively and efficiently meet the challenges it faces.

2. Imports—Strategic Approach

FDA continues to adjust its import program via the development of an Import Strategic Plan (ISP) to reflect the changing nature of risks and trade associated with imported goods. This approach encompasses and addresses the full "life-cycle" of imported products. As part of the ISP, FDA is assessing information derived from foreign and domestic inspectional operations, adverse events, consumer complaints, recall activities, and information technology. The goal of the ISP is to better protect the public health and safety by decreasing the risk that unsafe, ineffective, or violative products will enter U.S. commerce through our borders, ports, and other import hubs. Moreover, when implemented, the ISP will provide FDA with the critical flexibility it needs to shift resources as import trends alter the risks and change priorities for public health and safety protection.

Historically, the volume of U.S. imports of FDA-regulated products was relatively small and consisted of raw ingredients and bulk materials intended for further processing or incorporation into finished products. Therefore, FDA could rely more heavily on physical examination and domestic inspections to ensure that imported raw ingredients and bulk materials were properly handled, received, quarantined, released and processed according to good manufacturing practices and sanitation principles.

Even with the recent increases of personnel for counterterrorism efforts, border inspections cannot manage the changes in the nature of risks and trade. FDA is taking steps to implement a risk-based approach towards covering the importation of FDA-regulated goods. These proactive steps will assist FDA in identifying patterns of transportation while goods are in international streams of commerce; increase our ability to conduct effective, efficient foreign inspections; and will aid FDA in making admissibility decisions before goods enter domestic commerce. Moreover, the risk-based approaches we are contemplating include exploring the feasibility of forming regulatory partnerships to provide better information to FDA—and, ultimately, better protection to U.S. consumers.

FDA is supporting this enhanced import strategic plan by providing a greater import presence at our nation's borders. FDA is enhancing our capacity and capability to perform normal import operations such as sample collection and analysis, field examinations, and inspections across all agency programs. In 2001, FDA provided coverage at about 40 ports of entry. By 2002, FDA had more than doubled its presence to 90 ports of entry.

In addition, since 2001, FDA more than quintupled the number of food import examinations. In 2001, FDA conducted 12,000 food exams. FDA has conducted over 62,000 food exams already this fiscal year and has surpassed its 2003 year-end goal of 48,000 food exams. This increased coverage was due to redirecting resources dedicated to assure increased import coverage during Operation Liberty Shield when the nation was at a heightened security alert.

FDA is working to increase import filer evaluations to ensure integrity of importers and import entry data and to increase collections of samples for laboratory analysis.

FDA is working on additional enhancements to the Operational and Administrative System for Import Support (OASIS) to include real-time screening with multi-agency import databases to help target inspection resources.

3. Bioterrorism Act Regulations

The FDA published four major new regulations in accordance with provisions of the Bioterrorism Act. In May 2003, the FDA published in the *Federal Register* requirements, under the Bioterrorism Act, for manufacturers, processors, packers, transporters, distributors, receivers, holders, and importers of food to keep records identifying the immediate previous source from which they receive food, as well as the immediate subsequent recipient, to whom they sent food.

The FDA also published its new authority to detain any article of food for which there is credible evidence or information that the article poses a threat of serious adverse health consequences or death to humans or animals. The administrative detention authority granted to the FDA under the Bioterrorism Act is self-executing and currently in effect.

4. Industry Guidance and Preventive Measures

In 2002, the FDA published "Food Producers, Processors, and Transporters: Food Security Preventive Measures Guidance," designed to aid operators of food establishments, and "Importers and Filers: Food Security Preventive Measures Guidance," designed to help food importers. Each document recommends the types of preventive measures that companies can consider to minimize the risk that food under their control will be subject to tampering or criminal or terrorist actions. The FDA also notes,

> Consumers play a critical role in preventing illness due to food tampering. The FDA encourages consumers when shopping to carefully examine all food product packaging, check any anti-tampering devices on the packaging, not to purchase products if the packaging is open, torn, or damaged, not to buy products that are damaged or that look unusual and to check the "sell-by" dates. Consumers are also encouraged to carefully inspect products at home when opening the container and to never eat food from products that are damaged or that look unusual.

5. Vulnerability and Threat Assessments

Using the methodology called Operations Risk Management (ORM), FDA developed a vulnerability assessment for foods. The assessment evaluates the public health consequences of a range of product-agent scenarios associated with potential tampering, criminal, malicious, or terrorist activity. This relative risk ranking is designed to facilitate decision-making about the assignment of limited federal, state, and local public health resources to minimize such risks. It is also designed to assist the food industry in identifying areas where enhancements in preventive measures could increase the security of the food supply. This internal assessment identified a number of food/agent combinations that FDA is focusing on to implement shields for protecting those commodities. These shields will be implemented in partnership with FDA regulatory counterparts and industry.

FDA initiated and awarded a task order to the Institute of Food Technologists (IFT) to conduct an in-depth review of ORM and provide a critique on its application of Food Security. As part of this review, IFT was asked to apply ORM to food and to evaluate the relative public health consequences of a range of product-agent scenarios.

This review validated FDA's vulnerability assessment process and provided additional information on the public health consequences of a range of product, agent, and process scenarios. This assessment affirmed the food/agent combinations identified in the FDA ORM assessment and identified additional commodities to consider for shield implementation.

As an additional step, in 2003 FDA awarded an additional task order to IFT, requesting that IFT conduct an in-depth review of preventive measures that food processors may take to reduce the risk of an intentional act of terrorism or contamination. The review will assess ways to prevent or reduce the risk of contamination of processed food and will provide information on various research needs related to elimination or reduction of the risks. IFT will provide information on various processing technologies that might be used for eliminating or reducing the risk of an intentional act of terrorism or contamination for several commodity, agent, and processing combinations.

FDA also contracted with Battelle Memorial Institute to conduct a "Food and Cosmetics, Chemical, Biological, and Radiological Threat Assessment." The assessment affirmed the findings of the FDA/CFSAN Operational Risk Management Assessment, provided an additional decision-making tool for performing risk assessments, incorporating a Hazard Analysis Critical Control Points (HACCP) type approach, and made a number of recommendations about research needs, the need for enhanced laboratory capability and capacity, and the need for enhanced partnerships between federal, state, and local governments to ensure food security.

FDA provides regular updates to Congress about threat assessments and vulnerabilities related to the safety and security of the U.S. food supply. FDA will be providing to Congress the threat assessments conducted by FDA, IFT and the Battelle Memorial Institute.

FDA is conducting additional assessments of the vulnerability of FDA-regulated foods to intentional contamination with biological, chemical and radiological agents.

HACCP

Hazard Analysis Critical Control Points (HACCP) is an evaluation system to identify, monitor, and control contamination risks in food-service establishments.

These assessments use processes adapted from techniques developed by the U.S. Department of Defense for use in assessing the vulnerabilities of military targets to asymmetric threats. Results of the assessments will be used to develop countermeasures, identify research needs, and provide guidance to the private sector.

6. Operation Liberty Shield

In March 2003, the United States government launched Operation Liberty Shield to increase security and readiness in the United States at a time of elevated risk or a terrorist attack. Operation Liberty Shield, a comprehensive national plan of action to protect many of America's critical infrastructures, was a unified operation coordinated by the Department of Homeland Security that integrated selected national protective measures with the involvement and support of federal, state, local, and private responders and authorities from around the country. Operation Liberty Shield was designed to provide increased protection for America's citizens and infrastructure while maintaining the free flow of goods and people across our borders with minimal disruption to our economy and way of life. FDA has established protocols, trained staff and deployed supplies and equipment for future and similar elevated threat level actions. A key component of Operation Liberty Shield was increasing and targeting surveillance of both domestic and imported food. The agency initiated the following activities:

- FDA issued new industry guidance documents on security measures and encouraged industry to voluntarily assess their security measures in response to an increased threat level.
- FDA held a series of conference calls to brief state regulatory agencies, industry trade associations, consumer groups, and their federal counterparts on Operation Liberty Shield and to request their assistance in distributing the food security guidance documents to domestic facilities and the portion of the import community that handles food products.
- FDA increased its surveillance of the domestic food industry during Operation Liberty Shield, by conducting 844 inspections of domestic firms based on risk/threat assessments with a focus on enhancing awareness of food security at these facilities by providing copies of appropriate food security guidance documents. These investigations targeted examinations of specific commodities based on risk/threat assessments and sampled specific commodities based on risk/threat.
- FDA increased its monitoring of imported foods, during Operation Liberty Shield, by conducting increased examinations of specific imported commodities based on FDA's risk/threat assessments, enhancing the import communities' awareness of food security at ports by providing copies of FDA's food security guidance documents, and

sampling imported foods based on risk/threat assessments. FDA collected and analyzed 387 import samples for chemical and microbiological contaminants.

- FDA conducted domestic and import reconciliation exams to confirm that regulated
  commodities were what they purported to be, exposed unexplained differences between associated documentation and the product, and uncovered signs of tampering
  or counterfeiting.

- FDA increased joint activities with federal, state, and local partners to help ensure a
  safe and secure food supply, including working with the Centers for Disease Control
  and Prevention to ensure that outbreaks or unusual patterns of illness or injury are
  quickly investigated.

- Likewise, USDA undertook similar food security measures and activities for its regulated industries including meat, poultry and processed egg products. Thus, in combination, FDA and USDA comprehensively covered the U.S. food supply.

7. Emergency Preparedness and Response

FDA has established an Office of Crisis Management (OCM) to coordinate the preparedness and emergency response activities of the five FDA Centers, ORA and their
offices working with their federal, state and local counterparts that may be engaged in
a variety of different emergencies involving FDA regulated products and/or the need
to provide medical countermeasures. Within OCM, the FDA Emergency Operations
Center serves as the chief communications node and point of contact within FDA.

Over the past two years, FDA has participated in and conducted multiple emergency response exercises. Frequently, these exercises are coordinated with other federal and state agencies. In both exercises and everyday issues, the FDA's OCM works
closely with the Department of Health and Human Services/Office of Public Health
Emergency Preparedness (OPHEP) and the Secretary's Command Center (SCC).
This relationship facilitates communication between all HHS Operating Divisions,
the Department, and other federal agencies and Departments, including the Department of Homeland Security. In particular, FDA has focused on strengthening its
working relationship with USDA by joint testing of several response plans in an exercise environment. In May 2003, FDA participated in the TOPOFF 2 terrorism exercise, a national, full scale, fully functional exercise intended to simulate two
separate terrorist acts that had implications for food products (e.g., the possibility of
food contamination by radiation), as well as the ensuing response by federal, state,
and local governments.

FDA has also signed an Inter Agency Agreement (IAG) with the U.S. Army to design
and develop two mobile laboratories to the be deployed at borders, ports, or other locations, to provide timely and efficient analyses of samples being offered for import
into the U.S. and/or in the event of terrorist activity. . . .

Within current resources, FDA is assessing its ability to respond to high-risk product-agent scenarios and for what sustained period. This includes a review of our current scientific capabilities that may be available for extramural sources (academia, DoD, etc.) and efforts to enhance the nation's food laboratory capacity at federal, state and local facilities to conduct rapid, accurate tests to determine quickly the precise extent of food contamination in the event of an actual or suspected terrorist attack.

8. Laboratory Enhancements

Methods Development

FDA has redirected laboratory staff to develop laboratory methods for priority biological and chemical agents in food. Methods have been developed for the highest priority select agents.

FDA has reviewed and modified current regulatory analytical methods for their applicability to terrorism related samples. Methods have been modified to provide more rapid analysis while maintaining practical sensitivity.

FDA is enhancing its capacity to develop methods that can be used for rapid analysis of suspect foods for select agents or toxins, including the development of rapid methods that can be deployed and used in a field setting.

FDA is working to adapt an FDA toxin screening method for application as a surveillance tool.

FDA has established an IAG with Edgewood Arsenal and a task order contract with Midwest Research Institute for the validation of methods for the detection of microbiological agents in foods.

FDA has partnered with the Department of Defense to develop and validate methods to detect agents most likely to be used in a terrorist attack on the food supply, and engaged in interagency agreements that would allow the Department of Defense to provide laboratory support in the event of an attack.

Under contract to FDA, the New Mexico State University (NMSU) Physical Science Laboratory (PSL) is evaluating rapid test methods for microbiological analyses of produce samples. NMSU's evaluation includes the assessment of rapid test methods for a particular analyte(s) or food commodity—which is required prior to the agency adoption for any kit for use in the regulatory arena.

Network Development

FDC has worked with CDC, USDA, EPA, DOE and the states to initiate development of a nationwide Food Emergency Response Network (FERN). As mentioned earlier, FERN is a network of state and federal laboratories that is committed to analyzing food samples in the event of a biological, chemical, or radiological terrorist event in this country. Following the events of September 11, 2001, FDA took aggressive action to develop this network building on then-existing laboratory capabilities. FDA is working to add additional food laboratories to the FERN. Furthermore, FDA will work with CDC and the states to improve laboratory capacity to enhance response capability for food security concerns. With CDC grant funds, states are initiating additional additives to increase lab capacity for food-related emergencies.

FDA has made available methods for the isolation and detection of high-priority microorganisms and chemical agents not usually found in food that can be utilized by Laboratory Response Network (LRN) and FERN laboratories on a password protected Web site.

FDA has used emergency funding to purchase rapid method test kits for chemical and microbiological agents and has distributed the materials to laboratories within FERN.

Ninety-five laboratories representing 48 states are participating in the Electronic Laboratory Exchange Network (eLEXNET), the nation's first seamless, integrated, Web-based data exchange system for food testing information. Again, eLEXNET allows health officials at multiple government agencies engaged in food safety activities to compare, share, and coordinate laboratory analysis findings on food products. At its inception in 2000, eLEXNET included a mere eight labs from seven states and was capable of tracking a sole analyte. Where FERN laboratories were involved in the actual analysis of food samples, eLEXNET provides a forum for the exchange of laboratory data. FDA is continuing efforts to expand eLEXNET to provide better nationwide data on food product analyses by regulatory agencies.

Staff Development and Training

FDA has trained its staff as well as staff from USDA, state food laboratories and the CDC Laboratory Response Network public health laboratories in the analysis of foods for several microorganisms.

9. Research

The FDA focuses its food security research thrust on three broad areas: (1) development of prevention and mitigation technologies/strategies, (2) the elucidation of agent characteristics needed to develop these prevention technologies, and (3) the development of means for continuously assessing foods (raw or finished product) for contamination with chemical, microbiological, and radiological agents. This integrated program will draw upon all three components of the FDA's research infrastructure: its intramural research capabilities, its collaborative Centers of Excellence (e.g., National Center for Food safety and Technology, Joint Institute for Food Safety and Applied Nutrition, National Center for Natural Products Research), and extramural research programs that provide competitive research contracts and grants. Specific projects involve determining the stability of select chemical threat agents in foods and the impact of processing operations; the development of enrichment techniques for the isolation of select microbial agents from high priority foods; the development of prevention/mitigation strategies for intentional contamination of animal feed used for food-producing animals; the development of risk assessment tools for assessing critical control points within a food security/safety system; the development of methods for decontaminating food processing facilities, retail establishments, and transportation equipment that have been exposed to microbiological, chemical, or radiological agents as a result of a terrorism incident involving foods; the acceleration of the development of rapid, field deployable analytical methods for detecting selected agents in foods; and the development of a PC-based analytical modeling tool to facilitate rapid response to food security and safety emergencies.

10. Interagency and International Communication and Collaboration

Food security, like other aspects of protecting our nation's critical infrastructures, requires effective and enhanced coordination across many government agencies at the federal, state, and local level. FDA's activities in public health security are coordinated through the Department of Health and Human Services (DHHS) Secretary's Command Center. This relationship facilitates communication between all HHS Operating Divisions, the Department, and other federal agencies and departments, including Homeland Security.

BOTTOM LINE ON FDA'S APPROACH TO PROTECTING OUR FOOD SUPPLY

The FDA is using risk-based strategies to provide better information for and improve its collaborative efforts with other entities. This includes working with foreign authorities and manufacturers to improve production and shipping practices abroad as an alternative to detailed inspections at the border. The FDA is using better information on imports to focus border checks on products that present significant potential risks and is working with producers to improve checks on the integrity of ingredients and to implement common-sense steps to reduce security risks.

REFERENCES

CDC. 2007. *Animals*, at http://www.cdc.gov/ncidod/dpd/animals.htm (accessed July 02, 2007).

21 CFR Part 170. 2004. *Food and Human Consumption*. Washington, DC: Code of Federal Regulations.

CRS. 2003. *Mad Cow Disease and U.S. Beef Trade*. CRS Report for Congress, at http://www.ers .useda.gov/features/fse/index.htm (accessed July 05, 2007).

FDA. 2003. *Progress Report to Secretary Tommy G. Thompson: Ensuring the Safety and Security of the Nation's Food Supply*. Center for Food Safety and Applied Nutrition, July 23, at http://www.cfsan.fda.gov (accessed July 1, 2, and 4, 2007).

Mason, M. 2007. *Health: Tainted Food on the Menu throughout the Far East.* Associated Press Release.

OIE. 2003. *Terrestrial Animal Health Code,* 12th edition, at http://www.oie.int/eng/norms/ MCode/A_summry.htm.

Vallat, B. 2004. The OIE Paves the Way for a New Animal Disease Notification System, Editorial from the (OIE) Director General.

Foot-and-Mouth Disease: The Primary Threat

The foot-and-mouth disease virus (FMDV) is in the family Picornaviridae, genus *Aphthovirus*. There are 7 immunologically distinct serotypes and over 60 subtypes. New subtypes occasionally develop spontaneously. The FMDV is inactivated at a pH below 6.5 or above 11. The virus can survive in milk and milk products when regular pasteurization temperatures are used. However, it is inactivated by ultra high-temperature pasteurization procedures. Virus stability increases at lower temperatures and can survive in frozen bone marrow or lymph nodes. The virus can also survive drying and may persist for days to weeks in organic matter under moist and cool temperatures. It is inactivated on dry surfaces and by UV radiation (sunlight).

—*Fiebre Aftosa*

Knowles et al. (2005) note that risk assessments following the attacks of September 11, 2001, revealed stark vulnerabilities. Our agricultural landscape, products, methods, and program are exceptionally diverse, ranging from compact, intensive practices that lend themselves to control and security measures (i.e., poultry, swine) to open fields, pens, and pastures that would be virtually impossible to protect from intentional contamination. Consequently, there are many individual targets and threats to consider, each with its own set of potential challenges and countermeasures. For the sake of this book, concentration is placed on foot-and-mouth disease (FMD) the agricultural pathogen that has long been the most feared by U.S. authorities in the event of an accidental or purposeful introduction.

FMD is caused by a member of the picornaviradae family and is a serious disease of cloven-hoofed animals (e.g., cattle, sheep, swine, deer, and goats). The United States has been "FMD free" since 1929. Although it is possible for the virus to infect humans, clinical disease is very rare, and symptoms are generally mild. Consequently, FMD is

FMD: WHAT CAUSES IT?

The disease is caused by a virus. The virus survives in lymph nodes and bone marrow at neutral pH, but destroyed in muscle when in ph<6.0 (i.e., after rigor mortis). The virus can persist in contaminated fodder and the environment for up to one month, depending on the temperature and pH conditions.

There are at least seven separate types and many subtypes of the FMD virus. Immunity to one type does not protect an animal against other types. (USDA, 2002)

not considered a threat to humans and would not normally pose a personal health risk for perpetrators handling the agent (Knowles et al., 2005).

DISEASE CHARACTERISTICS

FMD is considered the most contagious virus known (some 20 times more infectious than smallpox virus) with reports of airborne transmission from animal to animal of up to fifty miles. This remarkable characteristic makes control of the agent in the presence of susceptible populations of animals especially daunting. The virus is also reported to be highly persistent in the environment, remaining viable in contaminated fodder or frozen animal tissues for months. Characteristic lesions of FMD involve blistering and vesicle formation on mucous membranes of the mouth and nose, on teats, and between the "claws" of the feet. Blisters rupture and become painful erosions in affected areas. Affected animals cannot walk, eat, drink, or be milked. FMD does not routinely cause high mortality (death) in infected adult animals but typically infects a high percentage of animals that are susceptible to disease. This infection results in decreased weight gains and milk production (mastitis), abortions, increased juvenile mortality, and hoof sloughing and deformation. In developing countries such as Afghanistan, endemic FMD can have a considerable negative economic and public health impact on those populations that heavily rely on domestic animals for nutrition and livelihood.

FMD WARNING SIGNS

Early warning signs of foot-and-mouth-disease (FMD) include excessive salivation, smacking of lips, severe lameness, fever, and loss of appetite.

HOW IT SPREADS

FMD viruses can be spread by animals, people, or materials that bring the virus into physical contact with susceptible animals. An outbreak can occur when:

- People wearing contaminated clothes or footwear or using contaminated equipment pass the virus to susceptible animals.
- Animals carrying the virus are introduced into susceptible herds.
- Contaminated facilities are used to hold susceptible animals.
- Contaminated vehicles are used to move susceptible animals.
- Raw or improperly cooked garbage containing infected meat or animal products is fed to susceptible animals.
- Susceptible animals are exposed to materials such as hay, feedstuffs, hides, or biologics contaminated with the virus.
- Susceptible animals drink common source contaminated water.
- A susceptible cow is inseminated by semen from an infected bull. (USDA, 2002)

Availability

Since FMD occurs naturally in cloven-hoofed animals in parts of Africa, Asia, the Middle East, and South America, with sporadic outbreaks in FMD-free areas, the virus is readily accessible to would-be terrorists. In the context of potential threats to U.S. interests, the ready availability of FMD-infected animals (a viable source of the virus) in many regions, including Southwest Asia, the Middle East and Afghanistan, greatly complicates strategies for protecting our national food animal herds.

Extent: Weapon of Mass Destruction

The unique characteristics of the FMD virus make it an ideal candidate for use as a weapon of mass destruction. Although it is not a human disease hazard, the economic, psychological, and symbolic effects of the intentional introduction of FMD would have the potential to be a national disaster. Fortunately, our agricultural programs are exceptionally productive and diverse, making it highly improbable that availability of enough food to feed our citizens would be a concern. The benefit for terrorists would be the scenes of chaos, mass euthanasia, funeral pyres, economic turmoil, and visual evidence of physical and emotional trauma to U.S. citizens on wall-to-wall media coverage (Knowles et al., 2005).

As mentioned earlier, agriculture accounts for a significant percentage of the U.S. gross national product (GNP), and even a limited outbreak of FMD in the United States would have a dramatic effect on the food animal industry and the economy. However, a widely dispersed outbreak perpetrated by terrorists could be disastrous on a number of levels. The national stock and commodities markets would likely tumble, regional unemployment would soar, regional agricultural interests heavily invested in the cattle or swine industry would be decimated, and allied agricultural and banking industries would suffer. The cost and effort required to kill and dispose of at-risk food animals would be immense. Additionally, there is the possibility that the virus could become established in such wildlife as deer, buffalo or elk, greatly complicating eradication. Dramatic images of a U.S. disaster (e.g., mass slaughter of animals and distraught owners) would likely achieve the symbolic or political goals of potential terrorists.

Vulnerabilities

U.S. agriculture excels at producing food that is safe, inexpensive, and plentiful as a result of many factors, including intensive industry practices that promote maximum efficiency. Although this a great advantage for the country and consumers, these production methods can greatly increase vulnerabilities to attack. The cattle industry is an extreme example of this vulnerability. A relatively compact geographical area of southwest Kansas, the Oklahoma panhandle, and north Texas accounts for 80 percent of the "fed" cattle in this country. These concentrations of millions of cattle in unprotected pastures and feedyards greatly increase our vulnerability to attack with a disease as deadly as FMD.

Delivery

FMD is easily obtained in many of the countries where declared opponents of U.S. interests and policies, such as al Qaeda, live and operate. The virus needs no complex technical weaponization and delivery systems. Consequently, technical capabilities that are problematic for many classical biowarfare or bioterrorist agents, such as anthrax and plague, are irrelevant for FMD. No technical capability is required. All that is needed is one infected animal and the intent to collect, transport, and use the virus to infect animals in another location. With current technologies and procedures, detection or interception of infectious materials at entry into the United States is exceptionally challenging and virtually impossible in the face of repeated attempts. Once in this country, the infectious virus would early overwhelm susceptible animals. Because of the exceptionally contagious nature of the virus, infected animals become a low-tech, but highly efficient, delivery system. With little strategic forethought, a terrorist could easily use the mobility of animals in our production systems to maximize terrorist goals by ensuring that the disease occurs in multiple locations throughout the country.

Countermeasure: Vaccination

FMD has seven immunological distinct serotypes and up to seventy subtypes. Although a number of different vaccines are available for FMD (the United States does not currently produce any FMD vaccines), different vaccines do not cross-protect against all serotypes and subtypes. Significantly, current vaccines may create a persistent carrier state in cattle that is indistinguishable form natural infection with the virus. Therefore, domestic use of current FMD vaccines as a preventive or deterrent could have the dramatic economic effect of immediately halting meat exports to FMD-free countries such as Japan. The use of available vaccines to help control an outbreak does have utility in a limited outbreak. However, the benefit of vaccination-control strategies is greatly reduced in the face of intentionally caused, widely spread outbreaks that could deplete available supplies of vaccine. Obviously, the vaccines that are available for use must be the right vaccine for the FMD serotype of subtype causing the disease.

Countermeasure: Quarantine, Isolation, and Slaughter

The current national strategy for responding to an FMD outbreak involves isolation of affected animals and systematic slaughter of at-risk animals. Rapid containment, quarantine, and euthanasia are essential to preventing the spreading of highly contagious disease such as FMD. This strategy is primarily designed to respond to an accidental introduction that would hopefully be limited in scope, and current technologies exist to execute this strategy. However, in the context of bioterrorism with potential for massive outbreaks of affected animals in the tens of millions, long-term reliance on such a countermeasure is highly problematic and flawed.

Profiling the Terrorists

Several categories of "terrorists" could be considered threats to the agricultural infrastructure. Although separated by motivation, ideology, and resources, each category of terrorists could be considered potential perpetrators of an agricultural event. Since formal state sponsorship is not a technical or political necessity, the threat of foot-and-mouth disease will be an enduring one for the United States.

There are four categories of potential terrorists:

1. **International terrorists:** Based on numerous threats and intelligence, international terrorists such as al Qaeda pose the most probable threat for introduction of a foreign animal disease.
2. **Economic opportunists:** An FMD outbreak in the U.S. would have a dramatic effect on markets and make virus introduction for the manipulation of markets for personal economic gain a possibility.
3. **Domestic terrorists:** Domestic terrorist groups could view the introduction of FMD as a blow against the federal government. In addition, an unbalanced individual or a disgruntled employee with many possible motivations could be the perpetrator of an attack.
4. **Militant animal rights activists:** Some animal rights activists believe that the use of animals for food is immoral. Militant elements, such as the Animal Liberation Front (ALF), could view an attack on the food animal industry as a positive event.

Terrorists have declared their intention to attack the United States in ways that were previously thought to be improbable, a declaration that has prompted both an evaluation of possible targets for terrorists and significant planning to protect those equities deemed at risk. Clearly, our agricultural infrastructure and food supply could be opportune targets for terrorists. FMD is by most accounts the most problematic of these threats. For many reasons, current strategies for countering an outbreak of FMD are inadequate, leaving this important component of our economy and national infrastructure vulnerable. In light of these vulnerabilities, the U.S must develop new response strategies and countermeasures to reduce the risk that terrorists could significantly damage it using FMD as a weapon.

NOTE

Much of the material presented in this chapter is adapted from a U.S Department of Justice funded report created by the National Institute of Justice, authored by Knowles et al. (2005).

REFERENCES

Aftosa, Fiebre. 2007. "Foot and Mouth Disease (FMD)." Center for Food Security and Public Health, Iowa State University, at www.cfsph.iastate.edu/factsheets/pdfs/foot_and_mouth_disease (accessed August 29, 2007).

Knowles, T., J. Lane, G. Bayens, N. Speer, J. Jaax, D. Carter, and A. Bannister. 2005. *Defining Law Enforcement's Role in Protecting American Agriculture from Agroterrorism.* Washington, DC: National Institute of Justice under contract with U.S. Department of Justice.

USDA. 2002. *Foot-and-Mouth Disease,* at APHIS.usda.gov.

USDA: Pre-Harvest Security Guidelines

The ability to feed its population effectively has always been a significant factor in the prosperity of a society. In fact, a persuasive case can be made that the United States, in part, owes its pre-eminent place in the hierarchy of world economic powers to its tremendous ability to produce and distribute food that is plentiful, inexpensive, and safe. Economists have calculated that U.S. wage earners spend approximately 10 percent of earned income to purchase food. Citizens of other countries cannot duplicate that efficiency and spend a proportionately larger amount of their income on food. The savings on food costs generate personal discretionary spending that propels our high national standard of living. Consequently, a significant attack on agricultural infrastructure could have potentially dire economic consequences, with a ripple effect that would go far beyond the direct cost of goods lost.

—*Knowles et al., 2005*

USDA (2006b) points out that "the protection and integrity of America's agricultural production and food supply are essential to the health and welfare of both the domestic population and the global community. While farm security presents unique challenges for producers, there are some basic and practical security measures that can be instituted at the farm level." Parts of the report are reproduced below.

FARM SECURITY

Threats to farm security are varied and numerous. The prevention of intentional or unintentional injury to crops or livestock is of primary concern in pre-harvest agricultural production. Risk assessments have great utility in the realm of prevention in that they help to identify hazards that need to be addressed and rank their importance. Information obtained from a facility-specific risk assessment can be a powerful tool. In addition to prevention, early identification to minimize damage should an event occur is also very important.

Producers can do some things to protect their facilities:

Awareness

- Periodically conduct random security checks along the perimeter of all fields and pastures for signs of suspicious activity or unauthorized entry.
- Encourage employees to report any suspicious activity or any unauthorized personnel on or near the facility.
- Educate employees and customers to be alert for signs of possible tampering with crops, livestock, supplies, equipment, and facilities.
- Alert all employees and family members to watch for sick animals, including wildlife, especially birds, or unusual changes in the appearance of crops.

Planning

- Develop or update a risk management plan and share it with employees, family, and local law enforcement.
- Identify areas or activities where threats might occur and increase security in those areas.
- Consult with experts when you are developing your plan. Include your veterinarian, crop consultant, Extension agent, university scientist, and state department of agriculture experts.
- Plan how to respond to threats or tampering with your animals, crops, equipment, chemicals, supplies, and energy and water sources.
- Update your plan regularly. Make sure you have contact names and telephone numbers. Include in your plan how you will notify appropriate local law enforcement officials, as well as federal and state agriculture officials.
- Develop a biosecurity plan that includes requirements for quarantining new stock, cleaning and disinfection procedures, and disposal of fallen stock.

Barriers

- Minimize the number of places where people can easily hide around the farm. Trim trees and shrubs that could provide concealment to criminals or block visibility of security patrols.
- Maintain fences in good repair.
- Secure hazardous materials, energy sources, and production inputs like feed and nutrients.
- Secure water wells or other water supplies, and identify alternative water sources as backups.

Community

- Get to know your neighbors.
- Initiate or join a community crime watch program.
- Don't advertise when you'll be away from your facility.

Inventory Control

- Maintain an up-to-date inventory of anhydrous ammonia, ammonium nitrate, bulk urea, pesticides, herbicides, and other hazardous materials and immediately investigate any discrepancies.
- Secure chemical containers inside buildings, whether they are empty or not.
- Make sure that all storage areas for hazardous chemicals and drugs are secured, reasonably isolated, and that they are built and vented according to national and state codes. Supervise employees with access to these materials.
- Inventory critical farm assets (e.g., trucks and tractors) and review your inventory regularly. Frequently inspect trucks, tractors, and other farm equipment of signs of tampering.
- Restrict access to computer data systems, secure on-line communications, and safeguard them with virus protection. Back-up all files at least weekly and store back-up files off-site.

Law Enforcement

- Talk with your local or county sheriff or state police office to find out if your farm or facility is subject to any specific risks based on its locality.
- Arrange to have a security survey of your facility by local law enforcement or your insurance agent.
- Request local law enforcement to routinely conduct patrols along your facility's perimeter.
- Immediately report any unusual or suspicious persons, vehicles, or activity to local law enforcement.

Lighting

- Make sure that the areas surrounding and within farm buildings are well lit.
- Install back-up lighting for emergencies.
- Install alarms, motion detection lights, cameras, and/or other appropriate security equipment as needed. Use electronic sensors around sensitive areas during times when no one should be working at these sites.

Locks

- Be sure your water supply system is secured with locks on wellheads and pump houses, water storage tanks, etc.
- Install entry prevention devices on exterior ladders, protecting the ladders from unauthorized use and preventing access to the top of bulk storage bins.
- Install locks on all doors and seal or lock all windows and vents on buildings that contain critical inventories and equipment.

- Lock all vehicles parked outside at night or during times of owner and employee absence.
- Use deadbolt locks on doors with a minimum of 1.5-inch throw.
- Padlock entry and discharge points of exterior liquid tanks (above and below ground) and all other storage areas when not in use.
- Keep padlocks locked on hasps while not in use.
- Distribute keys to employees on an as needed basis and verify when they are returned.

Signage
- Post signs in fields that direct visitors to a central sign-in area, away from fields, animal pens, and other restricted areas.
- Post alarm monitoring service signs in highly visible locations.
- Post "No Trespassing" signs along the perimeter of the property and "Do Not Enter" signs outside of all buildings.
- Periodically check the signs, and replace or repair them, as necessary.

Training
- Make an emergency preparation and response plan that includes all emergency phone numbers and information that may be needed by first responders (such as the type and location of all chemicals at the facility).
- Hold frequent safety and security meetings with all employees and family members who work or live on the farm/ranch.
- Make sure employees know how and where to report concerns or suspicious activities.

Visitors and Personnel
- Have only one (clearly marked) entryway for visitor use.
- Require all visitors to check in with a designated farm representative.
- Designate a specific area for visitor parking.
- Maintain a record of visitors' names/companies, arrival/departure times and purposes of the visit.
- Use visitor badges or identification cards if needed and explain disease prevention to visitors.
- Do not allow visitors, including delivery personnel, contract providers, and service support, to have unlimited access to the premises.
- Restrict visitor access to key areas such as gasoline, fertilizer, and pesticide storage.
- Require proof of identify for non-service visitors.
- Screen prospective employees, check with references, and consider regular background checks on all employees.
- Develop a system to identify employees and visitors.

PHYSICAL ASSET MONITORING AND CONTROL DEVICES (REPRINTED FROM SPELLMAN, 2007)

Aboveground, Outdoor Equipment Enclosures

An agricultural system consists of multiple components spread over a wide area, and typically includes feedlots, crop fields, silos, barns, machinery storage areas, as well as waste treatment ponds that are typically distributed (connected) to community wastewater treatment facilities. Because of need and use, designers typically favor placing critical equipment—especially assets that require regular use and maintenance—aboveground. One of the primary reasons for doing so is that locating equipment aboveground eliminates safety risks associated with confined space entry, which is often required for the maintenance of equipment located belowground. However, it should be pointed out that underground waste pits are quite common on farms and these spaces are people-killers—they should be only entered with great care and caution.

Many different system components can be installed outdoors and aboveground. Examples of these types of components could include:

- Backflow prevention devices
- Various piping systems
- Feedlots
- Pumps and motors
- Chemical storage and feed equipment
- Chicken coops
- Silos
- Instrumentation
- Farm machinery storage facility
- Miscellaneous outhouses
- Stock holding pens
- Ranch house
- Stables
- Greenhouses
- Nurseries
- Shops
- Manure storage/pits

One of the most effective security measures for protecting aboveground equipment is to place it inside a building. When/where this is not possible, enclosing the equipment or parts of the equipment using some sort of commercial or homemade add-on structure may help to prevent tampering with the equipment. These types of add-on structures or enclosures, which are designed to protect the equipment both from the elements and from unauthorized access or tampering, typically consist of a boxlike structure that is placed over the entire component, or over critical parts of the component (i.e., valves, etc.), and is then secured to delay or prevent intruders from tampering with the equipment. The enclosures are typically locked or otherwise anchored to a solid foundation, which makes it difficult for unauthorized personnel to remove the enclosure and access the equipment.

Standardized aboveground enclosures are available in a wide variety of materials, sizes, and configurations. Many options and security features are also available for each type of enclosure, and this allows system operators the flexibility to customize an enclosure for a specific application and/or price range. In addition, most manufacturers can custom-design enclosures if standard, off-the-shelf enclosures do not meet a user's needs.

Many of these enclosures are designed to meet certain standards. For example, the American Society of Sanitary Engineers (ASSE) has developed Standard #1060, *Performance Requirements for Outdoor Enclosures for Backflow Prevention Assemblies*. If an enclosure will be used to house a backflow preventer (used in some large operations to prevent liquid waste from entering the potable water system), this standard specifies the acceptable construction materials for the enclosure, as well as the performance requirements that the enclosure should meet, including specifications for freeze protection, drainage, air inlets, access for maintenance, and hinge requirements. ASSE #1060 also states that the enclosure should be lockable to enhance security.

Equipment enclosures can generally be categorized into one of four main configurations, which include:

- One-piece, drop-over enclosures
- Hinged or removable top enclosures
- Sectional enclosures
- Shelters with access locks

All enclosures, including those with integral floors, must be secured to a foundation to prevent them from being moved or removed. Un- or poorly anchored enclosures may be blown off the equipment being protected, or may be defeated by intruders. In either case, this may result in the equipment beneath the enclosure becoming exposed and damaged. Therefore, ensuring that the enclosure is securely anchored will increase the security of the protected equipment.

The three basic types of foundations that can be used to anchor the aboveground equipment enclosure are concrete footers, concrete slabs-on-grade, or manufactured fiberglass pads. The most common types of foundations utilized for equipment enclosures are standard or slab-on-grade footers; however, local climate and soil conditions may dictate whether either of these types of foundations can be used. These foundations can be either precast or poured in place at the installation site. Once the foundation is installed and properly cured, the equipment enclosure is bolted or anchored to the foundation to secure it in place.

An alternative foundation, specifically for use with smaller hot box enclosures, is a manufactured fiberglass pad known as the Glass PadTM. The Glass PadTM has the center cut out so that it can be dropped directly over the piece of equipment being enclosed. Once the pad is set level on the ground, it is backfilled over a two-inch flange located around its base. The enclosure is then placed on top of the foundation, and is locked in place with either a staple- or a slotted-anchor, depending on the enclosure configuration.

One of the primary attributes of a security enclosure is its strength and resistance to breaking and penetration. Accordingly, the materials from which the enclosure is constructed will be important in determining the strength of the enclosure, and thus its usefulness for security applications. Enclosures are typically manufactured from either fiberglass or aluminum. With the exception of the one-piece, drop-over enclosure, which is typically fabricated from fiberglass, each configuration described above can be constructed from either material. In addition, enclosures can be custom-manufactured from polyurethane, galvanized steel, or stainless steel. Galvanized or stainless steel is often offered as an exterior layer, or "skin," for an aluminum enclosure. Although they are typically utilized in underground applications, precast concrete structures can also be used as aboveground equipment enclosures. However, precast structures are much heavier and more difficult to maneuver than are their fiberglass and aluminum counterparts. Concrete is also brittle, and that can be a security concern; however, products (i.e., epoxy coating) can be applied to concrete structures to add strength and minimize security risks. Because precast concrete structures can be purchased from any concrete producers, this document does not identify specific vendors for these types of products.

In addition to the construction materials, enclosure walls can be configured or reinforced to give them added strength. Adding insulation is one option that can strengthen the structural characteristics of an enclosure; however, some manufacturers offer additional features to add strength to exterior walls. For example, while most enclosures are fabricated with a flat wall construction, some vendors manufacture fiberglass shelters with ribbed exterior walls. These ribs increase the structural integrity of the wall and allow the fabrication of standard shelters up to twenty feet in length. Another vendor has developed a proprietary process that uses a series of integrated fiberglass beams that are placed throughout a foam inner core to tie together the interior and exterior walls and roof. Yet another vendor constructs aluminum enclosures with horizontal and vertical redwood beams for structural support.

Other security features that can be implemented on aboveground, outdoor equipment enclosures include locks, mounting brackets, tamper-resistant doors, and exterior lighting.

Active Security Barriers (Crash Barriers)

Active security barriers (also known as crash barriers) are large structures that are placed in roadways at entrance and exit points to protected facilities to control vehicle access to these areas. In farm operations, these barriers could be used to protect entranceways to concentrated animal feeding operations (CAFO) and other farm stock/equipment areas. These barriers are placed perpendicular to traffic to block the roadway, so that the only way that traffic can pass the barrier is for the barrier to be moved out of the roadway. These types of barriers are typically constructed from sturdy materials, such as concrete or steel, such that vehicles cannot penetrate through them. They are also designed at a certain height off the roadway so that vehicles cannot go over them.

The key difference between active security barriers, which include wedges, crash beams, gates, retractable bollards, and portable barricades; and passive security barriers, which include nonmoveable bollards, jersey barriers, and planters, is that active security barriers are designed so that they can be raised and lowered or moved out of the roadway easily to allow authorized vehicles to pass them. Many of these types of barriers are designed so that they can be opened and closed automatically (i.e., mechanized gates, hydraulic wedge barriers), while others are easy to open and close manually (swing crash beams, manual gates). In contrast to active barriers, passive barriers are permanent, nonmovable barriers, and thus they are typically used to protect the perimeter of a protected facility, such as sidewalks and other areas that do not require vehicular traffic to pass them. Several of the major types of active security barriers such as wedge barriers, crash beams, gates, bollards, and portable/removable barricades are described below.

Wedge barriers are plated, rectangular steel buttresses approximately 2–3 feet high that can be raised and lowered from the roadway. When they are in the open position, they are flush with the roadway and vehicles can pass over them. However, when they are in the closed (armed) position, they project up from the road at a 45 degree angle, with the upper end pointing toward the oncoming vehicle and the base of the barrier away from the vehicle. Generally, wedge barriers are constructed from heavy-gauge steel, or concrete that contains an impact-dampening iron rebar core that is strong and resistant to breaking or cracking, thereby allowing them to withstand the impact from a vehicle attempting to crash through them. In addition, both of these materials help to transfer the energy of the impact over the barrier's entire volume, thus helping to prevent the barrier from being sheared off its base. In addition, because the barrier is angled away from traffic, the force of any vehicle impacting the barrier is distributed over the entire surface of the barrier and is not concentrated at the base, which helps prevent the barrier from breaking off at the base. Finally, the angle of the barrier helps hang up any vehicles attempting to drive over it.

Wedge barriers can be fixed or portable. Fixed wedge barriers can be mounted on the surface of the roadway ("surface-mounted wedges") or in a shallow mount in the road's surface, or they can be installed completely below the road surface. Surface-mounted wedge barricades operate by rising from a flat position on the surface of the roadway, while shallow-mount wedge barriers rise from their resting position just below the road surface. In contrast, below-surface wedge barriers operate by rising from beneath the road surface. Both the shallow-mounted and surface-mounted barriers require little or no excavation, and thus do not interfere with buried utilities. All three barrier mounting types project above the road surface and block traffic when they are raised into the armed position. Once they are disarmed and lowered, they are flush with the road, thereby allowing traffic to pass. Portable wedge barriers are moved into place on wheels that are removed after the barrier has been set into place.

Installing rising wedge barriers requires preparation of the road surface. Installing surface-mounted wedges does not require that the road be excavated; however, the road surface must be intact and strong enough to allow the bolts anchoring the wedge to the road surface to attach properly. Shallow-mount and below-surface wedge barricades require excavation of a pit that is large enough to accommodate the wedge structure, as well as any arming/disarming mechanisms. Generally, the bottom of the excavation pit is lined with gravel to allow for drainage. Areas not sheltered from rain or surface runoff can install a gravity drain or self-priming pump. Table 6.1 lists the pros and cons of wedge barriers.

Crash beam barriers consist of aluminum beams that can be opened or closed across the roadway. While there are several different crash beam designs, every crash beam system consists of an aluminum beam that is supported on each side by a solid footing or buttress, which is typically constructed from concrete, steel, or some other strong material. Beams typically contain an interior steel cable (typically at least one inch in diameter) to give the beam added strength and rigidity. The beam is connected by a heavy duty hinge or other mechanism to one of the footings so that it can swing or rotate out of the roadway when it is open, and can swing back across the road when it is in the closed (armed) position, blocking the road and inhibiting access by unauthorized vehicles. The nonhinged end of the beam can be locked into its footing, thus providing anchoring for the beam on both sides of the road and increasing the beam's resistance to any vehicles attempting to penetrate through it. In addition, if the crash beam is hit by a vehicle, the aluminum beam transfers the impact energy to the interior cable, which in turn transfers the impact energy through the footings and into

Table 6.1.   Pros and Cons of Wedge Barriers

Pros	Cons
Can be surface-mounted or completely installed below the roadway surface.	Installations below the surface of the roadway will require construction that may interfere with buried utilities.
Wedge barriers have a quick response time (normally 3.5–10.5 seconds, but can be 1–3 seconds in emergency situations). Because emergency activation of the barrier causes more wear and tear on the system than does normal activation, it is recommended for use only in true emergency situations. Surface or shallow-mount wedge barricades can be utilized in locations with a high water table and/or corrosive soils.	Regular maintenance is needed to keep wedge barrier fully operational.
	Improper use of the system may result in authorized vehicles being hung up by the barrier and damaged. Guards must be trained to use the system properly to ensure that this does not happen. Safety technologies may also be installed to reduce the risk of the wedge activating under an authorized vehicle.
All three wedge barrier designs have a high crash rating, thereby allowing them to be employed for higher security applications.	
These types of barrier are extremely visible, which may deter potential intruders.	

Source: U.S. EPA, 2005.

their foundation, thereby minimizing the chance that the impact will snap the beam and allow the intruding vehicle to pass through.

Crash beam barriers can employ drop-arm, cantilever, or swing beam designs. Drop-arm crash beams operate by raising and lowering the beam vertically across the road. Cantilever crash beams are projecting structures that are opened and closed by extending the beam from the hinge buttress to the receiving buttress located on the opposite side of the road. In the swing beam design, the beam is hinged to the buttress such that it swings horizontally across the road. Generally, swing beam and cantilever designs are used at locations where a vertical lift beam is impractical. For example, the swing beam or cantilever designs are utilized at entrances and exits with overhangs, trees, or buildings that would physically block the operation of the drop-arm beam design.

Installing any of these crash beam barriers involves the excavation of a pit approximately 48 inches deep for both the hinge and the receiver footings. Due to the depth of excavation, the site should be inspected for underground utilities before digging begins. Table 6.2 lists the pros and cons of crash beams.

In contrast to wedge barriers and crash beams, which are typically installed separately from a fence line, *gates* are often integrated units of a perimeter fence or wall around a facility. Gates are basically movable pieces of fencing that can be opened and

Table 6.2.   Pros and Cons of Crash Beams

Pros	Cons
Requires little maintenance, while providing long-term durability.	Crash beams have a slower response time (normally 9.5–15.3 seconds, but can be reduced to 7–10 seconds in emergency situations) than do other types of active security barriers, such as wedge barriers. Because emergency activation of the barrier causes more wear and tear on the system than does normal activation, it is recommended for use only in true emergency situations.
No excavation is required in the roadway itself to install crash beams.	All three crash beam designs possess a low crash rating relative to other types of barriers, such as wedge barriers, and thus they typically are used for lower security applications.
	Certain crash barriers may not be visible to oncoming traffic and therefore may require additional lighting and/or other warning markings to reduce the potential for traffic to accidentally run into the beam.

Source: U.S. EPA, 2005.

closed across a road. When the gate is in the closed (armed) position, the leaves of the gate lock into steel buttresses that are embedded in concrete foundation located on both sides of the roadway, thereby blocking access to the roadway. Generally, gate barricades are constructed from a combination of heavy gauge steel and aluminum that can absorb an impact from vehicles attempting to ram through them. Any remaining impact energy not absorbed by the gate material is transferred to the steel buttresses and their concrete foundation.

Gates can utilize a cantilever, linear, or swing design. Cantilever gates are projecting structures that operate by extending the gate from the hinge footing across the roadway to the receiver footing. A linear gate is designed to slide across the road on tracks via a rack and pinion drive mechanism. Swing gates are hinged so that they can swing horizontally across the road.

Installation of the cantilever, linear, or swing gate designs described above involve the excavation of a pit approximately 48 inches deep for both the hinge and receiver footings to which the gates are attached. Due to the depth of excavation, the site should be inspected for underground utilities before digging begins. Table 6.3 lists the pros and cons of gates.

Bollards are vertical barriers at least 3 feet tall and 1 to 2 feet in diameter that are typically set 4 to 5 feet apart from each other so that they block vehicles from passing

Table 6.3.   Pros and Cons of Gates

Pros	Cons
All three gate designs possesses an intermediate crash rating, thereby allowing them to be utilized for medium to higher security applications.	Gates have a slower response time (normally 10–15 seconds, but can be reduced to 7–10 seconds in emergency situations) than do other types of active security barriers, such as wedge barriers. Because emergency activation of the barrier causes more wear and tear on the system than does normal activation, it is recommended for use only in true emergency situations.
Requires very little maintenance.	
Can be tailored to blend in with perimeter fencing.	
Gate construction requires no roadway excavation.	
Cantilever gates are useful for roads with high crowns or drainage gutters.	
These types of barriers are extremely visible, which may deter intruders.	
Gates can also be used to control pedestrian traffic.	

Source: U.S. EPA, 2005.

between them. Bollards can either be fixed in place, removable, or retractable. Fixed and removable bollards are passive barriers that are typically used along building perimeters or on sidewalks to prevent vehicles from passing them, while allowing pedestrians to pass them. In contrast to passive bollards, retractable bollards are active security barriers that can easily be raised and lowered to allow vehicles to pass between them. Thus, they can be used in driveways or on roads to control vehicular access. When the bollards are raised, they protect above the road surface and block the roadway; when they are lowered, they sit flush with the road surface, and thus allow traffic to pass over them. Retractable bollards are typically constructed from steel or other materials that have a low weight-to-volume ratio so that they require low power to raise and lower. Steel is also more resistant to breaking than is a more brittle material, such as concrete, and is better able to withstand direct vehicular impact without breaking apart.

Retractable bollards are installed in a trench dug across a roadway—typically at an entrance or gate. Installing retractable bollards requires preparing the road surface. Depending on the vendor, bollards can be installed either in a continuous slab of concrete, or in individual excavations with concrete poured in place. The required excavation for a bollard is typically slightly wider and slightly deeper than the bollard height when extended aboveground. The bottom of the excavation is typically lined with gravel to allow drainage. The bollards are then connected to a control panel which controls the raising and lowering of the bollards. Installation typically requires mechani-

Table 6.4. Pros and Cons of Retractable Bollards

Pros	Cons
Bollards have a quick response time (normally 3–10 seconds, but can be reduced to 1–3 seconds in emergency situations).	Bollard installations will require construction below the surface of the roadway, which may interfere with buried utilities.
Bollards have an intermediate crash rating, which allows them to be utilized for medium to higher security applications.	Some maintenance is needed to ensure barrier is free to move up and down.
	The distance between bollards must be decreased (i.e., more bollards must be installed along the same perimeter) to make these systems effective against small vehicles (i.e., motorcycles).

Source: U.S. EPA, 2005.

cal, electrical, and concrete work; if utility personnel with these skills are available, then the utility can install the bollards themselves. Table 6.4 lists the pros and cons of retractable bollards.

Portable/removable barriers, which can include removable crash beams and wedge barriers, are mobile obstacles that can be moved in and out of position on a roadway. For example, a crash beam may be completely removed and stored off-site when it is not needed. An additional example would be wedge barriers that are equipped with wheels that can be removed after the barricade is towed into place.

When portable barricades are needed, they can be moved into position rapidly. To provide them with added strength and stability, they are typically anchored to buttress boxes that are located on either side of the road. These buttress boxes, which may or may not be permanent, are usually filled with sand, water, cement, gravel, or concrete to make them heavy and aid in stabilizing the portable barrier. In addition, these buttresses can help dissipate any impact energy from vehicles crashing into the barrier itself.

Because these barriers are not anchored into the roadway, they do not require excavation or other related construction for installation. In contrast, they can be assembled and made operational in a short period of time. The primary shortcoming to this type of design is that these barriers may move if they are hit by vehicles. Therefore, it is important to carefully assess the placement and anchoring of these types of barriers to ensure that they can withstand the types of impacts that may be anticipated at that location. Table 6.5 lists the pros and cons of portable/removable barricades.

Because the primary threat to active security barriers is that vehicles will attempt to crash through them, their most important attributes are their size, strength, and crash resistance. Other important features for an active security barrier are the mechanisms

Table 6.5.   Pros and Cons of Portable/Removable Barricades

Pros	Cons
Installing portable barricades requires no foundation or roadway excavation.	Portable barriers may move slightly when hit by a vehicle, resulting in a lower crash resistance.
Can be moved in and out of position in a short period of time.	Portable barricades typically require 7.75 to 16.25 seconds to move into place, and thus they are considered to have a medium response time when compared with other active barriers.
Wedge barriers equipped with wheels can be easily towed into place.	
Minimal maintenance is needed to keep barriers fully operational.	

Source: U.S. EPA, 2005.

by which the barrier is raised and lowered to allow authorized vehicle entry, and other factors, such as weather resistance and safety features.

Alarms

Common sense tells us that it would be extremely difficult to alarm hundreds or thousands of acres of farmland. However, for concentrated animal-feeding operations (CAFOs) and other farm operations, alarms may be appropriate; thus, they are discussed in the following.

An *alarm system* is a type of electronic monitoring system that is used to detect and respond to specific types of events—such as unauthorized access to an asset, or a possible fire. In large agribusiness operations, alarms are also used to alert operators (e.g. milking operations) when process operating or monitoring conditions go out of preset parameters (i.e., process alarms). These types of alarms are designed primarily to be integrated with process monitoring and reporting systems (i.e., SCADA systems) in some large agribusiness operations.

Alarm systems can be integrated with fire detection systems, IDSs (intrinsic detection systems), access control systems, or Closed Circuit Television (CCTV) systems, such that these systems automatically respond when the alarm is triggered. For example, a smoke detector alarm can be set up to automatically notify the fire department when smoke is detected; or an intrusion alarm can automatically trigger cameras to turn on in a remote location so that personnel can monitor that location.

An alarm system consists of sensors that detect different types of events; an arming station that is used to turn the system on and off; a control panel that receives information, processes it, and transmits the alarm; and an annunciator that generates a visual and/or audible response to the alarm. When a sensor is tripped it sends a signal to a control panel, which triggers a visual or audible alarm and/or notifies a central monitoring station. A more complete description of each of the components of an alarm system is provided below.

Detection devices (also called *sensors*) are designed to detect a specific type of event (such as smoke, intrusion, etc.). Depending on the type of event they are designed to detect, sensors can be located inside or outside of the facility or other asset. When an event is detected, the sensors use some type of communication method (such as wireless radio transmitters, conductors, or cables) to send signals to the control panel to generate the alarm. For example, a smoke detector sends a signal to a control panel when it detects smoke.

Alarms use either normally closed (NC) or normally open (NO) electric loops, or "circuits," to generate alarm signals. These two types of circuits are discussed separately below.

In NC loops or circuits, all of the system's sensors and switches are connected in series. The contacts are "at rest" in the closed (on) position, and current continually passes through the system. However, when an event triggers the sensor, the loop is opened, breaking the flow of current through the system and triggering the alarm. NC switches are used more often than are NO switches because the alarm will be activated if the loop or circuit is broken or cut, thereby reducing the potential for circumventing the alarm. This is known as a "supervised" system.

In NO loops or circuits, all of the system's sensors and switches are connected in parallel. The contacts are "at rest" in the open (off) position, and no current passes through the system. However, when an event triggers the sensor, the loop is closed. This allows current to flow through the loop, powering the alarm. NO systems are not "supervised" because the alarm will not be activated if the loop or circuit is broken or cut. However, adding an end-of-line resistor to an NO loop will cause the system to alarm if tampering is detected.

An *arming station*, which is the main user interface with the security system, allows the user to arm (turn on), disarm (turn off), and communicate with the system. How a specific system is armed will depend on how it is used. For example, while IDSs can be armed for continuous operation (24 hours/day), they are usually armed and disarmed according to the work schedule at a specific location so that personnel going about their daily activities do not set off the alarms. In contrast, fire protection systems are typically armed 24 hours a day.

A *control panel* receives information from the sensors and sends it to an appropriate location, such as to a central operations station or to a 24-hour monitoring facility. Once the alarm signal is received at the central monitoring location, personnel monitoring for alarms can respond (such as by sending security teams to investigate or by dispatching the fire department).

An *annunciator* responds to the detection of an event by emitting a signal. This signal may be visual, audible, electronic, or a combination of these three. For example, fire alarm signals will always be connected to audible annunciators, whereas intrusion alarms may not be.

Alarms can be reported locally, remotely, or both locally and remotely. Local and remotely (centrally) reported alarms are discussed in more detail below.

A *local alarm* emits a signal at the location of the event (typically using a bell or siren). A "local only" alarm emits a signal at the location of the event but does not transmit the alarm signal to any other location (i.e., it does not transmit the alarm to a central monitoring location). Typically, the purpose of a "local only" alarm is to frighten away intruders, and possibly to attract the attention of someone who might notify the proper authorities. Because no signal is sent to a central monitoring location, personnel can only respond to a local alarm if they are in the area and can hear and/or see the alarm signal.

Fire alarm systems must have local alarms, including both audible and visual signals. Most fire alarm signal and response requirements are codified in the National Fire Alarm Code, National Fire Protection Association (NFPA) 72. NFPA 72 discusses the application, installation, performance, and maintenance of protective signaling systems and their components. In contrast to fire alarms, which require a local signal when fire is detected, many IDSs do not have a local alert device, because monitoring personnel do not wish to inform potential intruders that they have been detected. Instead, these types of systems silently alert monitoring personnel that an intrusion has been detected, thus allowing monitoring personnel to respond.

In contrast to systems that are set up to transmit "local only" alarms when the sensors are triggered, systems can also be set up to transmit signals to a *central location,* such as to a control room or guard post at the utility, or to a police or fire station. Most fire/smoke alarms are set up to signal both at the location of the event and at a fire station or central monitoring station. Many insurance companies require that facilities install certified systems that include alarm communication to a central station. For example, systems certified by the Underwriters Laboratory (UL) require that the alarm be reported to a central monitoring station.

The main differences between alarm systems lie in the types of event detection devices used in different systems. *Intrusion sensors,* for example, consist of two main categories: perimeter sensors and interior (space) sensors. *Perimeter intrusion sensors* are typically applied on fences, doors, walls, windows, and so forth, and are designed to detect an intruder before he/she accesses a protected asset (i.e., perimeter intrusion sensors are used to detect intruders attempting to enter through a door, window, etc.). In contrast, *interior intrusion sensors* are designed to detect an intruder who has already accessed the protected asset (i.e., interior intrusion sensors are used to detect intruders once they are already within a protected room or building). These two types of detection devices can be complementary, and they are often used together to enhance security for an asset. For example, a typical intrusion alarm system might employ a perimeter glass-break detector that protects against intruders accessing a room

through a window, as well as an ultrasonic interior sensor that detects intruders that
have gotten into the room without using the window. Table 6.6 lists and describes types
of perimeter and interior sensors.

Fire detection/fire alarm systems consist of different types of fire detection devices
and fire alarm systems available. These systems may detect fire, heat, smoke, or a combination of any of these. For example, a typical fire alarm system might consist of heat

Table 6.6.   Perimeter and Interior Sensors

Type of Perimeter Sensor	*Description*
Foil	Foil is a thin, fragile, lead-based metallic tape that is applied to glass windows and doors. The tape is applied to the window or door, and electric wiring connects this tape to a control panel. The tape functions as a conductor and completes the electric circuit with the control panel. When an intruder breaks the door or window, the fragile foil breaks, opening the circuit and triggering an alarm condition.
Magnetic switches (reed switches)	The most widely used perimeter sensor. They are typically used to protect doors, as well as windows that can be opened (windows that cannot be opened are more typically protected by foil alarms).
Glass break detectors	Placed on glass and sense vibrations in the glass when it is disturbed. The two most common types of glass-break detectors are shock sensors and audio discriminators.
Type of Interior Sensor	*Description*
Passive infrared (PIR)	Presently the most popular and cost effective interior sensors. PIR detectors monitor infrared radiation (energy in the form of heat) and detect rapid changes in temperature within a protected area. Because infrared radiation is emitted by all living things, these types of sensors can be very effective.
Quad PIRs	Consist of two dual-element sensors combined in one housing. Each sensor has a separate lens and a separate processing circuitry, which allows each lens to be set up to generate a different protection pattern
Ultrasonic detectors	Emit high frequency sound waves, and sense movement in a protected area by sensing changes in these waves. The sensor emits sound waves that stabilize and set a baseline condition in the area to be protected. Any subsequent movement within the protected area by a would-be intruder will cause a change in these waves, thus creating an alarm condition.
Microwave detectors	Emit ultra high frequency radio waves, and the detector senses any changes in these waves as they are reflected throughout the protected space. Microwaves can penetrate through walls, and thus a unit placed in one location may be able to protect multiple rooms.
Dual technology devices	Incorporate two different types of sensor technology (such as PIR and microwave technology) together in one housing. When both technologies sense an intrusion, an alarm is triggered.

Source: U.S. EPA, 2005.

sensors, which are located throughout a facility and which detect high temperatures or a certain change in temperature over a fixed time period. A different system might be outfitted with both smoke and heat detection devices. A summary of several different types of fire/smoke/heat detection sensors is provided in table 6.7.

Once a sensor in an alarm system detects an event, it must communicate an alarm signal. The two basic types of alarm communication systems are hardwired and wireless. Hardwired systems rely on wire that is run from the control panel to each of the

Table 6.7. Fire/Smoke/Heat Detection Sensors

Detector Type	Description
Thermal detectors	Sense when temperatures exceed a set threshold (fixed temperature detectors) or when the rate of change of temperature increases over a fixed time period (rate-of-rise detectors).
Duct detector	Is located within the heating and ventilation ducts of the facility. This sensor detects the presence of smoke within the system's return or supply ducts. A sampling tube can be added to the detector to help span the width of the duct.
Smoke detectors	Sense invisible and/or visible products of combustion. The two principle types of smoke detectors are photoelectric and ionization detectors. The major differences between these devices are described below:
	• Photoelectric smoke detectors react to visible particles of smoke. These detectors are more sensitive to the cooler smoke with large smoke particles that is typical of smoldering fires.
	• Ionization smoke detectors are sensitive to the presence of ions produced by the chemical reactions that take place with few smoke particles, such as those typically produced by fast burning/flaming fires.
Multisensor detectors	Are a combination of photoelectric and thermal detectors. The photoelectric sensor serves to detect smoldering fires, while the thermal detector senses the heat given off from fast burning/flaming fires.
Carbon monoxide (CO) detectors	Are used to indicate the outbreak of fire by sensing the level of carbon monoxide in the air. The detector has an electrochemical cell which senses carbon monoxide, but not some or other products of combustion.
Beam detectors	Are designed to protect large, open spaces such as industrial warehouses. These detectors consist of three parts: the transmitter, which projects a beam of infrared light; the receiver, which registers the light and produces an electrical signal; and the interface, which processes the signal and generates fault signals. In the event of a fire, smoke particles obstruct the beam of light. Once a preset threshold is exceeded, the detector will go into alarm.
Flame detectors	Sense either ultraviolet (UV) or infrared (IR) radiation emitted by a fire.
Air-sampling detectors	Actively and continuously sample the air from a protected space and are able to sense the pre-combustion stages of incipient fire.

Source: U.S. EPA, 2005.

detection devices and annunciators. Wireless systems transmit signals from a transmitter to a receiver through the air—primarily using radio or other waves. Hardwired systems are usually lower cost, more reliable (they are not affected by terrain or environmental factors), and significantly easier to troubleshoot than are wireless systems. However, a major disadvantage of hardwired systems is that it may not be possible to hardwire all locations (for example, it may be difficult to hardwire remote locations). In addition, running wires to their required locations can be both time consuming and costly. The major advantage to using wireless systems is that they can often be installed in areas where hardwired systems are not feasible. However, wireless components can be much more expensive when compared to hardwired systems. In addition, in the past, it has been difficult to perform self-diagnostics on wireless systems to confirm that they are communicating properly with the controller. Presently, the majority of wireless systems incorporate supervising circuitry, which allows the subscriber to know immediately if there is a problem with the system (such as a broken detection device or a low battery), or if a protected door or window has been left open.

Exterior Intrusion Sensors

An exterior intrusion sensor is a detection device that is used in an outdoor environment to detect intrusions into a protected area. These devices are designed to detect an intruder, and then communicate an alarm signal to an alarm system. The alarm system can respond to the intrusion in many different ways, such as by triggering an audible or visual alarm signal, or by sending an electronic signal to a central monitoring location that notifies security personnel of the intrusion.

Intrusion sensors can be used to protect many kinds of assets. Intrusion sensors that protect physical space are classified according to whether they protect indoor, or "interior" space (i.e., an entire building or room within a building), or outdoor, or "exterior" space (i.e., a fence line or perimeter). Interior intrusion sensors are designed to protect the interior space of a facility by detecting an intruder who is attempting to enter, or who has already entered a room or building. In contrast, exterior intrusion sensors are designed to detect an intrusion into a protected outdoor/exterior area. Exterior protected areas are typically arranged as zones or exclusion areas placed so that the intruder is detected early in the intrusion attempt before the intruder can gain access to more valuable assets (e.g., into a building located within the protected area). Early detection creates additional time for security forces to respond to the alarm.

Exterior intrusion sensors are classified according to how the sensor detects the intrusion within the protected area. The three classes of exterior sensor technology include:

- Buried line sensors
- Fence-associated sensors
- Freestanding sensors

Buried-Line Sensors

As the name suggests, buried line sensors are sensors that are buried underground, and are designed to detect disturbances within the ground—such as disturbances caused by an intruder digging, crawling, walking, or running on the monitored ground. Because they sense ground disturbances, these types of sensors are able to detect intruder activity both on the surface and below ground. Individual types of exterior buried line sensors function in different ways, including detecting motion, pressure, or vibrations within the protected ground, or detecting changes in some type of field (e.g., magnetic field) that the sensors generate within the protected ground. Specific types of buried line sensors include pressure or seismic sensors, magnetic field sensors, ported coaxial cables, and fiber-optic cables. Details on each of these sensor types are provided below. Table 6.8 presents the distinctions between the four types of buried sensors.

- *Buried-line pressure* or *seismic sensors* detect physical disturbances to the ground—such as vibrations or soil compression—caused by intruders walking, driving, digging, or otherwise physically contacting the protected ground. These sensors detect disturbances from all directions and, therefore, can protect an area radially outward form their location; however, because detection may weaken as a function of distance from the disturbance, choosing the correct burial depth from the design area will be crucial. In general, sensors buried at a shallow depth protect a relatively small area but have a high probability of detecting intrusion within that area, while sensors buried at a deeper depth protect a wider area but have a lower probability of detecting intrusion into that area.
- *Buried line magnetic field sensors* detect changes in a local magnetic field that are caused by the movement of metallic objects within that field. This type of sensor can detect ferric metal objects worn or carried by an intruder entering a protected area on foot as well as vehicles being driven into the protected area.
- *Buried line ported coaxial cable sensors* detect the motion of any object (i.e., human body, metal, etc.) possessing high conductivity and located within close proximity to

Table 6.8. Types of Buried Sensors

Type	Description
Pressure or Seismic	Responds to disturbances in the soil.
Magnetic Field	Responds to a change in the local magnetic field caused by the movement of nearby metallic material.
Ported Coaxial Cables	Responds to motion of a material with a high dielectric constant or high conductivity near the cables.
Fiber-Optic Cables	Responds to a change in the shape of the fiber, which can be sensed using sophisticated sensors and computer signal processing.

Source: Adapted from Garcia, 2001.

the cables. An intruder entering into the protected space creates an active distur-bance in the electric field, thereby triggering an alarm condition.

- *Buried line fiber-optic cable sensors* detect changes in the attenuation of light signals transmitted within the cable. When the soil around the cable is compressed, the ca-ble is distorted, and the light signal transmitted through the cable changes, initiating an alarm. This type of sensor is easy to install because it can be buried at a shallow burial depth (only a few centimeters) and still be effective.

Fence-Associated Sensors

Fence-associated sensors are either attached to an existing fence, or are installed in such a way as to create a fence. These sensors detect disturbances to the fence—such as those caused by an intruder attempting to climb the fence, or by an intruder attempt-ing to cut or lift the fence fabric. Exterior fence-associated sensors include fence-dis-turbance sensors, taut-wire sensor fences, and electric field or capacitance sensors. Details on each of these sensor types are provided below.

- *Fence-disturbance sensors* detect the motion or vibration of a fence that can be caused by an intruder attempting to climb or cut through the fence. In general, fence dis-turbance sensors are used on chain link fences or on other fence types where a move-able fence fabric is hung between fence posts.
- *Taut-wire sensor fences* are similar to fence-disturbance sensors except that instead of attaching the sensors to a loose fence fabric, the sensors are attached to a wire that is stretched tightly across the fence. These types of systems are designed to de-tect changes in the tension of the wire rather than vibrations in the fence fabric. Taut-wire sensor fences can be installed over existing fences, or as stand-alone fence systems.
- *Electric field or capacitance sensors* detect changes in capacitive coupling between wires that are attached to, but electrically isolated from, the fence. As opposed to other fence-associated intrusion sensors, both electric-field and capacitance sensors generate an electric field that radiates out from the fence line, resulting in an ex-panded zone of protection relative to other fence-associated sensors, and allowing the sensor to detect an intruders' presence before they arrive at the fence line. Note: proper spacing is necessary during installation of the electric-field sensor to detect a would-be intruder from slipping between largely spaced wires.

Free-Standing Sensors

These sensors, which include active infrared, passive infrared, bistatic microwave, monostatic microwave, dual-technology, and video motion detection (VMD) sen-sors, consist of individual sensor units or components that can be set up in a variety of configurations to meet a user's needs. They are installed aboveground, and depending on how they are oriented relative to each other, they can be used to establish a protected perimeter or a protected space. More details on each of these sensor types are provided below.

- *Active infrared sensors* transmit infrared energy into the protected space, and monitor for changes in this energy caused by intruders entering that space. In a typical application, an infrared light beam is transmitted from a transmitter unit to a receiver unit. If an intruder crosses the beam, the beam is blocked, and the receiver unit detects a change in the amount of light received, triggering an alarm. Different sensors can see single- and multiple-beam arrays. Single-beam infrared sensors transmit a single infrared beam. In contrast, multiple-beam infrared sensors transmit two or more beams parallel to each other. This multiple-beam sensor arrangement creates an infrared "fence."
- *Passive infrared (PIR) sensors* monitor the ambient infrared energy in a protected area, and evaluate changes in that ambient energy that may be caused by intruders moving through the protected area. Detection ranges can exceed 100 yards on cold days with size and distance limitations dependent upon the background temperature. PIR sensors generate a nonuniform detection pattern (or "curtain") that has areas (or "zones") of more sensitivity and areas of less sensitivity. The specific shape of the protected area is determined by the detector's lenses. The general shape common to many detection patterns is a series of long "fingers" emanating from the PIR and spreading in various directions. When intruders enter the detection area, the PIR sensor detects differences in temperature due to the intruder's body heat, and triggers an alarm. While the PIR leaves unprotected areas between its fingers, an intruder would be detected if he passed from a nonprotected area to a protected area.
- *Microwave sensors* detect changes in received energy generated by the motion of an intruder entering into a protected area. Monostatic microwave sensors incorporate a transmitter and a receiver in one unit, while bistatic sensors separate the transmitter and the receiver into different units. Monostatic sensors are limited to a coverage area of 400 feet, while bistatic sensors can cover an area up to 1,500 feet. For bistatic sensors, a zone of no detection exists in the first few feet in front of the antennas. This distance from the antennas to the point at which the intruder is first detected is known as the offset distance. Due to this offset distance, antennas must be configured so that they overlap one another (as opposed to being adjacent to each other), thereby creating long perimeters with a continuous line of detection.
- *Dual-technology sensors* consist of two different sensor technologies incorporated together into one sensor unit. For example, a dual technology sensor could consist of a passive infrared detector and a monostatic microwave sensor integrated into the same sensor unit.

- *Video motion detection* (VMD) *sensors* monitor video images from a protected area for changes in the images. Video cameras are used to detect unauthorized intrusion into the protected area by comparing the most recent image against a previously established one. Cameras can be installed on towers or other tall structures so that they can monitor a large area.

Fences

When thinking about some picturesque rural setting containing a large farming complex, several buildings, farm animals, windbreaks and structures, split-rail fences comes to mind. A fence is a physical barrier that can be set up around the perimeter of an asset. Fences often consist of individual pieces (such as individual pickets in a wooden fence, or individual sections of a wrought iron fence) that are fastened together. Individual sections of the fence are fastened together using posts, which are sunk into the ground to provide stability and strength for the sections of the fence hung between them. Gates are installed between individual sections of the fence to allow access inside the fenced area. In farming, fences are generally put in place to keep livestock in place. Since September 11, 2001, however, placing fencing around critical infrastructure takes on new importance.

Many fences are used as decorative architectural features to separate physical spaces from each other. They may also be used to physically mark the location of a boundary (such as a fence installed along a properly line). However, a fence can also serve as an effective means for physically delaying intruders from gaining access to an agribusiness asset. For example, many farm operations install fences around their primary facilities, around food processing areas, around hazardous materials storage areas or around sensitive areas within a facility. Access to the area can be controlled through security at gates or doors through the fence (for example, by posting a guard at the gate or by locking it). In order to gain access to the asset, unauthorized persons would have to go either around or through the fence.

Fences are often compared with walls when determining the appropriate system for perimeter security. While both fences and walls can provide adequate perimeter security, fences are often easier and less expensive to install than walls. However, they do not usually provide the same physical strength that walls do. In addition, many types of fences have gaps between the individual pieces that make up the fence (i.e., the spaces between chain links in a chain link fence or the space between pickets in a picket fence). Thus, many types of fence allow the interior of the fenced area to be seen. This may allow intruders to gather important information about the locations or defenses of vulnerable areas within the facility.

There are numerous types of materials used to construct fences, including chain link, iron, aluminum, wood, or wire. Some types of fences, such as split rails or pickets, may not be appropriate for security purposes because they are traditionally low

Table 6.9. Comparison of Different Fence Types

Specifications	Chain Link	Iron	Wire (Wirewall)	Wood
Height limitations	12'	12'	12'	8'
Strength	Medium	High	High	Low
Installation Requirements	Low	High	High	Low
Ability to Remove/Reuse	Low	High	Low	High
Ability to Replace/Repair	Medium	High	Low	High

Source: U.S. EPA, 2005.

fences, and they are not physically strong. Potential intruders may be able to easily defeat these fences either by jumping or climbing over them or by breaking through them. For example, the rails in a split-rail fence may be able to be broken easily.

Important security attributes of a fence include the height to which it can be constructed, the strength of the material making up the fence, the method and strength of attaching the individual sections of the fence together at the posts, and the fence's ability to restrict the view of the assets inside the fence. Additional considerations should include the ease of installing the fence and the ease of removing and reusing sections of the fence. Table 6.9 provides a comparison of the important security and usability features of various fence types.

Some fences can include additional measures to delay, or even detect, potential intruders. Such measures may include the addition of barbed wire, razor wire, or other deterrents at the top of the fence. Barbed wire is sometimes employed at the base of fences as well. This can impede a would-be intruder's progress in even reaching the fence. Fences may also be fitted with security cameras to provide visual surveillance of the perimeter. Again, in a large farm operation, cameras would probably be positioned at or near important enclosed unit process areas. Finally, some facilities have installed motion sensors along their fences to detect movement on the fence. Several manufacturers have combined these multiple perimeter security features into one product and offer alarms, and other security features.

The correct implementation of a fence can make it a much more effective security measure. Security experts recommend the following when a facility constructs a fence:

- The fence should be at least seven to nine feet high.
- Any outriggers, such as barbed wire, that are affixed on top of the fence should be angled out and away from the facility, and not in toward the facility. This will make climbing the fence more difficult, and will prevent ladders from being placed against the fence.
- Other types of hardware can increase the security of the fence. This can include installing concertina wire along the fence (this can be done in front of the fence or

at the top of the fence), or adding intrusion sensors, cameras, or other hardware to the fence.

- All undergrowth should be cleared for several feet (typically six feet) on both sides of the fence. This will allow for a clearer view of the fence by any patrols in the area.
- Any trees with limbs or branches hanging over the fence should be trimmed so that intruders cannot use them to go over the fence. Also, it should be noted that fallen trees can damage fences, and so management of trees around the fence can be important. This can be especially important in areas where fence goes through a remote area.
- Fences that do not block the view from outside the fence to inside the fence allow patrols to see inside the fence without having to enter the facility.
- "No Trespassing" signs posted along a fence can be a valuable tool in prosecuting any intruders who claim that the fence was broken and that they did not enter through the fence illegally. Adding signs that highlight the local ordinances against trespassing can further dissuade simple troublemakers from illegally jumping/climbing the fence.

Locks

A lock is a type of physical security device that can be used to delay or prevent a door, a window, a manhole, a filing cabinet drawer, or some other physical feature from being opened, moved, or operated. Locks typically operate by connecting two pieces together—such as by connecting a door to a door jamb or a manhole to its casement. Every lock has two modes—engaged (or "locked"), and disengaged (or "opened"). When a lock is disengaged, the asset on which the lock is installed can be accessed by anyone, but when the lock is engaged the asset can not easily be accessed.

Locks are excellent security features because they have been designed to function in many ways and to work on many different types of assets. Locks can also provide different levels of security depending on how they are designed and implemented. The security provided by a lock is dependent on several factors, including its ability to withstand physical damage (i.e., can it be cut off, broken, or otherwise physically disabled) as well as its requirements for supervision or operation (i.e., combinations may need to be changed frequently so that they are not compromised and the locks remain secure). While there is no single definition of the "security" of a lock, locks are often described as minimum, medium, or maximum security. Minimum security locks are those that can be easily disengaged (or "picked") without the correct key or code, or those that can be disabled easily (such as small padlocks that can be cut with bolt cutters). Higher security locks are more complex and thus are more difficult to pick, or are sturdier and more resistant to physical damage.

Many locks, such as many door locks, only need to be unlocked from one side. For example, most door locks need a key to be unlocked only from the outside. A person opens such devices, called single-cylinder locks, from the inside by pushing a button or by turning a knob or handle. Double-cylinder locks require a key to be locked or unlocked from both sides.

SECURITY PLAN GUIDANCE—VOLUNTARY CHECKLIST

This voluntary checklist [USDA, 2006b] has been developed to provide the producer with information to consider when developing a security plan. Each producer should review all items and select those most appropriate to his or her operations. While it is difficult to address every contingency that may be encountered, instituting appropriate preventive and response measures will limit liability for farms and protect American agriculture.

The checklist that follows is divided into a general security and production-specific sections. The general security section is applicable to a wide variety of production facilities. Additional sections follow that focus upon particular types of production facilities.

General Security

- Procedures are in place for notifying appropriate law enforcement when a security threat is received, or when evidence of actual product tampering is observed.
- Procedures are in place for heightened awareness (especially when the Department of Homeland Security terrorism threat level is elevated) for unusual activities around the farm and increased disease symptoms among animals of crops.
- A current local, state, and federal government homeland security contact is maintained.
- All employees are encouraged to report any sign of product tampering.
- Facility boundaries are secured to prevent unauthorized entry.
- "No Trespassing" and "Restricted Entry" signs are posted appropriately.
- Alarms, motion detection lights, cameras, and/or other appropriate security equipment are used in key areas, as needed.
- Facility perimeter is regularly monitored for signs of suspicious activity or unauthorized entry.
- Doors, windows, gates, roof openings, vent openings, trailer bodies, railcars, and bulk storage tanks are secured at all times.
- Outside lighting is sufficient to allow detection of unusual activities.
- Fire, smoke, and heat detection devices are operable throughout the farm.
- Storage tanks for hazardous materials and potable water supply are protected from, and monitored for, unauthorized access.

- Wells and other water supplies are secured and routine testing is performed.
- Truck deliveries are verified against a roster of scheduled deliveries. Unscheduled deliveries are held away from facility premises pending verification of shipper and cargo.
- Records are maintained for all vehicles and equipment; make, mode, serial number, service date, etc.
- Vehicles and equipment are secured or immobilized when not in use; keys are never left in unattended vehicles.
- Machinery is removed from fields and stored appropriately; valuable equipment and tools are locked in a secure building.
- Entry into facility is controlled by requiring positive identification (i.e., picture ID).
- New employees are screened and references are checked.
- Visitors and guests are restricted to non-production areas unless accompanied by a facility employee.
- Where required by biosecurity procedures, visitors wear clean boots or coveralls (disposable boots and coveralls are provided for visitors).
- Areas are designated for check-in and check-out for visitors/deliveries (with a sign-in sheet for name, address, phone number, reason for visit).
- An inspection for signs of tampering or unauthorized entry is performed for all storage facilities regularly.
- Hazardous materials are purchased only from licensed dealers.
- A current inventory of hazardous or flammable chemicals (including drugs, chemicals, pesticides, fertilizers) or other products (including chemical trade names, product type, EPA numbers, quantity, and usage) is maintained and discrepancies are investigated immediately.
- A current inventory of stored fuel (diesel, gasoline fuel oil, propane, oxygen, acetylene, kerosene, etc.) is maintained.
- A disease surveillance plan is available.
- Risk management plans have been developed or updated and share with employees, family, visitors, customers, and local law enforcement. Plans include awareness of animal and plant health, as well as signs of tampering with crops, livestock, supplies, vehicles, equipment, and facilities.
- Orientation/training on security procedures is given to all facility employees at least annually.
- Passwords for USDA systems and programs are protected to prevent unauthorized user entry.

Dairy Security
- Appropriate sanitation measures are in place to ensure milk tanks and milk supply are not contaminated.

- Access to milking or milk storage areas is limited to essential personnel only. These areas are locked when an owner or employee is not present. (Arrangements must be made with state regulatory agencies, when applicable, to ensure that they have access to areas needed for routine inspections.)
- Any time a previously locked area is found to be unlocked or evidence of break-in or tampering is found, the cooperative or plant is notified immediately (the milk is held until an investigation determines that no tampering occurred).

Crop Security
- Aerial applicators are kept in locked hangars; anti-theft devices are installed.
- Access to pesticide storage areas or chemical and application equipment is controlled and limited to essential personnel only.
- All imported plant material, including seeds, meets phytosanitary import requirements.
- A stringent pest control program, using chemical or physical measures, is in effect.
- A disease outbreak or infection is limited through steam or chemical sterilization procedures, pasteurizing or sterilizing media, and disinfecting containers.
- Routine surveys are conducted for unusual pests (insects, disease, or weeds) or crop symptoms. Plant and soil samples are collected and submitted for diagnostics and verification.
- Greenhouses are locked and keys are available to essential personnel only.

PHYTOSANITARY CERTIFICATE

Phytosanitary certificates are issued to indicate that consignments of plants, plant products or other regulated articles meet specified phytosanitary import requirements and are in conformity with the certifying statement of the appropriate model certificate. Phytosanitary certificates should only be issued for this purpose.

Model certificates provide a standard wording and format that should be followed for the preparation of official phytosanitary certificates. This is necessary to ensure the validity of the documents, that they be easily recognized, and that essential information is reported.

Importing countries should only require phytosanitary certificates for regulated articles. These include commodities such as plants, bulbs and tubers, or seeds for prorogation, fruits and vegetables, cut flowers and branches, grain, and growing medium. Phytosanitary certificates may also be used for certain plant products that have been processed where such products, by their nature or that of their processing, have a potential for introducing regulated pests (e.g., wood, cotton). A phytosanitary certificate may also be required for other regulated articles where phytosanitary measures are technically justified (e.g., empty containers, vehicles, and organisms).

Importing countries should not require phytosanitary certificates for plant products that have been processed in such a way that they have no potential for introducing regulated pests, or for other articles that do not require phytosanitary measures.

(USDA, 2007)

- Signs are posted at the entries indicating that access is restricted.
- Benches are thoroughly cleaned and disinfected. (Solid concrete floors and drains facilitate cleaning and disinfection.)
- Routine maintenance is performed on ventilation and water systems.
- Records are maintained for plant health management, including invoices with dates, history of purchases, sources, arrival dates, etc.

Cattle Security

- Animal identification system is maintained (ear tags, horn brands, tattooing hoof brands freeze markings, micro-chipping, or other permanent markings, etc.).
- Records are maintained for animal health management, including vaccination dates, history of purchases, sources, arrival dates, etc.
- New additions to the herd are quarantined and inspected for disease symptoms.
- Quarantine area is at a sufficient distance from general population to prevent cross contamination of resident livestock.
- Cattle are transported in clean vehicles.
- Coveralls and boots are available for individuals coming in contact with animals.
- Equipment and clothing coming in contact with animals are cleaned and disinfected before it enters your property.
- Vaccinations are current and a parasite control plan is in place.
- Sick animals are isolated immediately and your veterinarian notified.
- Postmortem examinations are performed on every animal that dies unexpectedly and information on the situation is kept confidential until the diagnosis is confirmed.
- An emergency carcass disposal plan is available and provides approved burial sites, transportation routes, and/or composting or incineration facilities and plans.

THE NATIONAL POULTRY IMPROVEMENT PLAN (NPIP)

The National Poultry Improvement Plan (NPIP) was started in the 1930s to coordinate state programs aimed at the elimination of pullorum disease from commercial poultry. Pullorum is a bacterial disease of poultry that is transmitted from a hen to her chicks via the egg. By testing adult birds and eliminating disease carriers from the breeding flock, commercial chicken and turkey producers have eliminated this costly disease. (USDA, 2006a)

Poultry Security

- Chicks are selected from reliable sources and records are kept of all poultry purchased.
- Disease outbreaks are responded to quickly; sick birds are evaluated by a veterinarian; dead birds are removed immediately and stored for necropsy or buried or incinerated.
- Brooder houses are disinfected before a new shipment of chicks arrives.
- Vaccinations are given before chicks are introduced into flock.
- Vehicles entering and departing the area where poultry are housed are washed then sprayed with a disinfectant.
- Personnel with access to the flocks wear protective outer clothing, including boots and headgear.
- Disinfecting foot dips or footpads are at entrances and exits to poultry areas.
- Egg flats, racks, trolleys, and pallets are high-pressure and/or waterwashed and sanitized between uses at egg processing facilities.

Facility Map

A map and a list of emergency contacts are critical components for any farm security plan and can be particularly useful for first responders in the event of a fire, explosion, or biohazard incident. The map should include the following:

- The name and address or the owner/proprietor and relationship of the farm to adjacent fields or structures.
- Buildings/structures labeled, including houses, barns, greenhouses, nurseries, shops, outbuildings, silos, grain bins, chemical and fertilizer storage, manure storage/pits (indicate sizes and locations of entrances).

AVIAN INFLUENZA

Avian influenza—often referred to as "bird flu"—is a disease caused by a virus that infects domestic poultry, wild birds (such as quail, cranes, geese, and ducks) and pet birds such as parrots. There is a flu for birds, just as there is for humans, and as with people, some forms of flu are worse than others.

There are two types of avian influenza (AI) that are both identified as H5NI. A difference exists in the virus classification; one is low-pathogenicity (LPAI) and the other is high-pathogenicity (HPAI). Pathogenicity refers to the ability of the virus to produce disease. HPAI H5NI is the type causing worldwide concern. LPAI H5NI is relatively common and poses a lesser risk to both animal and human health.

HPAI, or highly pathogenic AI, spreads rapidly and is often fatal to chickens and turkeys. Millions of birds have died in countries where HPAI H5NI has been detected. This virus has also infected people, most of whom have had direct contact with infected birds. HPAI H5NI has not been detected in either birds or humans in the United States. However, other strains of HPAI have been detected in poultry and eradicated three times in the United States: In 1924, 1983 and 2004. No human illness resulted form these outbreaks.

In order to protect the poultry and bird populations, as well as the human population, from HPAI H5NI, it is critical that the United States have a strong surveillance plan to ensure an early detection and response plan to protect against the rapid spread of this virus. Controlling the disease in birds is a key component in protecting the public against a potential human pandemic of avian influenza.

To that end, USDA is the lead government agency in the government's efforts to combat avian influenza in birds. USDA recognizes that HPAI H5NI poses a significant threat to agriculture and potentially to human health. Accordingly, the USDA is taking steps to safeguard against the introduction of HPAI H5NI in the United States.

USDA is aggressively working overseas to slow the spread of the disease in poultry, while at the same time expanding our early warning system in the United States, and ensuring the preparedness to quickly and decisively respond to any eventual detection of HPAI H5NI in poultry in the Untied States. (Johanns, 2006)

- Transportation routes, including access roads, highways, crossroads, etc.
- Storage areas for machinery, equipment, airplanes
- Fences and gates (indicate dimensions)
- Well and/or municipal water supply, hydrants, ponds, streams, rivers, lakes, and wetland
- Electric, gas, and phone lines and shutoff
- Septic tanks, wastewater systems, cisterns
- Drainage ditches, culverts, surface drains
- Fields/pastures
- Fuel storage tanks
- Areas where animals and/or crops of concern are located

Emergency Contacts
- (Name and Phone Number)
- 911
- Fire Department
- Hospital
- Police Department
- Country Sheriff
- Country Extension Agent
- Doctor
- Poison Control Center
- Veterinarian
- Gas Company
- Electric Company
- Chemical Suppliers
- Feed Suppliers
- Vehicle/Equipment Dealers
- Ambulance

FARM-SECURITY RESOURCES AND REFERENCES

General Farm Security

Extension Disaster Emergency Network (EDEN):

http://www.agctr.lsu.edu/eden/

Guide for Security Practices in Transporting Agricultural and Food Commodities:

http://www.uada.gov/homlandsecurity/aftersecurguidefinal19.pdf

Michigan State University; Emergency Planning for the Farm:

http://www.pested.msu.edu/

National Association of State Departments of Agriculture:

http://www2.nasda.org/NASDS/

North Carolina Department of Agriculture and Consumer Services:
Farm Biosecurity Guidelines:

http://www.ncagr.comvet/Biosecurity.htm

NDSU Disaster Preparedness Lessons:

http://www.ag.ndsu.edu/prepare/

Purdue Pesticides Program:

http://www.btny.purdue.edu/Pubs/PPP/PPP-64.pdf

University of Arkansas Cooperative Extension Service; Farm and Home Biosecurity
Introduction:

http://www.uaex.edu/biosecurity/default.asp

Identity Theft:

http://www.consumer.gov/idtheft

Crop Security

American Phytopathological Society (APSnet):

http://www.apsenet.ogr/

Entomological Society of America:

http://www.entsoc.org/

National Agricultural Aviation Association:

http://www.agaviation.org/

Livestock Security

Farm & Ranch Biosecurity:

http://www.farmandranchbiosecurity.com/

Farm and Aquaculture Training:

http://www.hehd.clemson.edu/msp/farm_animal_training/

Farm Security—"Treat It Seriously": Security for Animal Agriculture:
Security Checklist:

http://www.est.vt.edu/pubs/farmsecurity/445-004/445-004.html

Nebraska Cooperative Extension:

http://ianrpubs.unl.edu/animaldisease/g1411.htm

Massachusetts Department of Agricultural Resources: Animal Health Information:

http://www.mass.gov/agr/animalhealth/Biosecurity%20for%20Commercial%20P
oultry%Facilities.pdf

Practical Biosecurity for Dairies: Where Is the Evidence, Does It Really Matter?:

http://www.vetmed.udavis.edu/vetext/INF-DA/PracticalBiosecurity.pdf

Security Guide for Pork Producers:

http://www.porkboard.ogr/docs/security%20book.pdf

Information for Employers

U.S. Department of Homeland Security Web Site
U.S. Citizenship and Immigration Services:

http://uscis.gov/graphics/services/employerinfo/index.htm

U.S. Department of Agriculture Web Sites
Animal and Plant Health Inspection Service (APHIS):

http://www.aphis.usda.gov/

Agricultural Research Service (ARS):

http://www.ars.usda.gov/main/main.htm

Cooperative State Research, Education, and Extension Service:

http://www.csrees.usda.go/qlingks/extension.html

Farm Service Agency (FSA):

http://www.fsa.usda.gov/pas/

Grain Inspection, Packers and Stockyards Administration (GIPSA):

http://www.gipsa.usda.gov

National Animal Health Laboratory Network:

http://www.crees.usda.gov/nea/ag_biosecurity/in_focus/apb_if_healthlab.html

National Plant Board:

http://www.phis.sda.gov/nph/

National Plant Diagnostic Network:

http://www.npdn.org/DesktopDefault.aspx

Rural Development

http://www.rurdev.usda.gov

U.S. Department of Agriculture:

http://www.usda.gov

U.S. Department of Agriculture; Homeland Security:

http://www.usda.gov/homlandsecurity/links.html

NOTE

Portions of this chapter are reproduced from USDA's *Pre-Harvest Security Guidelines Checklist 2006*, at http://www.peer.org/docs/usda/.

REFERENCES

Garcia, M. L., 2001. *The Design and Evaluation of Physical Protection Systems.* Boston: Butterworth-Heinemann.

IBWA, 2004. *Bottled Water Safety and Security.* Alexandria, VA: International Bottled Water Association.

Johanns, M. 2006. *USDA Pandemic Planning Report.* Washington, DC: United States Department of Agriculture.

Knowles, T., J. Lane, G. Bayens, N. Speer, J. Jaax, D. Carter, and A. Bannister. 2005. *Defining Law Enforcement's Role in Protecting American Agriculture from Agroterrorism.* Washington, DC: National Institute of Justice under contract with U.S. Department of Justice.

Spellman, F. R. 2007. *Water Infrastructure Protection and Homeland Security.* Rockville, MD: Government Institutes.

USDA. 2006a. *National Poultry Improvement Plan.* Washington, DC: U.S. Department of Agriculture.

USDA. 2006b. *Pre-harvest Security Guidelines Checklist 2006,* at http://www.peer.org/docs/usda/.

USDA. 2007. *Plant Export,* at http://www.aphis.usda.gov/import_export/plants (accessed June 9, 2007).

U.S. EPA. 2005. *Water and Wastewater Security Product Guide,* at http://cfpub.epa.gov.safewater/watersecurity/guide (accessed June 6, 2007).

From Farm to Fork: Transportation Issues

Farm managers must take the primary responsibility for maintaining the health of their herds and flocks. A major strategy in providing for healthy animals is biosecurity of the farming operation. The goal of biosecurity is to halt the spread of disease causing agents. An effective biosecurity program seeks to limit the introduction of disease causing agents onto the farm premises and to reduce the spread of those agents to healthy animals.

—*B. R. McKinnon (2002)*

In 2004, the USDA published a *Guide for Security Practices in Transporting Agricultural Food Commodities*, a voluntary security guide/checklist for agricultural transporters. The checklist is reproduced here:

America's trucking industry makes up 5 percent of GDP, and jobs related to the trucking industry employ 10.1 million people. The trucking industry's gross revenue in 2003 was $610 billion. Commercial agricultural transporters move the vast majority of all agricultural commodities shipped on a daily basis throughout the United States. When taken together, the agriculture, food, and transportation components of the American economy are vital to the nation's economy and public health. Since September 11, 2001, we are more aware of the possibility of a terrorist attack on our domestic infrastructure—including the food and agricultural sector. The protection and integrity of American's agricultural production and food supply are essential to the health and welfare of both the domestic population and the global community.

Guidance that assists commercial agricultural and food transporters is essential to addressing the security concerns of this portion of the farm-to-fork continuum. Agricultural transportation is a component common through the continuum, and therefore requires special attention from a security perspective. Contamination of the livestock population with a foreign animal disease could occur in a matter of seconds. Similarly, a tanker holding liquid products could also be contaminated in a matter of seconds. All that would be required in either case is for a terrorist to have the agent and access to the target. Products in transport provide significant opportunities for access. Therefore, planning for and implementing security-management practices in the commercial transportation of agricultural and food products will enhance efforts to ensure the contained safety and security of those products.

A company policy should be established to designate authorized personnel for the development and maintenance of security plans. The policy document should be maintained in company files. In addition to these guidelines, a company may provide employees with additional information and forms for use in operation of transportation equipment. Consult your legal counsel for guidance on related legal requirements concerning the transportation of agricultural and food commodities.

The American Transportation Research Institute (ATRI), as a part of the partnership between USDA and the AFTC, surveyed approximately 24,000 commercial agricultural and food transporters to identify potential security vulnerabilities during the transportation of agricultural and food products throughout the farm-to-fork continuum, and to evaluate appropriate countermeasures to mitigate those potential vulnerabilities. The survey findings and analysis have been provided to the U.S. Secretary of Agriculture and utilized in these guidelines, as appropriate. . . .

MANAGEMENT PRACTICES

A risk-based security management system for people, property, commodities, processes, information, and information systems throughout the commercial agricultural and food transportation industry is essential for the industry. A security management system contains the following management practices:

1. Leadership Commitment

Senior management commits to continuous improvement through accountability, published policies, and provisions for sufficient and qualified resources.

2. Threats, Vulnerabilities, and Exposures Assessment

Use approved Vulnerability and Threat Assessment Tool (VTA) methodologies, and prioritize and periodically analyze potential security threats, vulnerabilities, and consequences. The sponsors of this guide encourage commercial agricultural and food transportation companies to conduct vulnerability (risk) assessments using methods approved by recognized trade and professional associations and government agencies. . . .

3. Security Plan

Participating commercial agricultural commodity and food transporters are urged to develop and implement security plans based on identified exposures. . . .

4. Communications and Information Sharing

The commercial agricultural and food transportation industry should share information on effective security practices within the industry and with external, qualified security professionals. The commercial agricultural and food transportation industry should continue to expand the awareness of and commitment to enhanced security practices through the industry. . . .

GENERAL GUIDELINES FOR DRIVERS

This guide provides a list of security tips and checklists that may be voluntarily utilized to prevent contamination or disruption during the transportation of agricultural and food commodities. These voluntary guidelines also encourage controls for ensuring the safe condition of agricultural and food commodities shipped throughout the transportation process. Not all of these measures, or the degree to which they are implemented, will be appropriate or practical for every transporter or facility.

Security Watchwords for Drivers

- **Awareness**—Learn how terrorists act and the types of behaviors and events that can precede an attack. Know your company's security procedures and emergency response plans as they apply to you. Look for behaviors or events that might be tip-offs to a terrorist operation in progress.
- **Recognition**—When you see behavior or events that match the profiles you have been taught, make the mental connections between what you see and what it may mean to you if indeed it is a terrorist activity.
- **Communication**—Know who to call no matter where you are. Use 911 in emergencies, and use your company dispatcher and local FBI or law enforcement numbers if not an emergency. If you are a Highway Watch trained driver, use the national Call Center number.
- **Action**—Don't keep information to yourself. Report it to the people and agencies that have the expertise and training to react to information or to emergencies. If you are affected by an attack, take immediate action to protect yourself, your cargo, and your equipment.

Driver Security Checklists [Should Be Retained in Drivers' Vehicles].

I. Driver Pre-Departure Checklist

1. Observe the loading of your vehicle.
2. Note suspicious onlookers during the cargo loading and contact law enforcement immediately.
3. Using established communications ensure that route and immediate staging area appear clear.

4. Clean your cargo area—foreign animal disease and food contaminants can spread on contact.

5. Conduct a safety inspection; inspect tires, brakes, and radiator for damage.

6. Check to ensure that all tractor/trailer access panels/doors are locked and "seals" remain intact/uncompromised.

7. If equipped, check your vehicle electronic tracking system regularly, and notify dispatch when it is not working.

8. Establish an overdue time at your destination and have someone follow up if you are overdue.

II. Driver on-the-Road Checklist

1. When leaving your facility, be aware of any possible surveillance of your facility or your truck. Criminal surveillance often begins at, or within a mile of, your origin.

2. Follow company stopping and parking procedures. Do not leave animals in open trucks unattended.

3. Do not make any unscheduled stops.

4. Be aware of possible ruses. If you are unsure if a police officer is real, call 911 and ask.

5. Report any suspicious activities or emergencies to local police by calling 911, and then follow up with a call to Highway Watch at 1-877-USA-SAFE.

6. Also report any suspicious activities to dispatch.

7. Remain particularly observant for suspicious activities in and around refueling locations, railroad facilities, bridges, and tunnels.

8. Keep all tractor/trailer doors and access panels locked and windows rolled up or in a position to be raised rapidly.

9. Maintain regular communications with your dispatcher as required.

10. Vary your route when possible. If relevant, this should be a part of your pre-trip planning.

11. Do not discuss your cargo, destination, or trip specifics with people you don't know or on open channels—even with other drivers.

12. Do not discuss your route with any shipper personnel unless instructed to by your company.

13. When stopped at a traffic light or in traffic, be aware of anyone approaching your vehicle.

14. Go directly to your delivery point without making any stops.

15. Avoid being boxed in. Leave room in front and behind your truck to permit escape.

16. Do not pick up hitchhikers.

17. Be aware of vehicles that are following your truck and of strangers asking questions about your cargo, route, or destination.

III. Driver Stopping Checklist

1. Leave your truck in a secure parking lot or truckstop. Park units in a reputable truckstop or secure yard at all times. Facilities with video surveillance are recommended. Be especially vigilant with operating in "hot spots"—unsafe or high-crime areas.

2. When you stop or leave your vehicle, ensure that the rig is turned off and that all doors and access panels remain secure.

3. Before leaving/exiting your vehicle, look around and become familiar with your surroundings. Have a trusted person watch your vehicle.

4. If team driving, always leave one person with the truck.

5. Watch for individuals with spraying equipment or other possible contaminants (even a rag can spread a foreign animal disease and a small capsule can contaminate food).

6. Never leave your vehicle running with the keys in it; shut off the engine and lock the doors.

7. Do not stop in "hot spots"—unsafe or high-crime areas.

8. Park in areas where other truckers are present.

9. Do not stop on dark roadways or in deserted areas while waiting to make deliveries.

10. Don't take your load home or park in an unsecured area such as a parking lot or mall.

11. Drivers should check and use seals, padlocks, and other locks where appropriate.

12. Perform a quick walk-around to check your vehicle for foreign objects after all stops.

13. Drivers should never leave extra keys in the vehicle.

14. Drivers should utilize a "no-stop" policy while making local deliveries.

15. Drivers should have a 24-hour phone number of dispatch or management personnel who can be called in case of an emergency.

16. Keep your door locked and windows up at all stops, until the very instant you exit the vehicle. Then relock immediately. Upon returning to the vehicle, lock your doors immediately behind you.

IV. Driver Destination Checklist

1. Check to make sure the location of loading/unloading docks/warehouse looks safe.

2. Report your arrival time and location.

3. Note any suspicious onlookers observed during off-loading.

4. Confirm that recipient of the cargo is the intended recipient. Ask for identification.

5. If you exit your vehicle, ensure that all doors and access panels are locked and secured. Turn your tractor motor off.

6. Keep your doors locked and windows up at all stops until the very instant you exit the vehicle. Then relock immediately. Upon returning to the vehicle, lock your doors immediately behind you.

7. Observe the off-loading of your trailer and keep your tractor under observation at all times.

8. Have a communications device with you at all times.

V. Hijacking Prevention Tips for Drivers

1. Be watchful immediately after picking up a load. Most hijackings occur within a few miles of a pickup location. Interstate on-ramps and off-ramps are locations most often used by hijackers.

2. Look for vehicles following you, especially if there are three or more people in the car. If you believe you are being followed, call 911 and your dispatcher immediately.

3. Be suspicious of individuals asking you to stop as result of an alleged traffic accident. If unsure whether an accident has occurred, call the police or drive to a police station before stopping.

4. If you believe you are being hijacked, try to keep your truck moving.

5. If you think you are being followed, call 911. Keep moving and try to get to a public area.

6. When appropriate, keep windows secure and doors locked while in transit.

7. Avoid being boxed in. Where possible, leave room in front of and behind your truck.

8. Be aware of possible ruses. If you are unsure if an individual is a real police officer, call in and report it.

9. When stopped at a traffic light or in traffic, be aware of anyone approaching your vehicle.

10. If you are hijacked, watch and listen to the hijackers. You are law enforcement's best witness.

11. Drivers should carry information concerning the identification of the equipment they are driving. You will need license numbers, container and/or trailer numbers, and descriptions if equipment is stolen. (Law enforcement cannot make a stolen-vehicle report or cargo-theft report without this information.)

GENERAL GUIDELINES FOR COMPANIES

Security Watchwords for Companies

- Awareness: Accumulate and organize a knowledge base regarding the exposure of the trucking industry to terrorist acts and the types of behaviors and events that can warn of an event, and teach the workforce to be alert and observant.

- Recognition: Train employees and managers to make the logical connections between observed indicators and a specific company's operations that may signal an imminent act or increase a company's exposure to consequences.

- Communication: Build a network of time-sensitive systems through which information is routed to and among the internal and external decision-makers who need critical information in order to prevent or respond to terrorist actions.
- Action: Proactively deploy the correct measure of activity relating to the nature of the threat, the overall Homeland Security Advisory System (HSAS) threat-condition level, and the trucking operation's potential exposure.

Security Tips for Commercial Agricultural and Food Transporters

In the transportation of agricultural commodities and food products, consider the following steps to help prevent problems before they occur.

- Security measures should make it as difficult as possible for a troublemaker to tamper with agricultural commodities and food products or ingredients your company transports.
- If you hire someone from an outside vendor to work in the plant (e.g., plumber, pesticide applicator, maintenance), verify that he or she works for the company you hired.
- Establish contact with the local law enforcement offices so you know a specific contact in the case of emergencies or disasters.
- Be sure your water supply system is secure, with locks on wellheads and pump houses, water storage tanks, etc.
- Assess your facility for potential sabotage of bulk ingredients. Be sure connections for bulk systems are locked and secure. For example, other connections for liquid sugar, corn syrup, flour, etc., should be enclosed and locked at all times.
- Keep entry doors and other entrances secure and locked where fire codes permit.
- Restrict movement of non-employees (deliveries, outside repair, and maintenance personnel) to areas where they cannot contaminate food products or agricultural commodities.
- Have visitors sign in, show identification, and wear visitor passes. Maintain the visitor roster for 6–12 months.
- Personnel who move freely throughout the facility should watch for signs of sabotage. Make sure protective equipment such as screens, sifters, magnets, or metal detectors are in place and functioning.
- Remind employees to report anything unusual to their supervisors.
- If a telephone threat is received about a specific product or commodity, record or write down as nearly as possible every word said. Then segregate that product completely until the threat has been reported to the authorities, investigated, and confirmed or eliminated.

- Inventory any potential hazardous chemicals and the security for the same. Are they stored in a non-secure, non-supervised area? Are they stored outside? Are bulk delivery systems secure? Do you make it easy for a disgruntled employee, copycat tamperer, or terrorist to obtain chemicals and potentially add them to the commodities you transport?
- Restrict all personal items such as carry bags, extra clothing, purses, etc., from the loading and docking areas.
- Invite the local law enforcement agency to review your security measures.
- Routinely review, update, and exercise your emergency-response plan and procedures.
- Remind drivers to frequently inspect their trucks for signs of tampering.
- Establish security policies and procedures if you haven't already done so.
- Fence facilities where appropriate.
- Close and secure entrance and exit gates when not in use.
- Maintain well-lit facilities.
- Consider using surveillance and recording equipment at locations deemed necessary.
- Lock and seal all equipment parked in your facility.
- Provide a secured employee parking lot.
- Limit visitors and escort them to their destinations—know who you're letting in.
- Minimize who has access to computers. Use passwords and install firewalls.
- Where security patrols are used, vary patterns and schedules.
- Security should be present for weekends, evenings, and holidays as appropriate.
- Be diligent regarding your hiring practices. Beware of who you hire—verify all information such as employment history, education history, driving records, criminal records check, and social security numbers on all potential employees (including permanent, temporary, seasonal or contract workers, and cleaning crews).

Advance Planning for Emergency Management

- Establish a Crisis Management Team and identify a Crisis Coordinator or Team Leader with backup.
- Develop an action plan in case of a terrorist threat or tampering. Include an evacuation plan for facility employees and have a copy available in a secure compartment outside the facility for reference.
- List 24/7 contact information for internal and external communication in case of an emergency, identifying who should be notified, what triggers the notification, and in what order they are notified. Include who/when to contact law enforcement officials, regulatory inspectors, etc.
- Identify a list of resources you may need in a crisis situation: testing labs, medical experts, packaging consultants, legal counsel, public relations firm, insurance company, alternate emergency medical personnel, etc.

- Check that your recordkeeping system will allow you to trace commodities back and trace product forward.
- Practice using the action plan.
- Build security into your company operations plan so it is routinely monitored.

Security Measures for Truck Cleaning

Vehicle cleanliness is an important security factor in the transportation of agricultural and food commodities. Vehicles, accessories, and connections must be kept clean from any substances that may contaminate the commodities of food being transported. Cleaning and sanitation procedures should be maintained in writing and used as required. Proper cleaning and sanitation can mitigate the effects of intentional contamination by terrorists by reducing an agent's transmission across animals or products.

The following factors are important for vehicle cleanliness and sanitation:

- Use appropriate cleaning procedures for vehicles, based on the type of commodity being transported.
- Devices for loading vehicles, cargo pallets, and securing devices should be cleaned and sanitized, as necessary.
- Transfer equipment, such as lifts and hand trucks, should be regularly maintained, cleaned, and sanitized, as necessary.

Reporting Information

Call 911 with critical emergency information.

NOTE

It is important to note that the guidelines presented in this chapter are merely voluntary. As such, it is not guaranteed or warranted, expressly or by implication, that compliance with the guidelines will prevent damage, spoilage, accidents, or injuries to persons or property. It is the sole responsibility of the user of the information provided in this publication to ensure compliance with applicable local, state, and federal regulatory requirements.

REFERENCES

American Trucking Associations (ATA). 2007. *Statistics*, at www.Truckline.com/index (accessed July 9, 2007).

McKinnon, B. R. 2002. *Farm Security—"Treat It Seriously," Security for Animal Agriculture: Security Checklist*, at http://www.ext.vt.edu/pubs.farmsecurity/.

USDA. 2004. *Guide for Security Practices in Transporting Agricultural Food Commodities.* Washington, DC: U.S. Department of Agriculture.

8

Modified FDA *Bad Bug Book*

The FDA's *Bad Bug Book* provides basic facts regarding foodborne pathogenic microorganisms and natural toxins. The *Bad Bug Book* brings together in one place information from the Food and Drug Administration, the Centers for Disease Control and Prevention, the USDA Food Safety Inspection Service, and the National Institutes of Health.

Any person in charge of ensuring the security and/or safety of food (in any form, in any stage of production, in any stage of transportation, and/or in any stage of final use)

AVIAN FLU: TURKEYS ON FARM TEST POSITIVE

Associated Press Release July 10, 2007, Harrisonburg, VA

More than 50,000 turkeys on a farm west of Mount Jackson tested positive for avian flu antibodies, prompting additional testing and surveillance, officials said. The infected birds will be killed and composted on site, said Hobey Bauhan, President of the Virginian Poultry Federation. To prevent spread of the virus, more treating and surveillance will be conducted within a six-mile radius of the farm and at the more than 1,000 poultry farms in the Shenandoah Valley, Bauhan said. The turkeys, which were ready to be sent to the slaughterhouse, tested positive during a routine pre-slaughter test by the Virginia Department of Agriculture and Consumer Services on Friday, Bauhan said.

THE COOL RULE

On May 13, 2002, President Bush signed into law the Farm Security and Rural Investment Act of 2002, more commonly known as the 2002 Farm Bill. One of its many initiatives requires country of origin labeling [COOL Rule] for beef, lamb, pork, fish, perishable agricultural commodities and peanuts. On January 27, 2004, President Bush signed Public Law 108-199 which delays the implementation of Mandatory COOL for all covered commodities except wild and farm-raised fish and shellfish until September 30, 2006. On November 10, 2005, President Bush signed Public Law 109-97, which delays the implementation for all covered commodities except wild and farm-raised and shellfish until September 30, 2008. As described in the legislation, program implementation is the responsibility of USDA's Agricultural Marketing Service.

Source: USDA (2002)

should have ready access to USDA's *Bad Bug Book*, which is available online at http://www.cfsan.fda.gov/~mow/intro.html.

For the practical in-field usage of this text, an abbreviated *Bad Bug Book* is presented in this chapter, beginning with the table of contents.

CONTENTS OF THE *BAD BUG BOOK*

Pathogenic Bacteria

- *Salmonella* spp.
- *Clostridium botulinum*
- *Staphylococcus aureus*
- *Campylobacter jejuni*
- *Yersinia enterocolitica* and *Yersinia pseudotuberculosis*
- *Listeria monocytogenes*
- *Vibrio cholerae* O1
- *Vibrio cholera* non-O1
- *Vibrio parahaemolyticus* and other *vibrios*
- *Vibrio vunificus*
- *Clostridium perfringens*
- *Bacillus cereus*
- *Aeromonas hydrophila* and other spp.
- *Plesiomonas shigelloides*
- *Shigella* spp.
- Miscellaneous enteries
- *Streptococcus*

Enterovirulent Escherichia Coli Group (EEC Group)

- *Escherichia coli*—enterotoxigenic (ETEC)
- *Escherichia coli*—enteropathogenic (EPEC)
- *Escherichia coli*—O157:H7 enterohemorrhagic (EHEC)
- *Escherichia coli*—enteroinvasive (EIEC)

Parasitic Protozoa and Worms

- *Giardia lamblia*
- *Entamoeba histolytica*
- *Cryptosporidium parvum*
- *Cyclospora cayetanensis* (no data entered herein)
- *Anisakis* sp. and related worms
- *Diphyllobothrium* spp.
- *Nanophyetus* spp.

- *Eustrongylides* sp.
- *Ascanthamoeba* and other free-living amoebae
- *Ascaris lumbicoides* and *Trichuris trichiura*

Viruses
- Hepatitis A virus
- Hepatitis E virus
- Rotavirus
- Norwalk virus group
- Other viral agents

Natural Toxins
- Ciguatera poisoning
- Shellfish toxins (PSP, DSP, NSP, ASP)
- Scombroid poisoning
- Tetrodotoxin (Pufferfish)
- Mushroom toxins
- Aflatoxins
- Pyrrolizidine alkaloids
- Phytohaemagglutinin (Red kidney bean poisoning)
- Grayanotoxin (Honey intoxication)

Other Pathogenic Agents
- Prions

FROM THE *NEW YORK TIMES*, JULY 12, 2007

U.S. Records Point to Problems beyond China

Not Inspected: the FDA inspects only about 1 percent of the imports that fall under its jurisdiction. So the agency may miss many of the products that are contaminated or defective.

CLASSIFICATION

For the nonscience type, it is important at this point in the text to explain how organisms are classified. Thus, as an aid to understanding much of the material that follows, a simplified explanation of biological classification is provided.

The importance of classifying organisms cannot be overstated. The most important reason for classification is that a standardized system allows us to handle information efficiently—it makes the vastly diverse and abundant natural world less confusing.

For centuries, scientists classified the forms of life visible to the naked eye as either animal or plant. The Swedish naturalist Carolus Linnaeus organized much of the current knowledge about living things in 1735.

Linnaeus's classification system was extraordinarily innovative. His binomial system of nomenclature is still with us today. Under the binomial system, all organisms are generally described by a two-word scientific name, the genus and species. Genus and species are groups that are part of a hierarchy of groups of increasing size, based on their nomenclature (taxonomy). This hierarchy is:

Kingdom

Phylum

Class

Order

Family

Genus

Species

Using this hierarchy and Linnaeus's binomial system of nomenclature, the scientific name of any organism includes both the genus and the species name. The genus name is always capitalized, while the species name begins with a lowercase letter. On occasion, when little chance or confusion is present, the genus name is abbreviated to a single capital letter. The names are always in Latin, so they are usually printed in italics or underlined. Some organisms also have English common names. Some microbe names of interest, for example, are listed as follows:

Salmonella typhi—the typhoid bacillus

Escherichia coli—a coliform bacterium

Giardia lamblia—a protozoan

Note: *Escherichia coli* is commonly known as simply *E. coli*, while *Giardia lamblia* is usually referred to by only its genus name, *Giardia*.

KINGDOMS OF LIFE

Linnaeus classified all then-known (1700s) organisms into two large groups: the kingdoms Plantae and Animalia. In 1969, Robert Whittaker proposed five kingdoms: Monera, Protista, Fungi, Plantae, and Animalia. Other schemes involving an even greater number of kingdoms have lately been proposed; however, this text employs Whittaker's five kingdoms. Moreover, recent studies suggest that three domains (superkingdoms) be employed: Archaea, Bacteria, and Eukarya.

The basic characteristics of each kingdom are summarized in the following:

1. Kingdom Monera (10,000 species)—unicellular and colonial—including archaebacteria (from the Greek meaning "ancient") and eubacteria (meaning "true"). Archaebacteria include methanogens (producers of methane), halophiles (which live in bodies of concentrated salt water) and thermocidophiles (live in the hot acidic waters of sulfur springs). Eubacteria include heterotrophs (decomposers), autotrophs (which make food from photosynthesis), and proteobacteria (one of largest phyla of bacteria). All prokaryotic cells (without nuclei and membrane-bound organelles) are in this kingdom. Unicellular and colonial species reproduce by binary fission, but they do have some ways to recombine genes, allowing change (evolution) to occur.
2. Kingdom Protista (250,000 species)—unicellular protozoans and unicellular and multicellular (macroscopic) algae with cilia and flagella. Kingdom Protista contains all eukaryotes that are not plants, animal or fungi. Includes Amoebas and *Euglena*.
3. Kingdom Fungi (100,000 species)—eukaryotes, multicellular, and heterotrophic, having multinucleated cells enclosed in cells with cell walls. Fungi act either as decomposers or as parasites in nature. Includes molds, mildews, mushrooms, and yeast.
4. Kingdom Plantae (250,000 species)—immobile, eukaryotes, multicellular and carry out photosynthesis (autotrophs) and have cells encased in cellulose cell walls. Plants are important sources of oxygen, food, and clothing/construction materials, as well as pigments, spices, drugs, and dyes.
5. Kingdom Animalia (1,000,000)—multicellular, eukaryotes, heterotrophic, without photosynthetic pigment, and mostly move from place to place. Animal cells have no cell walls.

Note that recent practice is to place archaebacteria in a separate kingdom, Kingdom Archaebacteria. This is the case because data from DNA and RNA comparisons indicate that archaebacteria are so different that they should not even be classified with bacteria. Thus, a separate and distinct classification scheme higher than kingdom has been devised to accommodate the archaebacteria, called *domain*. In this new system, these organisms are now placed in the domain *Archaea*—the chemosynthetic bacteria. Other prokaryotes, including eubacteria, are placed in the domain *Bacteria*—the disease-causing bacteria. All the kingdoms of eukaryotes, including Protista, Fungi, Plantae, and Animalia, are placed in the domain *Eukarya*.

BACTERIA, PROTOZOA, AND VIRUSES: THE BASICS

Bacteria

The simplest wholly contained life systems are bacteria or prokaryotes, which are the most diverse group of microorganisms. Bacteria are primitive, unicellular (single-celled) organisms, possessing no well-defined nucleus, that present a variety of shapes and nutritional needs. Bacteria contain about 85 percent water and 15 percent ash or mineral matter. The ash is largely composed of sulfur, potassium, sodium, calcium, and chlorides, with small amounts of iron, silicon, and magnesium. Bacteria reproduce by binary fission, which occurs when one organism splits or divides into two or more new organisms.

Bacteria, once called the smallest living organisms (now it is known that smaller forms of matter exhibit many of the characteristics of life), range in size from 0.5 to 2 microns in diameter and are about 1–10 microns long. (A micron is a metric unit of measurement equal to 1 thousandth of a millimeter. To visualize the size of bacteria, consider that about 1,000 bacteria lying side-by-side would reach across the head of a straight pin.)

Bacteria are categorized into three general groups based on their physical form or shape (though almost every variation has been found; see table 8.1). The simplest form is the sphere. Spherical shaped bacteria are called cocci. Cocci mean "berries." They are not necessarily perfectly round, but may be somewhat elongated, flattened on one side, or oval. Rod shaped bacteria are called *bacilli*. Spiral-shaped bacteria (called *Spirilla*), which have one or more twists and are never straight, make up the third group (see page 180). Such formations are usually characteristic of a particular genus or species. Within these three groups are many different arrangements. Some exist as single cells; others as pairs, as packets of four or eight, as chains, and as clumps.

Most bacteria require organic food to survive and multiply. Plant and animal material that gets into the water provides the food source for bacteria. Bacteria convert the food to energy and use the energy to make new cells. Some bacteria can use inorganics (e.g., minerals such as iron) as an energy source and exist and multiply even when organics (pollution) are not available.

Table 8.1. Forms of Bacteria

| Form | Technical Name | | Example |
	Singular	Plural	
Sphere	Coccus	Cocci	Streptococcus
Rod	Bacillus	Bacilli	Bacillus typhosis
Curved or spiral	Spirillum	Spirilla	Spirillum cholera

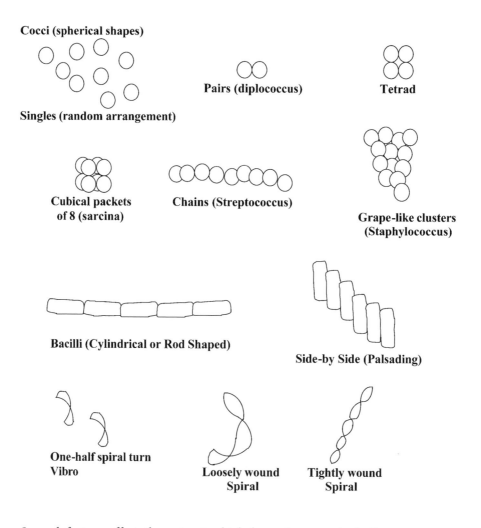

Cocci (spherical shapes)

Singles (random arrangement)

Pairs (diplococcus)

Tetrad

Cubical packets of 8 (sarcina)

Chains (Streptococcus)

Grape-like clusters (Staphylococcus)

Bacilli (Cylindrical or Rod Shaped)

Side-by Side (Palsading)

One-half spiral turn Vibro

Loosely wound Spiral

Tightly wound Spiral

Several factors affect the rate at which bacteria grow, including temperature, pH, and oxygen levels. The warmer the environment, the faster the rate of growth. Generally, for each increase of 10°C, the growth rate doubles. Heat can also be used to kill bacteria.

Most bacteria grow best at neutral pH. Extreme acidic or basic conditions generally inhibit growth, though some bacteria may require acidic and some require alkaline conditions for growth.

Bacteria are aerobic, anaerobic, or facultative. If aerobic, they require free oxygen in the aquatic environment. Anaerobic bacteria exist and multiply in environments that lack dissolved oxygen. Facultative bacteria (e.g., iron bacteria) can switch from an aerobic to anaerobic growth or grow in an anaerobic or aerobic environment.

Under optimum conditions, bacteria grow and reproduce very rapidly. As stated previously, bacteria reproduce by binary fission.

An important point to consider in connection with bacterial reproduction is the rate at which the process can take place. The total time required for an organism to reproduce and the offspring to reach maturity is called generation time. Bacteria growing under optimal conditions can double their number about every 20 to 30 minutes. Obviously, this generation time is very short compared with that of higher plants and animals. Bacteria continue to grow at this rapid rate as long as nutrients hold out— even the smallest contamination can result in a sizable growth in a very short time.

Protozoa

Protozoans (or "first animals") are a large group of eukaryotic organisms of more than 50,000 known species belonging to the Kingdom Protista that have adapted a form of cell to serve as the entire body. In fact, protozoans are one-celled animal-like organisms with complex cellular structures. In the microbial world, protozoans are giants, many times larger than bacteria. They range in size from 4 microns to 500 microns. The largest ones can almost be seen by the naked eye. Protozoa get their name because they employ the same type of feeding strategy as animals. That is, they are heterotrophic, meaning they obtain cellular energy from organic substances such as proteins. Most are harmless, but some are parasitic. Some forms have two life stages: active trophozoites (capable of feeding) and dormant cysts.

The major groups of protozoans are based on their method of locomotion (motility). For example, the Mastigophora are motile by means of one or more flagella (the whiplike projection that propels the free-swimming organisms—*Giardia lamblia* is a flagellated protozoan); the Ciliophora by means of shortened modified flagella called *cilia* (short hair-like structures that beat rapidly and propel the organisms through the water); the Sarcodina by means of amoeboid movement (streaming or gliding action—the shape of amoebae change as they stretch, then contract, from place to place); and the Sporozoa, which are nonmotile; they are simply swept along, riding the current of the water.

Protozoa consume organics to survive; their favorite food is bacteria. Protozoa are mostly aerobic or facultative in regards to oxygen requirements. Toxic materials, pH, and temperature affect protozoan rates of growth in the same way as they affect bacteria.

Most protozoan life cycles alternate between an active growth phase (trophozoites) and a resting stage (cysts). Cysts are extremely resistant structures that protect the organism from destruction when it encounters harsh environmental conditions— including chlorination.

The three protozoans and the waterborne diseases associated with them of most concern to the waterworks operator are:

Entamoeba histolytica—Amoebic dysentery

Giardia lamblia—Giardiasis

Cryptosporidium—Cryptosporidiosis

Viruses

Viruses are very different from the other microorganisms. Consider their size relationship, for example. Relative to size, if protozoans are the Goliaths of microorganisms, then viruses are the Davids. Stated more specifically and accurately, viruses are intercellular parasitic particles that are the smallest living infectious materials known—the midgets of the microbial world. Viruses are very simple life forms consisting of a central molecule of genetic material surrounded by a protein shell called a capsid—and sometimes by a second layer called an envelope. They contain no mechanisms by which to obtain energy or reproduce on their own; thus to live, viruses must have a host. After they invade the cells of their specific host (animal, plant, insect, fish, or even bacteria), they take over the host's cellular machinery and force it to make more viruses. In the process, the host cell is destroyed and hundreds of new viruses are released into the environment.

Smaller and different from bacteria, viruses are prevalent in water contaminated with sewage. Detecting viruses in water supplies is a major problem because of the complexity of nonroutine procedures involved, though experience has shown that the normal coliform index can be used as a rough guide for viruses as for bacteria. However, more attention must be paid to viruses whenever surface water supplies have been used for sewage disposal.

Viruses occur in many shapes, including long slender rods, elaborate irregular shapes, and geometric polyhedrals (see figure below).

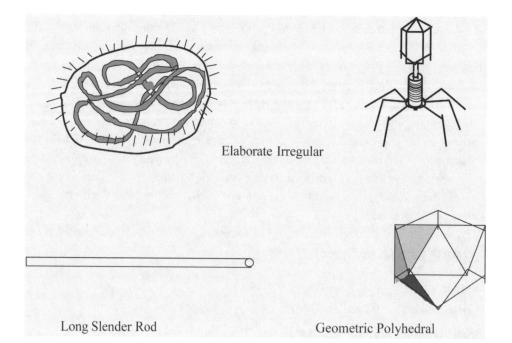

Elaborate Irregular

Long Slender Rod

Geometric Polyhedral

Viruses are difficult to destroy by normal disinfection practices, requiring increased disinfectant concentration and contact time for effective destruction. Viruses that infect bacterial cells cannot infect and replicate within cells of other organisms. It is possible to utilize the specificity to identify bacteria, a procedure called phage typing.

BAD BUGS

Salmonella spp

Salmonella spp. is a rod-shaped, motile bacterium—nonmotile exceptions *S. gallinarum* and *S. pullorum*—nonsporeforming and Gram-negative. There is a widespread occurrence in animals, especially in poultry and swine. Environmental sources of the organism include water, soil, insects, factory surfaces, kitchen surfaces, animal feces, raw meats, raw poultry, and raw seafoods, to name only a few.

Nature of Acute Disease

S. typhi and the paratyphoid bacteria are normally septicemic (in the bloodstream) and produce typhoid or typhoid-like fever in humans. Other forms of salmonellosis generally produce milder symptoms.

Nature of Disease

Acute symptoms—Nausea, vomiting, abdominal cramps, minal diarrhea, fever, and headache. Chronic consequences—arthritic symptoms may follow 3–4 weeks after onset of acute symptoms.

Onset time—6–48 hours.

Infective dose—As few as 15–20 cells; depends upon age and health of host, and strain differences among the members of the genus.

Duration of symptoms—Acute symptoms may last for 1–2 days or may be prolonged, again depending on host factors, ingested dose, and stain characteristics.

Cause of disease—Penetration and passage of Salmonella organisms from gut lumen into epithelium of small intestine where inflammation occurs; there is evidence that an enterotoxin may be produced, perhaps within the enterocyte.

Diagnosis of Human Illness

Serological identification of culture isolated from stool.

Associated Foods

Raw meats, poultry, eggs, milk and dairy products, fish, shrimp, frog legs, yeast, coconut, sauces and salad dressing, cake mixes, cream-filled desserts and toppings, dried gelatin, peanut butter, cocoa, and chocolate.

Various Salmonella species have long been isolated from the outside of egg shells. The present situation with *S. enteritidis* is complicated by the presence of the organism inside the egg, in the yolk. This and other information strongly suggest vertical transmission, i.e., deposition of the organism in the yolk by an infected layer hen prior to shell deposition. Foods other than eggs have also caused outbreaks of *S. enteritidis* disease.

Clostridium Botulinum

Clostridium botulinum is an anaerobic, Gram-positive, spore-forming rod that produces a potent neurotoxin. The spores are heat-resistant and can survive in foods that are incorrectly or minimally processed. Seven types (A, B, C, D, E, F and G) of botulism are recognized, based on the antigenic specificity of the toxin produced by each strain. Types A, B, E and F cause human botulism. Types C and D cause most cases of botulism in animals. Animals most commonly affected are wild fowl and poultry, cattle, horses and some species of fish. Although type G has been isolated from soil in Argentina, no outbreaks involving it have been recognized.

Food-borne botulism (as distinct from wound botulism and infant botulism) is a severe type of food poisoning caused by the ingestion of foods containing the potent neurotoxin formed during growth of the organism. The toxin is heat labile and can be destroyed if heated at 80°C for 10 minutes or longer. The incidence of the disease is low but the disease is of considerable concern because of its high mortality rate if not treated immediately and properly. Most of the up to 30 outbreaks that are reported annually in the United States are associated with inadequately processed, home-canned foods, but occasionally commercially produced foods have been involved in outbreaks. Sausages, meat products, canned vegetables and seafood products have been the most frequent vehicles for human botulism.

The organism and its spores are widely distributed in nature. They occur in both cultivated and forest soils, bottom sediments of steams, lakes, and coastal waters, and in the intestinal tracts of fish and mammals, and in the gills and viscera of crabs and other shellfish.

Foodborne botulism is the name of the disease (actually a foodborne intoxication) caused by the consumption of foods containing the neurotoxin produced by C. botulinum.

Infant botulism, first recognized in 1976, affects infants under 12 months of age. This type of botulism is caused by the ingestion of botulinum spores which colonize and produce toxins in the intestinal tract of infants (intestinal toxemia botulism). Of the various potential environmental sources such as soil, cistern water, dust and foods, honey is the dietary reservoir of *C. botulinum* spores thus far definitively linked to infant botulism by both laboratory and epidemiologic studies. The number of confirmed infant botulism cases has increased significantly as a result of greater awareness by health officials since its recognition in 1976. It is now internationally recognized, with cases being reported in more countries.

Wound botulism is the rarest form of botulism. The illness results when *C. botulinum* by itself or with other microorganisms infects a wound and produces toxins which reach other parts of the body via the blood system. Foods are not involved in this type of botulism

An undetermined category of botulism involves adult cases in which the specific food or wound source cannot be identified. It has been suggested that some cases of botulism assigned to this category may result from intestinal colonization in adults, with in vivo production of toxin. Reports in the medical literature suggest the existence of a form of botulism similar to infant botulism, but occurring in adults. In these cases, the patients had surgical alterations of the gastrointestinal tract and/or antibiotic therapy. It is proposed that these procedures may have altered the normal gut flora and allowed *C. botulinum* to colonize the intestinal tract.

Nature of the Disease

Infective dose—a very small amount (a few nanograms) of toxin can cause illness.

Onset

Onset of symptoms in foodborne botulism is usually 18 to 36 hours after ingestion of the food containing the toxin, although cases have varied from 4 hours to 8 days. Early signs of intoxication consist of marked lassitude, weakness and vertigo, usually followed by double vision and progressive difficulty in speaking and swallowing. Difficulty in breathing, weakness of other muscles, abdominal distention, and constipation may also be common symptoms.

Clinical symptoms of infant botulism consist of constipation that occurs after a period of normal development. This is followed by poor feeding, lethargy, weakness, pooled oral secretions, and wail or altered cry. Loss of head control is striking. Recommended treatment is primarily supportive care. Antimicrobial therapy is not recommended. Infant botulism is diagnosed by demonstrating botulinal toxins and the organism in the infant's stools.

Diagnosis of Human Illness

Although botulism can be diagnosed by clinical symptoms alone, differentiation from other diseases may be difficult. The most dire and effective way to confirm the clinical diagnosis of botulism in laboratory is to demonstrate the presence of toxin in the serum or feces of the patient or in the food which the patient consumed. Currently, the most sensitive and widely used method for detecting toxin is the mouse neutralization test. This text takes 48 hours. Culturing of specimens takes 5–7 days.

Associated Foods

The types of foods involved in botulism vary according to food preservation and eating habit in different regions. Any food that is conducive to outgrowth and toxin production, that when processed allows spore survival, and is not subsequently heated before consumption can be associated with botulism. Almost any type of food that is not very acidic (pH above 4.6) can support growth and toxin production by *C. botulinum*. Botulinal toxin has been demonstrated in a considerable variety of foods, such as canned corn, peppers, green beans, soups, beets, asparagus, mushrooms, ripe olives, spinach, tuna fish, chicken and chicken livers and liver pate, and luncheon meats, ham, sausage, stuffed eggplant, lobster, and smoked and salted fish.

Staphylococcus Aureus

Staphylococcus aureus is a spherical bacterium (coccus) which on microscopic examination appears in pairs, short chains, or bunched, grape-like clusters. These organisms are Gram-positive. Some strains are capable of producing a highly heat-stable protein toxin that causes illness in humans.

Staphylococcal food poisoning (staphyloenterotoxicosis; staphyloenterotoxemia) is the name of the condition caused by the enterotoxins which some strains of *S. aureus* produce.

Nature of the Disease

The onset of symptoms in staphylococcal food poisoning is usually rapid and in many cases acute, depending on individual susceptibility to the toxin, the amount of contaminated food eaten, the amount of toxin in the food ingested, and the general health of the victim. The most common symptoms are nausea, vomiting, retching, abdominal cramping, and prostration. Some individuals may not always demonstrate all the symptoms associated with the illness. In more severe cases, headache, muscle cramping, and transient changes in blood pressure and pulse rate may occur. Recovery generally takes two days; however, it is not unusual for complete recovery to take three days and sometimes longer in severe cases.

Infective dose—a toxin dose of less than 1.0 microgram in contaminated food will produce symptoms of staphylococcal intoxication. This toxin level is reached when *S. aureus* populations exceed 100,000 per gram.

Diagnosis of Human Illness

In the diagnosis of staphylococcal foodborne illness, proper interviews with the victims and gathering and analyzing epidemiological data are essential. Incriminated foods should be collected and examined for staphylococci. The presence of relatively large numbers of enterotoxigenic staphylococci is good circumstantial evidence that the food contains toxin. The most conclusive test is the linking of an illness with a specific food or in cases where multiple vehicles exist, the detection of toxin in the food sample(s). In cases where the food may have been treated to kill the staphylococci, as in pasteurization or heating, direct microscopic observation of the food may be an aid in the diagnosis. A number of serological methods for determining the enterotoxigenicity of *S. aureus* isolated from foods as well as methods for the separation and detection of toxins in foods have been developed and used successfully to aid in the diagnosis of the illness. Phage typing may also be useful when viable staphylococci can be isolated from the incriminated food, from victims, and from suspected carriers such as food handlers.

Foods Incriminated

Foods that are frequently incriminated in staphylococcal food poisoning include meat and meat products; poultry and egg products; salads such as egg, tuna, chicken, potato, and macaroni; bakery products such as cream-filled pastries, cream pies, and chocolate éclairs; sandwich fillings; and milk and dairy products. Foods that require considerable handling during preparation and that are kept at slightly elevated temperatures after preparation are frequently involved in staphylococcal food poisoning.

Staphylococci exist in air, dust, sewage, water, milk, and food or on food equipment, environmental surface, humans, and animals. Humans and animals are the primary reservoirs. Staphylococci are present in the nasal passages and throats and on the hair and skin of 50 percent or more or healthy individuals. This incidence is even higher for those who associate with or who came in contact with sick individuals and hospital environments. Although food handlers are usually the main source of food contamination in food poisoning outbreaks, equipment and environmental surfaces can also be sources of contamination with *S. aureus*. Human intoxication is caused by ingesting enterotoxins produced in food by some strains of *S. aureus*, usually because the food has not been kept hot enough (60° C, 140° F, or above) or cold enough (7.2° C, 45° F, or below).

Campylobacter Jejuni

Campylobacter jejuni (formerly known as *Campylobacter fetus subsp. Jejuni*) is a Gram-negative, slender, curved, and motile rod. It is a microaerophilic organism, which means it has a requirement for reduced levels of oxygen. It is relatively fragile, and sensitive to environmental stresses (e.g., 21 percent oxygen, drying, heating, disinfectants, acidic conditions). Because of its microaerophilic characteristics the organism required 3 to 5 percent oxygen and 2 to 10 percent carbon dioxide for optimal growth conditions. This bacterium is now recognized as an important enteric pathogen. Before 1972, when methods were developed for its isolation from feces, it was believed to be primarily an animal pathogen causing abortion and enteritis in sheep and cattle. Surveys have shown that *C. jejuni* is the leading cause of bacterial diarrheal illness in the United States. It causes more disease than *Shigella* spp. and *Salmonella* spp. combined.

Although *C. jejuni* is not carried by healthy individuals in the United States and Europe, it is often isolated from healthy cattle, chickens, birds, and even flies. It is sometimes present in nonchlorinated water sources such as streams and ponds.

Because the pathogenic mechanisms of *C. jejuni* are still being studied, it is difficult to differentiate pathogenic from nonpathogenic strains. However, it appears that many of the chicken isolates are pathogens.

Name of Disease

Campylobacteriosis is the name of the illness caused by *C. jejuni*. It is also often known as *campylobacter enteritis* or *gastroenteritis*.

Major Symptoms

C. jejuni infection causes diarrhea, which may be watery or sticky and can contain blood (usually occult) and fecal leukocytes (white cells). Other symptoms often present are fever, abdominal pain, nausea, headache, and muscle pain. The illness usually occurs 2–5 days after ingestion of the contaminated food or water. Illness generally lasts 7–10 days, but relapses are not uncommon (about 25 percent of cases). Most infections are self-limiting and are not treated with antibiotics. However, treatment with erythromycin does reduce the length of time that infected individuals shed the bacteria in their feces.

The infective dose of *C. jejuni* is considered to be small. Human feeding studies suggest that about 400–500 bacteria may cause illness in some individuals, while in others, greater numbers are required. A conducted volunteer human feeding study suggests that host susceptibility also dictates infectious dose to some degree. The pathogenic mechanisms of *C. jejuni* are still not completely understood, but it does produce a heat-labile toxin that may cause diarrhea. *C. jejuni* may also be an invasive organism.

Isolation Procedures

C. jejuni is usually present in high numbers in the diarrheal stools of individuals, but isolation requires special antibiotic-containing media and a special microaerophilic atmosphere (5 percent oxygen). However, most clinical laboratories are equipped to isolate Campylobacter spp. if requested.

Associated Foods

C. jejuni frequently contaminates raw chicken. Surveys show that 20 to 100 percent of retail chickens are contaminated. This is not overly surprising since many healthy chickens carry these bacteria in their intestinal tracts. Raw milk is also a source of infections. The bacteria are often carried by healthy cattle and by flies on farms.

Nonchlorinated water may also be a source of infections. However, properly cooking chicken, pasteurizing milk, and chlorinating drinking water will kill the bacteria.

Yersinia Enterocolitica

Yersinia enterocolitica (and *Yersinia pseudotuberculosis*) is a small, rod-shaped, Gram-negative bacteria, often isolated from clinical specimens such as wounds, feces, sputum, and mesenteric lymph nodes. However, it is not part of the normal human flora. *Y. pseudotuberculosis* has been isolated from the diseased appendix of humans.

Both organisms have often been isolated from such animals as pigs, birds, beavers, cats, and dogs. Only *Y. enterocolitica* has been detected in environmental and food sources, such as ponds, lakes, meats, ice cream, and milk. Most isolates have been found not to be pathogenic.

Name of Disease

Yersiniosis is the name of the disease caused by *Yersinia enterocolitica.*

There are three pathogenic species in the genus Yersinia, but only *Y. enterocolitica* and *Y. pseudotuberculosis* cause gastroenteritis. To date, no foodborne outbreaks caused by *Y. pseudotuberculosis* have been reported in the United States, but human infections transmitted via contaminated water and foods have been reported in Japan. *Y. pestis*, the causative agent of the plague, is genetically very similar to *Y. pseudotuberculosis* but infects humans by routes other than food.

Nature of Disease

Yersiniosis is frequently characterized by such symptoms as gastroenteritis with diarrhea and/or vomiting; however, fever and abdominal pain are the hallmark symptoms. *Yersinia* infections mimic appendicitis and mesenteric lymphadenitis, but the bacteria may also cause infections of other sites such as wounds, joints, and the urinary tract.

Infective dose—Unknown.

Onset—Illness onset is usually between 24 and 48 hours after ingestion, which (with food or drink as vehicle) is the usual route of infection.

Diagnosis of Human Illness

Diagnosis of Yersiniosis begins with isolation of the organism from the human host's feces, blood, or vomit, and sometimes at the time of appendectomy. Confirmation occurs with the isolation, as well as biochemical and serological identification, of *Y. enterocolitica* from both the human host and the ingested foodstuff. Diarrhea is reported to occur in about 80 percent of cases; abdominal pain and fever are the most reliable symptoms.

Because of the difficulties in isolating *yersiniae* from feces, several countries rely on serology. Acute and convalescent patient sera are titered against the suspect serotype of *Yersinia spp.*

Yersiniosis has been misdiagnosed as Crohn's disease (regional enteritis) as well as appendicitis.

Associated Foods

Strains of *Y. enterocolitica* can be found in meats (pork, beef, lamb, etc.), oysters, fish, and raw milk. The exact cause of the food contamination is unknown. However, the prevalence of this organism in the soil and water and in animals such as beavers, pigs, and squirrels, offers ample opportunities for it to enter our food supply. Poor sanitation and improper sterilization techniques by food handlers, including improper storage, cannot be overlooked as contributing to contamination.

Listeria Monocytogenes

Listeria monocytogenes is a Gram-positive bacterium, motile by means of flagella. Some studies suggest that 1 to 10 percent of humans may be intestinal carriers of *L. monocytogenes*. It has been found in at least 37 mammalian species, both domestic and feral, as well as at least 17 species of birds and possibly some species of fish and shellfish. It can be isolated from soil, silage, and other environmental sources. *L. monocytogenes* is quite hardy and resists the deleterious effects of freezing, drying, and heat remarkably well for a bacterium that does not form spores. Most *L. monocytogenes* are pathogenic to some degree.

Name of the Disease

Listeriosis is the name of the general group of disorders caused by *L. monocytogenes*.

Nature of Disease

Listeriosis is clinically defined when the organism is isolated from flood, cerebrospinal fluid, or an otherwise normally sterile site (e.g. placenta, fetus).

The manifestations of Listeriosis include septicemia, meningitis (or meningoencephalitis), encephalitis, and intrauterine or cervical infections in pregnant women, which may result in spontaneous abortion (2nd/3rd trimester) or stillbirth. The onset of the aforementioned disorders is usually preceded by influenza-like symptoms including persistent fever. It was reported that gastrointestinal symptoms such as nausea, vomiting, and diarrhea may precede more serious forms of Listeriosis or may be the only symptoms expressed. Gastrointestinal symptoms were epidemiologically associated with use of antacids or cimetidine. The onset time to serious forms of listeriosis is unknown but may range from a few days to three weeks. The onset time to gastrointestinal symptoms is unknown but is probably greater than 12 hours.

The infective dose of *L. monocytogenes* is unknown but is believed to vary with the strain and susceptibility of the victim. From cases contracted through raw or supposedly pasteurized milk, it is safe to assume that in susceptible persons, fewer than 1,000 total organisms may cause disease. *L. monocytogenes* may invade the gastrointestinal epithelium. Once the bacterium enters the host's monocytes, macrophages, or polymorphonuclear leukocytes, it is bloodborne (septicemic) and can grow. Its presence intracellularly in phagocytic cells also permits access to the brain and probably transplacental migration to the fetus in pregnant women. The pathogenesis of L. monocytogenes centers on its ability to survive and multiply in phagocytic host cells.

Diagnosis of Human Illness

Listeriosis can only be positively diagnosed by culturing the organism from blood, cerebrospinal fluid, or stool (although the latter is difficult and of limited value).

Associated Foods

L. monocytogenes has been associated with such foods as raw milk, supposedly pasteurized fluid milk, cheeses (particularly soft-ripened varieties), ice cream, raw vegetables, fermented raw-meat sausages, raw and cooked poultry, raw meats (all types), and raw and smoked fish. Its ability to grow at temperatures as low as 3º C permits multiplication in refrigerated foods.

Vibrio Cholerae Serogroup O1

Vibrio cholerae Serogroup O1 bacterium is responsible for Asiatic or epidemic cholera. No major outbreaks of this disease have occurred in the United States since 1911. However, sporadic cases occurred between 1973 and 1991, suggesting the possible reintroduction of the organism into the U.S. marine and estuarine environment. The cases between 1973 and 1991 were associated with the consumption of raw shellfish or of shellfish either improperly cooked or recontaminated after proper cooking. Environmental studies have demonstrated that strains of this organism may be found in the temperate estuarine and marine coastal areas surrounding the United States.

In 1991 cholera was reported for the first time in this century in South America, starting in Peru. The outbreaks quickly grew to epidemic proportions and spread to other South American and Central American countries, and into Mexico. 1,099,882 cases and 10,453 deaths were reported in the Western Hemisphere between January 1991 and July 1995.

Although the South American strain of V. Cholera O1 has been isolated from Gulf Coast waters, presumably transmitted by ships off-loading contaminated ballast water, no cases of cholera have been attributed to fish or shellfish harvested from U.S. waters. However, over 100 cases of cholera caused by the South American strain have been reported in the United States. These cases were travelers returning from South America, or were associated with illegally smuggled, temperature-abused crustaceans from South America.

In the autumn of 1993, a new strain, a non-O1 never before identified, was implicated in outbreaks of cholera in Bangladesh and India. The organism, V. cholerae Serogroup O139 (Bengal), causes characteristic severe cholera symptoms. Previous illness with V. cholerae O1 does not confer immunity and the disease is now endemic. In the U.S., V. cholerae O139 has been implicated in one case, a traveler returning from India. The strain has not been reported in U.S. waters or shellfish.

Nature of Acute Disease

Cholera is the name of the infection caused by *V. cholerae*.

Nature of Disease

Symptoms of Asiatic cholera may vary from a mild, watery diarrhea to an acute diarrhea, with characteristic rice-water stools. Onset of the illness is generally sudden, with incubation periods varying from six hours to five days. Abdominal cramps, nausea, vomiting, dehydration, and shock may occur. After severe fluid and electrolyte loss, death may occur. Illness is caused by the ingestion of viable bacterial, which attach to the small intestine and produce cholera toxin. The production of cholera toxin by the attached bacteria results in the watery diarrhea associated with this illness.

Infective dose—Human volunteer feeding studies utilizing healthy individuals have demonstrated that approximately one million organisms must be ingested to cause illness. Antacid consumption markedly lowers the infective dose.

Diagnosis of Human Illness

Cholera can be confirmed only by the isolation of the causative organism from the diarrheic stools of infected individuals.

Associated Foods

Cholera is generally a disease spread by poor sanitation, resulting in contaminated water supplies. This is clearly the main mechanism for the spread of cholera in poor communities in South America. The excellent sanitation facilities in the U.S. are responsible for the near eradication of epidemic cholera. Sporadic cases occur when shellfish harvested from fecally polluted coastal waters are consumed raw. Cholera may also be transmitted by shellfish harvested from nonpolluted waters since V. Cholera O1 is part of the autochthonous microbiota of these waters.

Vibrio Cholerae Serogroup Non-O1

Vibrio cholera Serogroup Non-O1 is a bacterium that infects only humans and other primates. It is related to *V. cholerae* Serogroup O1, the organism that causes Asiatic or epidemic cholera, but causes a disease reported to be less severe than cholera. Both pathogenic and nonpathogenic strains of the organism are normal inhabitants of marine and estuarine environments of the United States. This organism has been referred to as non-cholera vibrio (NVC) and nonagglutinable vibrio (NAG) in the past, although at least 139 O serogroups have been identified.

Nature of Acute Disease

Non-O1 V. cholerae gastroenteritis is the name associated with this illness. Although rare, septicemic infections have been reported and deaths have resulted. Some cases are similar to the primary septicemia caused by V. vulnificus.

Nature of Disease

Diarrhea, abdominal cramps, and fever are the predominant symptoms associated with this illness, with vomiting and nausea occurring in approximately 25 percent of infected individuals. Approximately 25 percent of infected individuals will have blood and mucus in their stools. Diarrhea may, in some cases, be quite severe, lasting six to seven days. Diarrhea will usually occur within 48 hours following ingestion of the organism. It is unknown how the organism causes the illness, although an enterotoxin is suspected as well as an invasive mechanism. Disease is caused when the organism attaches itself to the small intestine of infected individuals and perhaps subsequently invades.

Disease caused by V. cholerae O139 is distinguishable from cholera caused by V. cholerae O1.

Infective dose—It is suspected that large numbers (more than one million) of the organism must be ingested to cause illness.

Diagnosis of Human Illness

Diagnosis of a V. cholerae non-01 infection is made by culturing the organism from an individual's diarrheic stool or from the blood of patients with septicemia.

Associated Foods

Shellfish harvested from U.S. coastal waters frequently contain V. cholerae serogroup non-O1. Consumption of raw, improperly cooked, or cooked but recontaminated shellfish may lead to infection.

Vibrio Parahaemolyticus

Vibrio parahaemolyticus (and other marine Vibrio spp.) is a bacterium that is frequently isolated from the estuarine and marine environment of the United States. Both pathogenic and nonpathogenic forms of the organism can be isolated from marine and estuarine environments and from fish and shellfish dwelling in these environments.

Nature of Acute Disease

V. parahaemolyticus–associated gastroenteritis is the name of the infection caused by this organism.

Nature of Disease

Diarrhea, abdominal cramps, nausea, vomiting, headache, fever, and chills may be associated with infections caused by this organism. The illness is usually mild or moderate, although some cases may require hospitalization. The median duration of the illness is 2.5 days. The incubation period is 4 to 96 hours after the ingestion of the organism, with a mean of 15 hours. Disease is caused when the organism attaches itself to an individual's small intestine and excretes an as yet unidentified toxin.

Infective dose—A total dose of greater than one million organisms may cause disease; this dose may be markedly lowered by coincident consumption of antacids (or presumably by food with buffering capacity).

Diagnosis of Human Illness

Diagnosis of gastroenteritis caused by this organism is made by culturing the organism from the diarrheic stools of an individual.

Associated Foods

Infections with this organism have been associated with the consumption of raw, improperly cooked, or cooked but recontaminated fish and shellfish. A correlation exists between the probability of infection and warmer months of the year. Improper refrigeration of seafoods contaminated with this organism will allow its proliferation, which increases the possibility of infection.

Vibrio Vulnificus

Vibrio vulnificus, a lactose-fermenting, halophilic, Gram-negative, opportunistic pathogen, is found in estuarine environments and associated with various marine species such as plankton, shellfish (oysters, calms, and crabs), and finfish. It is found in all of the coastal waters of the United States. [Cases of illness have also been associated with brackish lakes in New Mexico and Oklahoma.] Environmental factors responsible for controlling members of V. vulnificus in seafood and in the environment include temperature, pH, salinity, and increased dissolved organics.

Nature of Acute Disease

This organism causes wound infection, gastroenteritis, or a syndrome known as "primary septicemia."

Nature of Disease

Wound infections result either from contaminating an open wound with seawater harboring the organism, or by lacerating part of the body on coral, fish, and so forth, followed by contamination with the organism. The ingestion of *V. vulnificus* by healthy individuals can result in gastroenteritis. The "primary septicemia" form of the disease follows consumption of raw seafood containing the organism by individuals with underlying chronic disease, particularly liver disease. In these individuals, the microorganism enters the blood stream, resulting in septic shock, rapidly followed by death in many cases (about 50 percent). Over 70 percent of infected individuals have distinctive bulbous skin lesions.

Infective dose—The infective dose for gastrointestinal symptoms in healthy individuals is unknown but for predisposed persons, septicemia can presumably occur with a dose of less than 100 total organisms.

Diagnosis of Human Illness

The culturing of the organism from wounds, diarrheic stools, or blood is diagnostic of this illness.

Associated Foods

This organism has been isolated from oysters, clams, and crabs. Consumption of these products raw or recontaminated may result in illness.

KEY DEFINITION: HALOPHILIC

Organisms that require a salty environment.

Clostridium Perfringens

Clostridium perfringens is an anaerobic, Gram-positive, sporeforming rod (anaerobic means unable to grow in the presence of free oxygen). It is widely distributed in the environment and frequently occurs in the intestines of humans and many domestic and feral animals. Spores of the organism persist in soil, sediments, and areas subject to human or animal fecal pollution.

Nature of Acute Disease

Perfringens food poisoning is the term used to describe the common foodborne illness caused by *C. perfringens*. A more serious but rare illness is also caused by ingesting food contaminated with Type C strains. The latter illness is known as enteritis necroticans or pig-bel disease.

Nature of Disease

The common form of perfringens poisoning is characterized by intense abdominal cramps and diarrhea which begin 8–22 hours after consumption of foods containing large numbers of those *C. perfringens* bacteria capable of producing the food poisoning toxin. The illness is usually over within 24 hours but less severe symptoms may persist in some individuals for 1–2 weeks. A few deaths have been reported as a result of dehydration and other complications.

Necrotic enteritis (pig-bel) caused by *C. perfringens* is often fatal. This disease also begins as a result of ingesting large numbers of the causative bacteria in contaminated foods. Deaths from necrotic enteritis (pig-bel syndrome) are caused by infection and necrosis of the intestines and from resulting septicemia. This disease is very rare in the U.S.

Infective dose—The symptoms are caused by ingestion of large numbers (greater than 10 to the 8th) of vegetative cells. Toxin production in the digestive tract (or in test tubes) is associated with sporulation. This disease is a food infection; only one episode has ever implied the possibility of intoxication (i.e. disease from preformed toxin).

Diagnosis of Human Illness

Perfringens is diagnosed by its symptoms and the typical delayed onset of illness. Diagnosis is confirmed by detecting the toxin in feces of patient. Bacteriological confirmation can also be done by finding exceptionally large numbers of the causative bacteria in implicated foods or in the feces of patients.

Associated Foods

In most instances, the actual cause of poisoning by *C. perfringens* is temperature abuse of prepared foods. Small numbers of the organism are often present after cooking and multiply to food poisoning levels during cooldown and storage of prepared foods. Meats, meat products, and gravy are the foods most frequently implicated.

Bacillus Cereus and other Bacillus spp.

Bacillus cereus is a Gram-positive, facultatively aerobic sporeformer whose cells are large rods and whose spores do not swell the sporangium. These and other characteristics, including biochemical features, are used to differentiate and confirm the presence of *B. cereus*, although these characteristics are shared with *B. cereus* var. mycoides, *B. thuringiensis*, and *B. anthracis*. Differentiation of these organisms depends upon determination of motility (most B. cereus are motile), presence of toxin crystals (B. thuringiensis), hemolytic activity (B. cereus and others are beta hemolytic whereas B. anthracis is usually nonhemolytic), and rhizoid growth which is characteristic of B. cereus var. mycoides.

Nature of Acute Disease

B. cereus food poisoning is the general description, although two recognized types of illness are caused by two distinct metabolites. The diarrheal type of illness is caused by a large molecular weight protein, while the vomiting emetic type of illness is believed to be caused by a low molecular weight, heat-stable peptide.

Nature of Disease

The symptoms of B. cereus diarrheal type food poisoning mimic those of *Clostridium perfringens* food poisoning. The onset of watery diarrhea, abdominal cramps, and pain occurs 6–15 hours after consumption of contaminated food. Nausea may accompany diarrhea, but vomiting (emesis) rarely occurs. Symptoms persist for 24 hours in most instances.

The emetic type of food poisoning is characterized by nausea and vomiting within 0.5 to 6 hours after consumption of contaminated foods. Occasionally, abdominal cramps and/or diarrhea may also occur. Duration of symptoms is generally less than 24 hours. The symptoms of this type of food poisoning parallel those caused by *Staphylococcus aureus* foodborne intoxication. Some strains of *B. subtilis* and *B. licheniformis* have been isolated from lamb and chicken incriminated in food poisoning episodes. These organisms demonstrate the production of a highly heat-stable toxin which may be similar to the vomiting type toxin produced by *B. cereus*.

The presence of large numbers of *B. cereus* (grater than10^6 organisms/g) in a food is indicative of active growth and proliferation of the organism and is consistent with a potential hazard to health.

Diagnosis of Human Illness

Confirmation of *B. cereus* as the etiologic agent in a foodborne outbreak requires either (1) isolation of strains of the same serotype from the suspect food and feces or vomitus of the patient, (2) isolation of large numbers of a *B. cereus* serotype known to cause foodborne illness from the suspect food or from the feces or vomitus of the

---

KEY DEFINITION: SEPTICEMIA

The presence of bacteria in the blood.

---

patient, or (3) isolation of *B. cereus* from suspect foods and determining their entero-toxigenicity by serological (diarrheal toxin) or biological (diarrheal and emetic) tests. The rapid onset time to symptoms in the emetic form of disease, coupled with some food evidence, is often sufficient to diagnose this type of food poisoning.

Associated Foods

A wide variety of foods including meats, milk, vegetables, and fish have been associated with the diarrheal type food poisoning. The vomiting-type outbreaks have generally been associated with rice products; however, other starchy foods such as potato, pasta, and cheese products have also been implicated. Food mixtures such as sauces, puddings, soups, casseroles, pastries, and salads have frequently been incriminated in food-poisoning outbreak.

Aeromonas Hydrophila

Aeromonas hydrophila (*Aeromonas caviae*, *Aeromonas sobria*) is a species of bacterium that is present in all freshwater environments and in brackish water. Some strains of *A. hydrophila* are capable of causing illness in fish and amphibians as well as in humans who may acquire infections through open wounds or by ingestion of a sufficient number of the organisms in food or water.

Not as much is known about the other Aeromonas spp., but they too are aquatic microorganisms and have been implicated in human disease.

Nature of Acute Disease

A. hydrophila may cause gastroenteritis in healthy individuals or septicemia in individuals with impaired immune systems or various malignancies.

A. caviae and *A. sobria* also may cause enteritis in anyone or septicemia in immunocompromised persons or those with malignancies.

Nature of Disease

At the present time, there is controversy as to whether *A. hydrophila* is a cause of human gastroenteritis. Although the organism possesses several attributes which could make it pathogenic for humans, volunteer human feeding studies, even with enormous numbers of cells (i.e., 10^{11}), have failed to elicit human illness. Its presence in the stools of individuals with diarrhea, in the absence of other known enteric pathogens, suggests that it has some role in disease.

Likewise, *A. caviae* and *A. sobria* are considered by many as "putative pathogens," associated with diarrheal disease, but as of yet they are unproven causative agents.

Two distinct types of gastroenteritis have been associated with *A. hydrophila*: a cholera-like illness with a watery (rice and water) diarrhea and a dysenteric illness characterized by loose stools containing blood and mucus. The infectious dose of this organism is unknown, but SCUBA divers who have ingested small amounts of water have become ill, and A. hydrophila has been isolated from their stool.

A general infection in which the organisms spread through the body has been observed in individuals with underlying illness (septicemia).

Diagnosis of Human Illness

A. hydrophila can be cultured from stools or from blood by plating the organisms on an agar medium containing sheep blood and the antibiotic ampicillin. Ampicillin prevents the growth of most competing microorganisms. The species identification is confirmed by a series of biochemical tests. The ability of the organism to produce the enterotoxins believed to cause the gastrointestinal symptoms can be confirmed by tissue culture assays.

Associated Foods

A. hydrophila has frequently been found in fish and shellfish. It has also been found in market samples of red meats (beef, pork, lamb) and poultry. Since little is known about the virulence mechanisms of *A. hydrophila*, it is presumed that not all strains are pathogenic, given the ubiquity of the organism.

Plesiomonas Shigelloides

Plesiomonas shigelloides is a Gram-negative, rod-shaped bacterium which has been isolated from freshwater, freshwater fish and shellfish, and from many types of animals including cattle, goats, swine, cats, dogs, monkeys, vultures, snakes, and toads.

Most human *P. shigelloides* infections are suspected to be waterborne. The organism may be present in unsanitary water which has been used as drinking water, recreational water, or water used to rinse foods that are consumed without cooking or heating. The ingested *P. shigelloides* organism does not always cause illness in the host animal but may reside temporarily as a transient, noninfectious member of the intestinal flora. It has been isolated from the stools of patients with diarrhea, but is also sometimes isolated from healthy individuals (0.2–3.2 percent of population).

It cannot yet be considered a definite cause of human disease, although its association with human diarrhea and the virulence factors it demonstrates make it a prime candidate.

Nature of Acute Disease

Gastroenteritis is the disease with which *P. shigelloides* has been implicated.

Nature of Disease

P. shigelloides gastroenteritis is usually a mild self-limiting disease with fever, chills, abdominal pain, nausea, diarrhea, or vomiting; symptoms may begin 20–24 hours after consumption of contaminated food or water; diarrhea is watery, nonmucoid, and non-bloody; in severe cases, diarrhea may be greenish-yellow, foamy, and blood tinged; duration of illness in healthy people may be one to seven days. The infectious dose is presumed to be quite high, at least greater than one million organisms.

Diagnosis of Human Illness

The pathogenesis of *P. Shigelloides* infection is not known. The organism is suspected of being toxigenic and invasive. Its significance as an enteric (intestinal) pathogen is presumed because of its predominant isolation from stools of patients with diarrhea. It is identified by common bacteriological analysis, serotyping, and antibiotic sensitivity testing.

Associated Foods

Most *P. shigelloides* infections occur in the summer months and correlate with environmental contamination of freshwater (rivers, streams, ponds, etc.). The usual route of transmission of the organism in sporadic or epidemic cases is by ingestion of contaminated water or raw shellfish.

Shigella spp.

Shigella spp. (*Shigella sonnei*, *S. boydii*, *S. flexneri*, and *S. dysenteriae*) are Gram-negative, nonmotile, nonsporeforming rod-shaped bacteria. The illness caused by *Shigella* (shigellosis) accounts for less than 10 percent of the reported outbreaks of foodborne illness in this country. *Shigella* rarely occurs in animals; it is principally a disease of humans except for other primates such as monkeys and chimpanzees. The organism is frequently found in water polluted with human feces.

Nature of Acute Disease

Shigellosis (bacillary dysentery).

KEY DEFINITION: DYSENTERY

An infectious disease characterized by inflammation of the intestine, abdominal pain, and diarrhea with stools that often contain blood.

Nature of Disease

Symptoms—Abdominal pain; cramps; diarrhea; fever; vomiting; blood, pus, or mucus in stools; tenesmus.

Onset time—12 to 50 hours.

Infective dose—As few as 10 cells depending on age and condition of host. The Shigella spp. are highly infectious agents that are transmitted by the fecal-oral route.

The disease is caused when virulent *Shigella* organisms attach to, and penetrate, epithelial cells of the intestinal mucosa. After invasion, they multiply intracellularly, and spread to contiguous epithelial cells resulting in tissue destruction. Some strains produce enterotoxin and Shiga toxin (very much like the verotoxin of E. coli O157:H7).

Diagnosis of Human Illness

Serological identification of culture isolated from stool.

Associated Foods

Salads (potato, tuna, shrimp, macaroni, and chicken), raw vegetables, milk and dairy products, and poultry. Contamination of these foods is usually through the fecal-oral route. Fecally contaminated water and unsanitary handling by food handlers are the most common causes of contamination.

KEY DEFINITION: TENESMUS

Painful straining to pass stool.

Miscellaneous Enterics

Miscellaneous enterics, Gram-negative genera including *Klebsiella, Enterobacter, Proteus, Citrobacter, Aerobacter, Providencia,* and *Serratia* are rod-shaped enterics (intestinal bacteria) that have been suspected of causing acute and chronic gastrointestinal disease. The organisms may be recovered from natural environments such as forests and freshwater as well as from farm produce (vegetables) where they reside as normal microflora.

Nature of Acute Disease

Gastroenteritis is name of the disease occasionally and sporadically caused by these genera.

Nature of Disease

Acute gastroenteritis is characterized by two or more of the symptoms of vomiting, nausea, fever, chills, abdominal pain, and watery (dehydrating) diarrhea occurring 12 to 24 hours after ingestion of contaminated food or water. Chronic diarrheal disease is characterized by dysenteric symptoms: Foul-smelling, mucous-containing, diarrheic stool with flatulence and abdominal distention. The chronic disease may continue for months and require antibiotic treatment.

Infectious dose—Unknown. Both the acute and chronic forms of the disease are suspected to result from the elaboration of enterotoxins. These organisms may become transiently virulent by gaining mobilizable genetic elements from other pathogens. For example, pathogenic *Citrobacter freundii* which elaborated a toxin identical to E. coli heat-stable toxin was isolated from the stools of ill children.

Diagnosis of Human Illness

Recovery and identification methods for these organisms from food, water, or diarrheal specimens are based upon the efficacy of selective media and results of microbiological and biochemical assays. The ability to produce enterotoxin(s) may be determined by cell culture assay and animal bioassays, serological methods, or genetic probes.

Associated Foods

These bacteria have been recovered from dairy products, raw shell fish, and fresh raw vegetables. The organisms occur in soils used for crop production and shellfish harvesting waters and, therefore, may pose a health hazard.

Streptococcus spp.

The genus *Streptococcus* is comprised of Gram-positive, microaerophilic cocci (round), which are not motile and occur in chains or pains. The genus is defined by a combination of antigenic, hemolytic, and physiological characteristics into Groups A, B, C, D, F, and G. Groups A and D can be transmitted to humans via food.

Nature of Acute Disease

Group A: one species with 40 antigenic types (*S. pyogenes*).

Group D: five species (*S. faecalis, S. faecium, S. durans, S. avium,* and *S. bovis*).

Nature of Disease

Group A: Sore and red throat pain on swallowing, tonsillitis, high fever, headache, nausea, vomiting, malaise, rhinorrhea; occasionally a rash occurs, onset 1–3 days; the infectious dose is probably quite low (less than 1,000 organisms).

Group D: Diarrhea, abdominal cramps, nausea, vomiting, fever, chills, dizziness in 2–36 hours. Following ingestion of suspect food, the infectious dose is probably high (greater than 107 organisms).

Diagnosis of Human Illness

Group A: Culturing of nasal and throat swabs, pus, sputum, blood, suspect food, environmental samples.

Group D: Culturing of stool samples, blood, and suspect food.

Associated Foods

Group A: Food sources include milk, ice cream, eggs, steamed lobster, ground ham, potato salad, egg salad, custard, rice pudding, and shrimp salad. In almost all cases, the foodstuffs were allowed to stand at room temperature for several hours between preparation and consumption. Entrance into the food is the result of poor hygiene, ill food handlers, or the use of unpasteurized milk.

Group D: Food sources include sausage, evaporated milk, cheese, meat croquettes, meat pie, pudding, raw milk, and pasteurized milk. Entrance into the food chain is due to underprocessing and/or poor and unsanitary food preparation.

Enterotoxigenic *Escherichia Coli* (ETEC)

Currently, there are four recognized classes of enterovirulent *E. coli* (collectively referred to as the EEC group) that cause gastroenteritis in humans. Among these are the enterotoxigenic (ETEC) strains. They comprise a relatively small proportion of the species and have been etiologically associated with diarrheal illness of all age groups from diverse global locations. The organism frequently causes diarrhea in infants in less developed countries and in visitors there from industrialized countries. The etiology of this cholera-like illness has been recognized for about 20 years.

Nature of Acute Disease

Gastroenteritis is the common name of the illness caused by ETEC, although travelers' diarrhea is a frequent sobriquet.

Nature of Disease

The most frequent clinical syndrome of infection includes watery diarrhea, abdominal cramps, low-grade fever, nausea, and malaise.

Infective dose—Volunteer feeding studies indicate that a relatively large dose (100 million to 10 billion bacteria) of enterotoxigenic *E. coli* is probably necessary to establish colonization of the small intestine, where these organisms proliferate and produce toxins, which induce fluid secretion. With high infective dose, diarrhea can be induced within 24 hours. Infants may require fewer organisms for infection to be established.

Diagnosis of Human Illness

During the acute phase of infection, large numbers of enterotoxigenic cells are excreted in feces. These strains are differentiated from nontoxigenic *E. coli* present in the bowel by a variety of in vitro immunochemical, tissue culture, or gene probe tests designed to detect either the toxins or genes that encode for these toxins. The diagnosis can be completed in about three days.

Associated Foods

ETEC is not considered a serious foodborne disease hazard in countries having high sanitary standards and practices. Contamination of water with human sewage may lead to contamination of foods. Infected food handlers may also contaminate foods. These organisms are infrequently isolated from dairy products such as semisoft cheeses.

Enteropathogenic *Escherichia Coli*

Currently, there are four recognized classes of enterovirulent *E. coli* (collectively referred to as the EEC group) that cause gastroenteritis in humans. Among these are the enteropathogenic (EPEC) strains. EPEC are defined as *E. coli* belonging to serogroups epidemiologically implicated as pathogens but whose virulence mechanism is unrelated to the excretion of typical *E. coli* enterotoxins. *E. coli* are Gram-negative, rod-shaped bacteria belonging to the family Enterobacteriaceae. Source(s) and prevalence of EPEC are controversial because foodborne outbreaks are sporadic. Humans, bovines, and swine can be infected, and the latter often serve as common experimental animal models. *E. coli* are present in the normal gut flora of these mammals. The proportion of pathogenic to nonpathogenic strains, although the subject of intense research, is unknown.

Nature of Acute Disease

Infantile diarrhea is the name of the disease usually associated with EPEC.

Nature of Disease

EPEC cause either a watery or bloody diarrhea, the former associated with the attachment to, and physical alteration of, the integrity of the intestine. Bloody diarrhea is associated with attachment and an acute tissue-destructive process, perhaps caused by a toxin similar to that of *Shigella dysenteriae*, also called verotoxin. In most of these strains the shiga-like toxin is cell-associated rather than excreted.

Infective dose—EPEC are highly infectious for infants and the dose is presumably very low. In the few documented cases of adult disease, the dose is presumably similar to other colonizers (greater than 10^6 total dose).

Diagnosis of Human Illness

The distinction of EPEC from other groups of pathogenic *E. coli* isolated from patients' stools involves serological and cell culture assays. Serotyping, although useful, is not strict for EPEC.

Associated Foods

Common foods implicated in EPEC outbreaks are raw beef and chicken, although any food exposed to fecal contamination is strongly suspect.

Escherichia Coli O157:H7

Currently, there are four recognized classes of enterovirulent *E. coli* (collectively referred to as the EEC group) that cause gastroenteritis in humans. Among these is the enterohemorrhagic (EHEC) strain designated *E. coli* O157:H7. *E. coli* is a normal inhabitant of the intestines of all mammals, including humans. When aerobic culture methods are used, *E. coli* is the dominant species found in feces. Normally *E. coli* serves a useful function in the body by suppressing the growth of harmful bacterial species and by synthesizing appreciable amounts of vitamins. A minority of *E. coli* strains are capable of causing human illness by several different mechanisms. *E. coli* serotype O157:H7 is a rare variety of *E. coli* that produces large quantities of one or more related, potent toxins that cause severe damage to the lining of the intestine. These toxins [verotoxin (VT), shiga-like toxin] are closely related or identical to the toxin produced by *Shigella dysenteriae*.

Nature of Acute Disease

Hemorrhagic colitis is the name of the acute disease caused by *E. coli* O157:H7.

Nature of Disease

The illness is characterized by severe cramping (abdominal pain) and diarrhea that is initially watery but becomes grossly bloody. Occasionally vomiting occurs. Fever is either low-grade or absent. The illness is usually self-limited and lasts for an average of eight days. Some individuals exhibit watery diarrhea only.

Infective dose—Unknown, but from a compilation of outbreak data, including the organism's ability to be passed person-to-person in the day-care setting and nursing homes, the dose may be similar to that of *Shigella* spp. (as few as 10 organisms).

Diagnosis of Human Illness

Hemorrhagic colitis is diagnosed by isolation of *E. coli* of serotype O157:H7 or other verotoxin-producing *E. coli* from diarrheal stools. Alternatively, the stools can be tested directly for the presence of verotoxin. Confirmation can be obtained by isolation of *E. coli* of the same serotype from the incriminated food.

Associated Foods

Undercooked or raw hamburger (ground beef) has been implicated in many of the documented outbreaks, however E. coli O157:H7 outbreaks have implicated alfalfa sprouts, unpasteurized fruit juices, dry-cured salami, lettuce, game meat, and cheese curds. Raw milk was the vehicle in a school outbreak in Canada.

Enteroinvasive *Escherichia Coli* (EIEC)

It is unknown what foods may harbor these pathogenic enteroinvasive (EIEC) strains responsible for a form of bacillary dysentery.

Nature of Acute Disease

Enteroinvasive *E. coli* (EIEC) may produce an illness known as bacillary dysentery. The EIEC strains responsible for this syndrome are closely related to *Shigella* spp.

Nature of Disease

Following the ingestion of EIEC, the organisms invade the epithelial cells of the intestine, resulting in a mild form of dysentery, often mistaken for dysentery caused by *Shigella* species. The illness is characterized by the appearance of blood and mucus in the stools of infected individuals.

Infective dose—The infectious dose of EIEC is thought to be as few as 10 organisms (same as *Shigella*).

Diagnosis of Human Illness

The culturing of the organism from the stools of infected individuals and the demonstration of invasiveness of isolates in tissue culture or in a suitable animal model is necessary to diagnose dysentery caused by this organism.

More recently, genetic probes for the invasiveness genes of both EIEC and Shigella spp. have been developed.

Associated Foods

It is currently unknown what foods may harbor EIEC, but any food contaminated with human feces from an ill individual, either directly or via contaminated water, could cause disease in others. Outbreaks have been associated with hamburger meat and unpasteurized milk.

Giardia Lamblia

Giardia lamblia (intestinalis) is a single-celled animal, that is, a protozoa, that moves with the aid of five flagella.

Nature of Acute Disease

Giardiasis is the most frequent cause of nonbacterial diarrhea in North America.

Nature of Disease

Organisms that appear identical to those that cause human illness have been isolated from domestic animals (dogs and cats) and wild animals (beavers and bears). A related but morphologically distinct organism infects rodents, although rodents may be infected with human isolates in the laboratory. Human giardiasis may involve diarrhea within one week of ingestion of the cyst, which is the environmental survival form and infective stage of the organism.

Normally illness lasts for one to two weeks, but there are cases of chronic infections lasting months to years. Chronic cases, both those with defined immune deficiencies and those without, are difficult to treat.

The disease mechanism is unknown. Some investigators report that the organism produces a toxin, while others are unable to confirm its existence. The organism has been demonstrated inside host cells in the duodenum, but most investigators think this is such an infrequent occurrence that it is not responsible for disease symptoms. Mechanical obstruction of the absorptive surface of the intestine has been proposed as a possible pathogenic mechanism, as has a synergistic relationship with some of the intestinal flora.

Giardia can be excysted, cultured and encysted in vitro; new isolates have bacterial, fungal, and viral symbionts. Classically the disease was diagnosed by demonstration of the organism in stained fecal smear.

Several strains of *G. lamblia* have been isolated and described through analysis of their proteins and DNA; type or strain, however, is not consistently associated with disease severity. Different individuals show various degrees of symptoms during the course of the disease.

Infectious dose—Ingestion of one or more cysts may cause disease, as contrasted to most bacterial illnesses where hundreds to thousands of organisms must be consumed to produce illness.

Diagnosis of Human Illness

Giardia lamblia is frequently diagnosed by visualizing the organism, either the trophozoite (active reproducing form) or the cyst (the resting stage that is resistant to adverse environmental conditions) in stained preparations or unstained wet mounts with the aid of a microscope. A commercial fluorescent antibody kit is available to stain the organism. Organism may be concentrated by sedimentation or flotation; however, these procedures reduce the number of recognizable organism in the sample. An enzyme linked immunosorbant assay (ELISA) that detects excretory secretory products of the organism is also available. So far, the increased sensitivity of indirect serological detection had not been consistently demonstrated.

Associated Foods

Giardiasis is most frequently associated with the consumption of contaminated water. Five outbreaks have been traced to food contamination by infected or infested food handlers, and the possibility of infections from contaminated vegetables that are eaten raw cannot be excluded. Cool moist conditions favor the survival of the organism.

Entamoeba Histolytica

Entamoeba histolytica is a single-celled parasitic animal, that is, a protozoa, that infects predominantly humans and other primates. Diverse mammals such as dogs and cats can become infected but usually do not shed cysts (the environmental survival form of the organism) with their feces, and thus do not contribute significantly to transmission. The active (trophozoite) stage exists only in host and in fresh feces; cysts survive outside the host in water and soils and on foods, especially under moist conditions on the latter. When swallowed they cause infections by excysting (to the trophozoite stage) in the digestive tract.

Nature of Acute Disease

Amebiasis (or amoebiasis) is the name of the infection caused by E. histolytica.

Nature of Disease

Infections that sometimes last for years may be accompanied by (1) no symptoms, (2) vague gastrointestinal distress, (3) dysentery (with blood and mucus). Most infections occur in the digestive tract but other tissues may be invaded. Complications include (4) ulcerative and abscess pain and, rarely, (5) intestinal blockage. Onset time is highly variable. It is theorized that the absence of symptoms or their intensity varies with such factors as (1) strain of amoeba, (2) immune health of the host, and (3) associated bacteria and, perhaps, viruses. The amoeba's enzymes help it to penetrate and digest human tissues; it secretes toxic substances.

Infectious dose—Theoretically, the ingestion of one viable cyst can cause an infection.

Diagnosis of Human Illness

Human cases are diagnosed by finding cysts shed with the stool; various flotation or sedimentation procedures have been developed to recover the cysts from fecal matter; strains (including fluorescent antibody) help to visualize the isolated cysts for microscopic examination. Since cysts are not shed constantly, a minimum of three stools should be examined. In heavy infections, the motile form (the trophozoite) can be seen in fresh feces. Serological tests exist for long-term infections. It is important to distinguish the E. histolytica cyst from the cysts of nonpathogenic intestinal protozoa by its appearance.

Associated Foods

Amebiasis is transmitted by fecal contamination of drinking water and foods, but also by direct contact with dirty hands or objects as well as by sexual contact.

Cryptosporidium Parvum

Cryptosporidium parvum, a single-celled animal, that is, a protozoa, is an obligate intracellular parasite. It has been given additional species names when isolated from different hosts. It is currently thought that the form infecting humans is the same species that causes disease in young calves. The forms that infect avian hosts and those that infect mice are not thought capable of infecting humans. *Cryptosporidium* sp. infects many herd animals (cows, goats, sheep among domesticated animals, and deer and elk among wild animals). The infective stage of the organism, the oocyst is 3 μm in diameter or about half the size of a red blood cell. The sporocysts are resistant to most chemical disinfectants, but are susceptible to drying and the ultraviolet portion of sunlight. Some strains appear to be adapted to certain hosts but cross-strain infectivity occurs and may or may not be associated with illness. The species or strain infecting the respiratory system is not currently distinguished from the form infecting the intestines.

Nature of Acute Disease

Intestinal, tracheal, or pulmonary cryptosporidiosis.

Nature of Disease

Intestinal cryptosporidiosis is characterized by severe watery diarrhea but may, alternatively, be asymptomatic. Pulmonary and tracheal cryptosporidiosis in humans is associated with coughing and frequently a low-grade fever; these symptoms are often accompanied by severe intestinal distress.

Infective dose—Fewer than 10 organisms and, presumably, one organism can initiate an infection. The mechanism of disease is not known; however, the intracellular stages of the parasite can cause severe tissue alternation.

Diagnosis of Human Illness

Oocysts are shed in the infected individual's feces. Sugar flotation is used to concentrate the organisms and acid fast stain is used to identify them. A commercial kit is available that uses fluorescent antibody to stain the organisms isolated from feces. Diagnosis has also been made by staining the trophozoites in intestinal and biopsy specimens. Pulmonary and tracheal cryptosporidiosis are diagnosed by biopsy and staining.

Associated Foods

Cryptosporidium sp. could occur, theoretically, on any food touched by a contaminated food handler. Incidence is higher in child day-care centers that serve food. Fertilizing salad vegetables with manure is another possible source of human infection. Large outbreaks are associated with contaminated water supplies.

Anisakis Simplex and Related Worms

Anisakis simplex (herring worm), *Pseudoterranova* (*Phocanema, Terranova*) *decipiens* (cod or seal worm), *Contracaecum* spp., and *Hysterothylacium* (*Thynnascaris*) spp. are anisakid nematodes (roundworms) that have been implicated in human infections caused by the consumption of raw or undercooked seafood. To date, only *A. simplex* and *P. decipiens* are reported from human cases in North America.

Nature of Acute Disease

Anisakiasis is generally used when referring to the acute disease in humans. Some purists utilize generic names (e.g., contracaeciasis) in referring to the disease, but the majority considers that the name derived from the family is specific enough. The range of clinical features is not dependent on species of anisakid parasite in cases reported to date.

Nature of Disease

In North America, anisakiasis is most frequently diagnosed when the affected individual feels a tingling or tickling sensation in the throat and coughs up or manually extracts a nematode. In more severe cases there is acute abdominal pain, much like acute appendicitis accompanied by a nauseous feeling. Symptoms occur from as little as an hour to about two weeks after consumption of raw or undercooked seafood. One nematode is the usual number recovered from a patient. With their anterior ends, these larval nematodes from fish or shellfish usually burrow into the wall of the digestive tract to the level of the muscularis mucosae (occasionally they penetrate the intestinal wall completely and are found in the body cavity). They produce a substance that attracts eosinophils (white blood cells; easily stained) and other host white blood cells to the area. The infiltrating host cells form a granuloma (mass of inflamed tissue) in the tissues surrounding the penetrated worm. In the digestive tract lumen, the worm can detach and reattach to other sites on the wall. Anisakids rarely reach full maturity in humans and usually are eliminated spontaneously from the digestive tract lumen within three weeks of infection. Penetrated worms that die in the tissues are eventually removed by the host's phagocytic cells.

Diagnosis of Human Illness

In cases where the patient vomits or cough up the worm, the disease may be diagnosed by morphological examination of the nematode. (*Ascaris lumbricoides*, the large roundworm of humans, is a terrestrial relative of anisakines and sometimes these larvae also crawl up into the throat and nasal passages.) Other cases may require a fiber optic device that allows the attending physician to examine the inside of the stomach and the first part of the small intestine. These devices are equipped with a mechanical forceps that can be used to remove the worm. Other cases are diagnosed upon finding a granulomatous lesion with a worm on laparotomy. A specific radioallergosorbent test has been developed for anasakiasis, but is not yet commercially marketed.

Associated Foods

Seafoods are the principal sources of human infections with these larval worms. The adults of *A. simplex* are found in the stomachs of whales and dolphins. Fertilized eggs from the female parasite pass out of the host with the host's feces. In seawater, the eggs embryonate, developing into larvae that hatch in sea water. These larvae are infective to copepods (minute crustaceans related to shrimp) and other small invertebrates. The larvae grow in the invertebrate and become infective for the next host, a fish or larger invertebrate host such as a squid. The larvae may penetrate through the digestive tract into the muscle of the second host. Some evidence exists that the nematode larvae move from the viscera to the flesh if the fish hosts are not gutted promptly after catching. The life cycles of all the other anisakid genera implicated in human infections are similar. These parasites are known to occur frequently in the flesh of cod, haddock, fluke, pacific salmon, erring, flounder, and monkfish.

Diphyllobothrium spp.

Diphyllobothrium latum and other members of the genus are broad fish tapeworms reported from humans. They are parasitic flatworms.

Nature of Acute Disease

Diphyllobothriasis is the name of the disease caused by broad fish tapeworm infections.

Nature of Disease

Diphyllobothriasis is characterized by abdominal distention, flatulence, intermittent abdominal cramping, and diarrhea with onset about 10 days after consumption of raw or insufficiently cooked fish. The tapeworm larva that infects people, a "plerocercoid," is frequently encountered in the viscera of freshwater and marine fishes. *D. latum* is sometimes encountered in the flesh of firewater fish or fish that are anadromous (migrating from salt water to fresh water for breeding). Bears and humans are the final or definitive hosts for this parasite. *D. latum* is a broad, long tapeworm, often growing to lengths of 1–2 meters (3–7 feet) and potentially capable of attaining 10 meters (32 feet); the closely related *D. pacificum* normally matures in seals or other marine mammals and reaches only about half and length of *D. latum*. Treatment consists of administration of the drug niclosamide, which is available to physicians through the Centers for Disease Control's Parasitic Disease Drug Service.

Diagnosis of Human Illness

The disease is diagnosed by finding operculate eggs (egg with a lid) in the patient's feces on microscopical examination. These eggs may be concentrated by sedimentation but not by flotation. They are difficult to distinguish from the eggs of *Nanophyetus* spp.

Associated Foods

The larvae of these parasites are sometimes found in the flesh of fish.

Nanophyetus spp.

Nanophyetus salmincola or *N. schikhobalowi* are the names, respectively, of the North American and Russian troglotrematoid trematodes (or flukes). These are parasitic flatworms.

Nature of Acute Disease

Nanophyetiasis is the name of the human disease caused by these flukes. At least one newspaper referred to the disease as "fish flu." N. salmincola is responsible for the transmission of Neorickettsia helmithoeca, which causes an illness in dogs that may be serious or even fatal.

Nature of Disease

Knowledge of nanophyetiasis is limited. The first reported cases are characterized by an increase of bowel movements or diarrhea, usually accompanied by increased numbers of circulating eosinophils, abdominal discomfort and nausea. A few patients reported weight loss and fatigue, and some were asymptomatic. The rickettsia, though fatal to 80 percent of untreated dogs, is not known to infect humans.

Diagnosis of Human Illness

Detection of operculate eggs of the characteristic size and shape in the feces is indicative of nanophyetiasis. The eggs are difficult to distinguish from those of *Diphyllobothrium latum*.

Associated Foods

There have been no reported outbreaks of nanophyetiasis in North America; the only scientific reports are of 20 individual cases referred to in one Oregon clinic. A report in the popular press indicates that the frequency is significantly higher. It is significant that two cases occurred in New Orleans well outside the endemic area. In Russia's endemic area the infection rate is reported to be greater than 90 percent and the size of the endemic area is growing.

Eustrongylides sp.

Larval *Eustrongylides* sp. are large, bright red roundworms (nematodes), 25–150 mm long, 2 mm in diameter. They occur in freshwater fish, brackish water fish and in marine fish. The larvae normally mature in wading birds such as herons, egrets, and flamingos.

Nature of Acute Disease

If the larvae are consumed in undercooked or raw fish, they can attach to the wall of the digestive tract. In the five cases for which clinical symptoms have been reported, the penetration into the gut wall was accompanied by severe pain. The nematodes can perforate the gut wall and probably other organs. Removal of the nematodes by surgical resection or fiber optic devices with forceps is possible if the nematodes penetrate accessible areas of the gut.

Nature of Disease

One live larva can cause an infection.

Diagnosis of Human Illness

In three of the five reported cases, the worms were diagnosed by surgical resection of the intestine. In one case, there was no clinical data and in one other, the patient was treated medically and recovered in four days.

Associated Foods

Fish from fresh, brackish, or salt water.

Acantamoeba spp., Naegleria Fowleri and Other Amoebae

Acanthamoeba spp. and *Naegleria fowleri* are the principal examples of protozoa commonly referred to as pathogenic free-living amoebae.

Nature of Acute Disease

Primary amoebic meningoencephalitis (PAM), *Naegleria fowleri* and granulomatious amoebic encephalitis (GAE), acanthamoebic keratitis, or acanthamoebic uveitis.

These organisms are ubiquitous in the environment, in soil, water, and air. Infections in humans are rare and are acquired through water entering the nasal passages (usually during swimming) and by inhalation. They are discussed here because the FDA receives inquiries about them.

Nature of Disease

PAM occurs in persons who are generally healthy prior to infection. Central nervous system involvement arises from organisms that penetrate the nasal passages and enter the brain through the cribriform plate. The organisms can multiply in the tissues of the central nervous system and may be isolated from spinal fluid. In untreated cases death occurs within one week of the onset of symptoms. Amphotercin B is effective in the treatment of PAM. At least four patients have recovered when treated with Amphotercin B alone or in combination with micronazole administered both intravenously and intrathecally or intraventrically.

GAE occurs in persons who are immunodeficient in some way; the organisms cause granulomatous encephalitis that leads to death in several weeks to a year after the appearance of symptoms. The primary infection site is thought to be the lungs, and the organisms in the brain are generally associated with blood vessels, suggesting vascular dissemination. Treatment with sulfamethazine may be effective in controlling the amoebae.

Prior to 1985 amoebae had been reported isolated from diseased eyes only rarely; cases were associated with trauma to the eye. In 1985–1986, 24 eye cases were reported to CDC and most of these occurred in wearers of contact lenses. It has been demonstrated that many of these infections resulted from the use of home-made saline solutions with the contact lenses. Some of the lenses had been heat treated and others had been chemically disinfected. The failure of the heat treatment was attributed to faulty equipment, since the amoebae are killed by 65°C (149°F) for 30 minutes. The failure of the chemical disinfection resulted from insufficient treatment or rinsing the lenses in contaminated saline after disinfection. The following agents have been used to successfully eliminate the amoebic infection in the eye: ketoconazole, microconazole, and propamidine isothionate; however, penetrating keratoplasty has been necessary to restore useful vision.

Diagnosis of Human Illness

PAM is diagnosed by the presence of amoebae in the spinal fluid. GAE is diagnosed by biopsy of the lesion. Ocular amoebic keratitis may be diagnosed by culturing corneal scrapings on nonnutrient agar overlaid with viable *Escherichia coli*; amoebae from PAM and GAE may be cultured by the same method. Clinical diagnosis by experienced practitioners is based on the characteristic stromal infiltrate.

Associated Foods

Transmission is through water-based fluids or the air.

Ascaris Lumbricoides and *Trichuris Trichiura*

Humans worldwide are infected with *Ascaris lumbricoides* and *Trichuris trichiura*; the eggs of these roundworms (nematode) are "sticky" and may be carried to the mouth by hands, other body parts, fomites (inanimate objects), or foods.

Nature of Acute Disease

Ascariasis and trichuriasis are the scientific names of these infections. Ascariasis is also known commonly as the "large roundworm" infection and trichuriasis as "whip worm" infection.

Nature of Disease

Infection with one or a few *Ascaris* sp. may be inapparent unless noticed when passed in the feces, or, on occasion, crawling up into the throat and trying to exit through the mouth or nose. Infection with numerous worms may result in a pneumonitis during the migratory phase, when larvae that have hatched from the ingested eggs in the lumen of the small intestine penetrate into the tissues and by way of the lymph and blood systems reach the lungs. In the lungs, the larvae break out of the pulmonary capillaries into the air sacs, ascend into the throat and descend to the small intestine again where they grow, becoming as large as 31 × 4 cm. Molting (ecdysis) occurs at various points along this path and typically for roundworms, the male and female adults in the intestine are 5th-stage nematodes. Vague digestive tract discomfort sometimes accompanies the intestinal infection, but in small children with more than a few worms there may be intestinal blockage because of the worms' large size. Not all larval or adult worms stay on the path that is optimal for their development; those that wander may locate in diverse sites throughout the body and cause complications. Chemotherapy with anthelimintics is particularly likely to cause the adult worms in the intestinal lumen to wander; a not unusual escape route for them is into the bile duct, which may occlude. The larvae of ascarid species that mature in hosts other than humans may hatch in the human intestine and are especially prone to wander; they may penetrate into tissues and locate in various organ systems of the human body, perhaps eliciting a fever and diverse complications.

Trichuris sp. larvae do not migrate after hatching but molt and mature in the intestine. Adults are not as large as *A. lumbricoides*. Symptoms range from inapparent through vague digestive tract distress to emaciation with dry skin and diarrhea (usually mucoid). Toxic or allergic symptoms may also occur.

Diagnosis of Human Illness

Both infections are diagnosed by finding the typical eggs in the patient's feces; on occasion the larval or adult worms are found in the feces or, especially for *Ascaris* sp., in the throat, mouth, or nose.

Associated Foods

The eggs of these worms are found in insufficiently treated sewage-fertilizer and in soils where they embryonate (i.e., larvae develop in fertilized eggs). The eggs may contaminate crops grown in soil or fertilized with sewage that has received nonlethal treatment; humans are infected when such produce is consumed raw. Infected foodhandlers may contaminate a wide variety of foods.

Hepatitis A Virus

Hepatitis A virus (HAV) is classified with the enterovirus group of the Picornaviridae family. HAV has a single molecule of RNA surrounded by a small (27 nm diameter) protein capsid and a buoyant density in CsCl of 1.33 g/ml. Many other picornaviruses cause human disease, including polioviruses, coxsachieviruses, echoviruses, and rhinoviruses (cold viruses).

Nature of Acute Disease

The term hepatitis A (HA) or type A viral hepatitis has replaced all previous designations: infectious hepatitis, epidemic hepatitis, epidemic jaundice, catarrhal jaundice, infectious icterus, Botkins disease, and MS-1 hepatitis.

Nature of Disease

Hepatitis A is usually a mild illness characterized by sudden onset of fever malaise, nausea, anorexia, and abdominal discomfort, followed in several days by jaundice. The infectious dose is unknown but presumably is 10–100 virus particles.

Diagnosis of Human Illness

Hepatitis A is diagnosed by finding IgM-class anti-HAV in serum collected during the acute or nearly convalescent phase of disease. Commercial kits are available.

Associated Foods

HAV is excreted in feces of infected people and can produce clinical disease when susceptible individuals consume contaminated water or foods. Cold cuts and sandwiches, fruits and fruit juices, milk and milk products, vegetables, salads, shellfish, and iced drinks are commonly implicated in outbreaks. Water, shellfish, and salads are the most frequent sources. Contamination of foods by infected workers in food processing plants and restaurants is common.

Hepatitis E Virus

Hepatitis E. Virus (HEV) has a particle diameter of 32–34 nm, a buoyant density of 1.29 g/ml in KTar/GLY gradient, and is very labile. Serologically related smaller (27–30 nm) particles are often found in feces of patients with Hepatitis E and are presumed to represent degraded viral particles. HEV has a single-stranded polyadenylated RNS genome of approximately 8 kb. Based on its physicochemical properties it is presumed to be a calici-like virus.

Nature of Acute Disease

The disease caused by HEV is called hepatitis E, or enterically transmitted non-A non-B hepatitis (ET-NANGH). Other names include fecal-oral non-A non-B hepatitis, and A-like non-A non-B virus.

Note: This disease should not be confused with hepatitis C, also called parenterally transmitted non-A non-B hepatitis (PT-NANBH), or B-like non-A non-B hepatitis, which is a common cause of hepatitis in the U.S.

Nature of Disease

Hepatitis caused by HEV is clinically indistinguishable from hepatitis A disease. Symptoms include malaise, anorexia, abdominal pain, arthralgia, and fever. The infective dose is not known.

Diagnosis of Human Illness

Diagnosis of HEV is based on the epidemiological characteristics of the outbreak and by exclusion of hepatitis A and B viruses by serological tests. Confirmation requires identification of the 2–34 nm virus-like particles by immune electron microscopy in feces of acutely ill patients.

Associated Foods

HEV is transmitted by the fecal-oral route. Waterborne and person-to-person spread have been documented. The potential exists for foodborne transmission.

Rotavirus

Rotaviruses are classified with the Reoviridae family. They have a genome consisting of 11 double-standard RNA segments surrounded by a distinctive two-layered protein capsid. Particles are 70 nm in diameter and have a buoyant density of 1.36 g/ml in CsCl. Six serological groups have been identified, three of which (groups A, B, and C) infect humans.

Nature of Acute Disease

Rotaviruses cause acute gastroenteritis. Infantile diarrhea, winter diarrhea, acute nonbacterial infectious gastroenteritis, and acute viral gastroenteritis are names applied to the infection caused by the most common and widespread group A rotavirus.

Nature of Disease

Rotavirus gastroenteritis is a self-limiting, mild to severe disease characterized by vomiting, watery diarrhea, and low-grade fever. The infective dose is presumed to be 10–100 infectious viral particles. Because a person with rotavirus diarrhea often excretes large numbers of virus (10^8–10^{10} infectious particles/ml of feces), infection doses can be readily acquired through contaminated hands, objects, or utensils. Asymptomatic rotavirus excretion has been well documented and may play a role in perpetuating endemic disease.

Diagnosis of Human Illness

Specific diagnosis of the disease is made by identification of the virus in the patient's stool. Enzyme immunoassay (EIA) is the test most widely used to screen clinical specimens, and several commercial kits are available for group A. rotavirus. Electron microscopy (EM) and polyacrylamide gel electrophoresis (PAGE) are used in some laboratories in addition or as an alternative to EIA. A reverse transcription-polymerase chain reaction (RT-PCR) has been developed to detect and identify all three groups of human rotaviruses.

Associated Foods

Rotaviruses are transmitted by the fecal-oral route. Person-to-person spread through contaminated hands is probably the most important means by which rotaviruses are transmitted in close communities such as pediatric and geriatric wards, day-care centers and family homes. Infected food handlers may contaminate foods that require handling and not further cooking, such as salads, fruits, and hors d'oeuvres. Rotaviruses are quite stable in the environment and have been found in estuary samples at levels as high as 1–5 infectious particles/gal. Sanitary measures adequate for bacteria and parasites seem to be ineffective in endemic control of rotavirus, as similar incidence of rotavirus infection is observed in countries with both high and low health standards.

The Norwalk Virus Family

Norwalk virus is the prototype of a family of unclassified small round structured viruses (SRSVs) which may be related to the caliciviruses. They contain a positive strand RNA genome of 7.5 kb and a single structural protein of about 60 kDa. The 27–32 nm viral particles have buoyant density of 1.39–1.40 g/ml in CsCl. The family consists of several serologically distinct groups of viruses that have been named after the places where the outbreaks occurred. In the U.S., the Norwalk and Montgomery County agents are serologically related but distinct from the Hawaii and Snow Mountain agents. The Taunton, Moorcroft, Barnett, and Amulree agents were identified in the U.K., and the Sapporo and Otofuke agents in Japan. Their serological relationships remain to be determined.

Nature of Acute Disease

Common names of the illness caused by the Norwalk and Norwalk-like viruses are viral gastroenteritis, acute nonbacterial gastroenteritis, food poisoning, and food infection.

Nature of Disease

The disease is self-limiting, mild, and characterized by nausea, vomiting, diarrhea, and abdominal pain. Headache and low-grade fever may occur. The infectious dose is unknown but presumed to be low.

Diagnosis of Human Illness

Specific diagnosis of the disease can only be made by a few laboratories possessing reagents for human volunteer studies. Identification of the virus can be made on early stool specimens using immune electron microscopy and various immunoassays. Confirmation often requires demonstration of seroconverison, the presence of specific IgM antibody, or a fourfold rise in antibody titer to Norwalk virus on paired acute-convalescent sera.

KEY DEFINITION: TITER

Concentration/strength of a substance in solution determined by titration.

KEY DEFINITION: TITRATION

The process or method of determining the concentration of a substance in solution by adding to it a standard reagent of known concentration in carefully measured amounts until a reaction of definite and known proportion is completed, as shown by a color change or by electrical measurement, and then calculating the unknown concentration.

Associated Foods

Norwalk gastroenteritis is transmitted by the fecal-oral route via contaminated water and foods. Secondary person-to-person transmission has been documented. Water is the most common source of outbreaks and may include water from municipal supplies, wells, recreational lakes, swimming pools, and water stored on board cruise ships.

Shellfish and salad ingredients are the foods most often implicated in Norwalk outbreaks. Ingestion of raw or insufficiently steamed clams and oysters poses a high risk for infection with Norwalk virus. Foods other than shellfish are contaminated by ill food handlers.

Other Gastroenteritis Viruses

Although the rotavirus and the Norwalk family of viruses are the leading causes of viral gastroenteritis, a number of other viruses have been implicated in outbreaks, including astroviruses, caliciviruses, enteric adenoviruses, and parvovirus. Astroviruses, caliciviruses, and the Norwalk family of viruses possess well-designed surface structures and are sometimes identified as "small round structured viruses" or SRSVs. Viruses with smooth edges and no discernible surface structure are designated "featureless viruses" or "small round viruses" (SRVs). These agents resemble enterovirus or parvovirus, and may be related to them.

Astroviruses are unclassified viruses that contain a single positive strand of RNA of about 7.5 kb surrounded by a protein capsid of 28–30 nm diameter. A five- or six-pointed star shape can be observed on the particles under the electron microscope. Mature virions (complete viral particles) contain two major coat proteins of about 33 kDa each and have a buoyant density in CsCl of 1.38–1.40 g/ml. At least five human serotypes have been identified in England. The Marin County agent found in the U.S. is serologically related to astrovirus type 5.

Caliciviruses are classified in the family Caliciviridae. They contain a single stand of RNA surrounded by a protein capsid of 31–40 nm diameter. Mature virions have cup-shaped indentations which give them a "Star of David" appearance in the electron microscope. The particles contain a single major coat protein of 60 kDa and have a buoyant density in CsCl of 1.36–1.39 g/ml. Four serotypes have been identified in England.

Enteric adenoviruses represent serotypes 40 and 41 of the family Adenoviridae. These viruses contain a double-stranded DNA surrounded by a distinctive protein capsid of about 70 nm diameter. Mature virions have a buoyant density in CsCl of about 1.345 g/ml.

Parvoviruses belong to the family Parvoviridae, the only group of animal viruses to contain linear single-stranded DNA. The DNA genome is surrounded by a protein capsid of about 22 nm diameter. The buoyant density of the particle in CsCl is 1.39–1.42 g/ml. The Ditchling, Wollan, Paramatta, and cockle agents are candidate parvoviruses associated with human gastroenteritis.

Nature of Acute Disease

Common names of the illness caused by these viruses are acute nonbacterial infectious gastroenteritis and viral gastroenteritis.

Nature of Disease

Viral gastroenteritis is usually a mild illness characterized by nausea, vomiting, diarrhea, malaise, abdominal pain, headache, and fever. The infectious dose is not known but is presumed to be low.

Diagnosis of Human Illness

Specific diagnosis of the disease can be made by some laboratories possessing appropriate reagents. Identification of the virus present in early acute stool samples is made by immune electron microscopy and various enzyme immunoassays. Confirmation often requires demonstration of seroconversion to the agent by serological tests on acute and convalescent serum pairs.

Associated Foods

Viral gastroenteritis is transmitted by the fecal-oral route via person-to-person contact or ingestion of contaminated foods and water. Ill food handlers may contaminate foods that are not further cooked before consumption. Enteric adenovirus may also be transmitted by the respiratory route. Shellfish have been implicated in illness caused by a parvo-like virus.

Ciguatera—Fish Poisoning

Nature of Acute Disease

Ciguatera is a form of human poisoning caused by the consumption of subtropical and tropical marine finfish that have accumulated naturally occurring toxins through their diet. The toxins are known to originate from several dinoflagellate (algae) species that are common to ciguatera endemic regions in the lower latitudes.

Nature of Disease

Manifestations of ciguatera in humans usually involves a combination of gastrointestinal, neurological, and cardiovascular disorders. Symptoms defined within these general categories vary with the geographic origin of toxic fish.

Diagnosis of Human Illness

Clinical testing procedures are not presently available for the diagnosis of ciguatera in humans. Diagnosis is based entirely on symptomology and recent dietary history. An enzyme immunoassay (EIA) designed to detect toxic fish in field situations is under evaluation by the Association of Official Analytical Chemists (AOAC) and may provide some measure of protection to the public in the future.

Associated Foods

Marine finfish most commonly implicated in ciguatera fish poisoning include the groupers, barracudas, snappers, jacks, mackerel, and triggerfish. Many other species of warm-water fishes harbor ciguatera toxins. The occurrence of toxic fish is sporadic, and not all fish of a given species or from a given locality will be toxic.

CIGUATOXIN (CTX-1)

Toxin produced by the Dinoflagellate *Gambierdiscus toxicus* and isolated from the flesh and viscera of ciguatoxic fish.

Various Shellfish-Associated Toxins

Shellfish poisoning is caused by a group of toxins elaborated by planktonic algae (dinoflagellates, in most cases) on which the shellfish feed. The toxins are accumulated and sometimes metabolized by the shellfish. The 20 toxins responsible for paralytic shellfish poisonings (PSP) are all derivatives of saxitoxin. Diarrheic shellfish poisoning (DSP) is presumably caused by a group of high molecular weight polyethers, including okadaic acid, the dinophysis toxins, the pectenotoxins, and yessotoxin. Neurotoxic shellfish poisoning (NSP) is the result of exposure to a group of polyethers called brevetoxins. Amnesic shellfish poisoning (ASP) is caused by the unusual amino acid, domoic acid, as the contaminant of shellfish.

Nature of Acute Disease

Types of Shellfish Poisoning.

Paralytic Shellfish Poisoning (PSP)

Diarrheic Shellfish Poisoning (DSP)

Neurotoxic Shellfish Poisoning (NSP)

Amnesic Shellfish Poisoning (ASP)

Nature of Disease

Ingestion of contaminated shellfish results in a wide variety of symptoms, depending on the toxin(s) present, their concentrations in the shellfish and the amount of contaminated shellfish consumed. In the case of PSP, the effects are predominantly neurological and include tingling, burning, numbness, drowsiness, incoherent speech, and respiratory paralysis. Less well characterized are the symptoms associated with DSP, NSP, and ASP. DSP is primarily observed as a generally mild gastrointestinal disorder, that is, nausea, vomiting, diarrhea, and abdominal pain accompanied by chills, headache, and fever. Both gastrointestinal and neurological symptoms characterize NSP, including tingling and numbness of lips, tongue, and throat, muscular aches, dizziness, reversal of the sensations of hot and cold, diarrhea, and vomiting. ASP is characterized by gastrointestinal disorders (vomiting, diarrhea, abdominal pain) and neurological problems (confusion, memory loss, disorientation, seizure, coma).

Diagnosis of Human Illness

Diagnosis of shellfish poisoning is based entirely on observed symptomatology and recent dietary history.

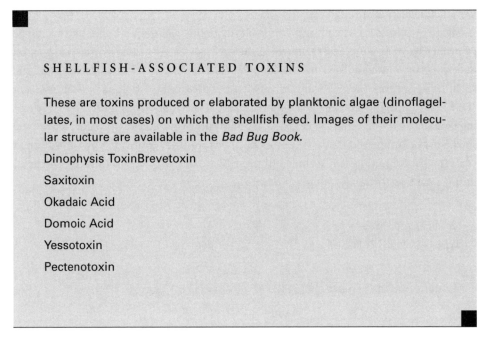

SHELLFISH-ASSOCIATED TOXINS

These are toxins produced or elaborated by planktonic algae (dinoflagellates, in most cases) on which the shellfish feed. Images of their molecular structure are available in the *Bad Bug Book.*

Dinophysis ToxinBrevetoxin

Saxitoxin

Okadaic Acid

Domoic Acid

Yessotoxin

Pectenotoxin

Associated Foods

All shellfish (filter-feeding molluscs) are potentially toxic. However, PSP is generally
associated with mussels, clams, cockles, and scallops; NSP with shellfish harvested
along the Florida coast and the Gulf of Mexico; and DSP with mussels, oysters, and
scallops, and ASP with mussels.

Scombrotoxin

Nature of Acute Disease

Scombroid Poisoning (also called Histamine Poisoning) is caused by the ingestion
of foods that contain high levels of histamine and possibly other vasoactive amines and
compounds. Histamine and other amines are formed by the growth of certain bacteria and the subsequent action of their decarboxylase enzymes on histidine and other
amino acids in food, either during the production of a product such as Swiss cheese or
by spoilage of foods such as fishery products, particularly tuna or mahi mahi. However, any food that contains the appropriate amino acids and is subjected to certain
bacterial contamination and growth may lead to scombroid poisoning when ingested.

Nature of Disease

Initial symptoms may include a tingling or burning sensation in the mouth, a rash
on the upper body and a drop in blood pressure. Frequently, headaches and itching of

the skin are encountered. The symptoms may progress to nausea, vomiting, and diarrhea and may require hospitalization, particularly in the case of elderly or impaired patients.

Diagnosis of Human Illness

Diagnosis of the illness is usually based on the patient's symptoms, time of onset, and the effect of treatment with antihistamine medication. The suspected food must be analyzed within a few hours for elevated levels of histamine to confirm a diagnosis.

Associated Foods

Fishery products that have been implicated in scombroid poisoning include the tunas (e.g., skipjack and yellowfin), mahi mahi, bluefish, sardines, mackerel, amberjack, and abalone. Many other products also have caused the toxic effects. The primary cheese involved in intoxications has been Swiss cheese. The toxin forms in a food when certain bacteria are present and time and temperature permit their growth. Distribution of the toxin within an individual fish fillet or between cans in a case lot can be uneven, with some sections of a product causing illnesses and others not. Neither cooking, canning, nor freezing reduces the toxic effect. Common sensory examination by the consumer cannot ensure the absence or presence of the toxin. Chemical testing is the only reliable test for evaluation of a product.

Tetrodotoxin

Tetrodotoxin is also called anhydrotetrodotoxin 4-epitetrootoxin and tetrodonic acid.

Nature of Acute Disease

Pufferfish Poisoning, Tetradon Poisoning, Fugu Poisoning

Nature of Disease

Fish poisoning by consumption of members of the order Tetraodontiformes is one of the most violent intoxications from marine species. The gonads, liver, intestines, and skin of Pufferfish can contain levels of tetrodotoxin sufficient to produce rapid and violent death. The flesh of many pufferfish may not usually be dangerously toxic. Tetrodotoxin has also been isolated from widely differing animal species, including the California newt. Parrotfish frogs of the genus Atelopus, the blue-ringed octopus, starfish, angelfish, and xanthid crabs. The metabolic source of tetrodotoxin is uncertain. No algal source has been identified, and until recently tetrodotoxin was assumed to be a metabolic product of the host. However, recent reports of the production of tetrodotoxin/anhydrotetrodotoxin by several bacterial species, including strains of the family Vibrionaceae, *Pseudomonas* sp., and Photobacterium phosphoreum, point toward a bacterial origin of this family of toxins. These are relatively common marine bacteria that are often associated with marine animals. If confirmed, these findings may have some significance in toxicoses that have more directly related to these bacterial species.

Diagnosis of Human Illness

The diagnosis of pufferfish poisoning is based on the observed symptomology and recent dietary history.

Associated Foods

Poisonings from tetrodotoxin have been almost exclusively associated with the consumption of pufferfish from waters of the Indo-Pacific ocean regions. Several reported cases of poisonings, including fatalities, involved pufferfish from the Atlantic Ocean, Gulf of Mexico, and Gulf of California. There have been no confirmed cases of poisoning from the Atlantic pufferfish, Spheroides maculates. However, in one study, extracts from fish of this species were highly toxic in mice. The trumpet shell Charonia sauliae has been implicated in food poisonings, and evidence suggests that it contains a tetrodotoxin derivative. There have been several reported poisonings from mislabeled pufferfish and at least one report of a fatal episode when an individual swallowed a California newt.

Mushroom Toxins

The organisms include Amanitin, Gyromitrin, Orellanine, Muscarine, Ibotenic Acid, Muscimol, Psilocybin, and Coprine.

Nature of Acute Disease

Mushroom poisoning is caused by the consumption of raw or cooked fruiting bodies (mushrooms, toadstools) of a number of species of higher fungi. The term "toadstool" (from the German *Todesstuhl*, death's stool) is commonly given to poisonous mushrooms, but for individuals who are not experts in mushroom identification there are generally no easily recognizable differences between poisonous and nonpoisonous species. Old wives' tales notwithstanding, there is no general rule of thumb for distinguishing edible mushrooms and poisonous toadstools. The toxins involved in mushroom poisoning are produced naturally by the fungi themselves, and each individual specimen of a toxic species should be considered equally poisonous. Most mushrooms that cause human poisoning cannot be made nontoxic by cooking, canning, freezing, or any other means of processing. Thus, the only way to avoid poisoning is to avoid consumption of the toxic species. Poisonings in the United States occurs most commonly when hunters of wild mushrooms (especially novices) misidentify and consume a toxic species, when recent immigrants collect and consume a poisonous American species that closely resemble an edible wild mushroom from their native land, or when mushrooms that contain psychoactive compounds are intentionally consumed by persons who desire these effects.

Nature of Disease

Mushroom poisonings are generally acute and are manifested by a variety of symptoms and prognoses, depending on the amount and species consumed. Because the chemistry of many of the mushroom toxins (especially the less deadly ones) is still unknown and positive identification of the mushrooms is often difficult or impossible, mushroom poisonings are generally categorized by their physiological effects. There are four categories of mushroom toxins: protoplasmic poisons (poisons that result in generalized destruction of cells, followed by organ failure); neurotoxin (compounds that cause neurological symptoms such as profuse sweating, coma, convulsions, hallucinations, excitement, depression, spastic colon); gastrointestinal irritants (compounds that produce rapid, transient nausea, vomiting, abdominal cramping, and diarrhea); and disulfiram-like toxins. Mushrooms in this last category are generally nontoxic and produce no symptoms unless alcohol is consumed within 72 hours after eating them, in which case a short-lived acute toxic syndrome is produced.

Diagnosis of Human Illness

A clinical testing procedure is currently available only for the most serious types of mushroom toxins, the amanitins. The commercially available method uses a 3H-radioimmunoassay (RIA) test kit an can detect subnanogram levels of toxin in urine and plasma. Unfortunately, it requires a two-hour incubation period, and this is an excruciating delay in a type of poisoning which the clinician generally does not see until a day or two has passed. A 125I-based kit which overcomes this problem has recently been reported, but has not yet reached the clinic. A sensitive and rapid HPLC technique has been reported in the literature even more recently, but it has not yet been reported in the literature even more recently, but it has not yet seen clinical application. Since most clinical laboratories in this country do not use even the older RIA technique, diagnosis is based entirely on symptomology and recent dietary history. Despite the fact that cases of mushroom poisoning may be broken down into a relatively small number of categories based on symptomatology, positive botanical identification of the mushroom species consumed remains the only means of unequivocally determining the particular type of intoxication involved, and it is still vitally important to obtain such accurate identification as quickly as possible. Cases involving ingestion of more than one toxic species in which one set of symptoms masks or mimics another set are among many reasons for needing this information. Unfortunately, a number of factors (not discussed here) often make identification of the causative mushroom impossible. In such cases, diagnosis must be based on symptoms alone. In order to rule out other types of food poisoning and to conclude that the mushrooms eaten were the cause of the poisoning, it must be established that everyone who ate the suspect mushrooms became ill and that no one who did not eat the mushrooms became ill. Wild mushrooms eaten raw, cooked, or processed should always be regarded as primary suspects. After ruling out other sources of food poisoning and positively implicating mushrooms as the cause of the illness, diagnosis may proceed in two steps.

As described above, the protoplasmic poisons are the most likely to be fatal or to cause irreversible organ damage. In the case of poisoning by the deadly Amanitas, important laboratory indicators of liver (elevated LDH, SGOT, and bilirubin levels) and kidney (elevated uric acid, creatinine, and BUN levels) damage will be present. Unfortunately, in the absence of dietary history, these signs could be mistaken for symptoms of liver or kidney impairment as the result of other causes (e.g., viral hepatitis). It is important that this distinction be made as quickly as possible, because the delayed onset of symptoms will generally mean that the organ has already been damaged. The importance of rapid diagnosis is obvious: victims who are hospitalized and given aggressive support therapy almost immediately after ingestion have a mortality rate of only 10 percent, where those admitted 60 or more hours after ingestion have a 50–90 percent mortality rate.

Associated Foods

Mushroom poisonings are almost always caused by ingestion of wild mushrooms that have been collected by nonspecialists (although specialists have also been poisoned). Most cases occur when toxic species are confused with edible species, and a useful question to ask of the victims of their mushroom-picking benefactors is the identity of the mushroom they thought they were picking. In the absence of a well-preserved specimen, the answer to this question could narrow the possible suspects considerably. Intoxication has also occurred when reliance was placed on some folk method of distinguishing poisonous and safe species. Outbreaks have occurred after ingestion of fresh, raw mushrooms, stir-fried mushrooms, home-canned mushrooms, mushrooms cooked in tomato sauce (which rendered the sauce itself toxic, even when no mushrooms were consumed), and mushrooms that were blanched and frozen at home. Cases of poisoning by home-canned and frozen mushrooms are especially insidious because a single outbreak may easily become a multiple outbreak when the preserved toadstools are carried to another location and consumed at another time.

Specific cases of mistaken mushroom identity appear frequently. The Early False Morel *Gyromitra esculenta* is easily confused with the true Morel *Morchella esculenta* and poisonings have occurred after consumption of fresh or cooked Gyromitra. Gy-

MUSHROOM TOXINS

Amatoxin—Toxin produced by several mushroom species, including the Death Cap or Destroying Angel (*Amanita phalloides, A. virosa*), the Fool's Mushroom (*A. verna*) and several of their relatives, along with the Autumn Skullcap (*Galerina autumnalis*) and some of its relatives.

Orellanine—Toxin produced by the Sorrel Webcap mushroom (*Cortinarius orellanus*) and some of its relatives.

Muscarine—Toxin produced by any number of *Inocybe* or *Clitocybe* species (e.g., *Inocybe gephylla, clitocybe dealbata*).

Ibotenic Acid—Toxin produced by Fly Agaric (*Amanita muscaria*) and Pantherscap (*Amanita pantherina*) mushrooms.

Muscimol—Toxin produced by Fly Agaric (*Amanita muscaria*) and Panthercap (*Amanita pantherina*) mushrooms.

Psilocybin—Toxin produced by a number of mushrooms belonging to the genera *Psilocybe, Panaeolus, Copelandia, Gymnopilus, Conocybe,* and *Pluteus.*

Gyromitrin—Toxin produced by certain species of False Morel (*Gyromitra esculenta* and *G. gigas*).

Coprine—Toxin produced by the Inky Cap Mushroom (*Coprinus atramentarius*).

romitra poisonings have also occurred after ingestion of commercially available "morels" contaminated with G. esculenta. The commercial sources for these fungi (which have not yet been successfully cultivated on a large scale) are field collection of wild morels by semiprofessionals. Cultivated commercial mushrooms of whatever species are almost never implicated in poisoning outbreaks unless there are associated problems such as improper canning (which led to bacterial food poisoning).

Aflatoxins

Nature of Acute Disease

Aflatoxicosis is poisoning that results from ingestion of aflatoxins in contaminated food or feed. The aflatoxins are a group of structurally related toxic compounds produced by certain strains of the fungi *Aspergillus flavus* and *A. parasiticus*. Under favorable conditions of temperature and humidity, these fungi grow on certain foods and feeds, resulting in the production of aflatoxins. The most pronounced contamination as been encountered in tree nuts, peanuts, and other oilseeds, including corn and cottonseed. The major aflatoxins of concern are designated B1, B2, G1, and G2. These toxins are usually found together in various foods and feeds in various proportions; however, aflatoxin B1 is usually predominant and is the most toxic. When a commodity is analyzed by thin-layer chromatography, the aflatoxins separate into the individual components in the order given above; however, the first two fluoresce blue when viewed under ultraviolet light and the second two fluoresce green. Aflatoxin M a major metabolic product of aflatoxin B1 in animals and is usually excreted in the milk and urine of dairy cattle and other mammalian species that have consumed aflatoxin-contaminated food or feed.

Nature of Disease

Aflatoxins produce acute necrosis, cirrhosis, and carcinoma of the liver in a number of animal species; no animal species is resistant to the acute toxic effects of aflatoxins; hence it is logical to assume that humans may be similarly affected. A wide variation in DL50 values has been obtained in animal species tested with single doses of aflatoxins. For most species, the LD50 value ranges form 0.5 to 10 mg/kg body weight. Animal species respond differently in their susceptibility to the chronic and acute toxicity of aflatoxins. The toxicity can be influenced by environmental factors, exposure level, and duration of exposure, age, health, and nutritional status of diet. Aflatoxin B1 is a very potent carcinogen in many species, including nonhuman primates, birds, fish, and rodents. In each species, the liver is the primary target organ of acute injury. Metabolism plays a major role in determining the toxicity of aflatoxin B1; studies show that this aflatoxin requires metabolic activation to exert its carcinogenic effect, and these effects can be modified by induction or inhibition of the mixed function oxidase system.

Diagnosis of Human Illness

Aflatoxicosis in humans has rarely been reported; however, such cases are not always recognized. Aflatoxicosis may be suspected when a disease outbreak exhibits the following characteristics:

- the cause is not readily identifiable
- the condition is not transmissible
- syndromes may be associated with certain batches of food
- treatment with antibiotics or other drugs has little effect
- the outbreak may be seasonal, that is, weather conditions may affect mold growth

---

KEY DEFINITION: AFLATOXIN B₁ AND M₁

Toxin produced by certain strains of the fungi *Aspergillus flavus* and *A. parasiticus.*

KEY DEFINITION: AFLATOXIN G₁

Toxin produced by certain strains of the fungi *Aspergillus flavus* and *A. parasiticus.*

The adverse effects of aflatoxins in animals (and presumably in humans) have been categorized in two general forms:

A. (Primary) Acute Aflatoxicosis is produced when moderate to high levels of aflatoxins are consumed. Specific, acute episodes of disease ensure many include hemorrhage, acute liver damage, edema, alteration in digestion, absorption and/or metabolism of nutrients, and possibly death.

B. (Primary) Chronic Aflatoxicosis results from ingestion of low to moderate levels of aflatoxins. The effects are usually subclinical and difficult to recognize. Some of the common symptoms are impaired food conversion and slower rates of growth with or without the production of an overt aflatoxin syndrome.

Associated Foods

In the United States, aflatoxins have been identified in corn and corn products, peanuts and peanut products, cottonseed, milk, and tree nuts such as Brazil nuts, pecans, pistachio nuts, and walnuts. Other grains and nuts are susceptible but less prone to contamination.

Pyrrolizidine Alkaloids

Pyrrolizidine alkaloid intoxication is caused by consumption of plant material containing these alkaloids. The plants may be consumed as food, for medicinal purposes, or as contaminants of other agricultural crops. Cereal crops and forage crops are sometimes contaminated with pyrrolizidine-producing weeds, and the alkaloids find their way into flour and other foods, including milk from cows feeding on these plants. Many plants for the Boraginaceae, Compositae, and Leguminosae families contain well over 100 hepatotoxic pyrrolizidine alkaloids.

Nature of Disease

Most cases of pyrrolizidine alkaloid toxicity result in moderate to severe liver damage. Gastrointestinal symptoms are usually the first sign of intoxication, and consist predominantly of abdominal pain with vomiting and the development of ascites. Death may ensue from two weeks to more than two years after poisoning, but patients may recover almost completely if the alkaloid intake is discontinued and the liver damage has not been too severe.

Diagnosis of Human Illness

Evidence of toxicity may not become apparent until sometime after the alkaloid is ingested. The acute illness has been compared to the Budd-Chiari syndrome (thrombosis of hepatic veins, leading to liver enlargement, portal hypertension, and ascites). Early clinical signs include nausea and acute upper gastric pain, acute abdominal distension with prominent dilated veins on the abdominal wall, fever, and biochemical evidence of liver disfunction. Fever and jaundice may be present. In some cases the lungs are affected; pulmonary edema and pleural effusions have been observed. Lung damage may be prominent and has been fatal. Chronic illness from ingestion of small amounts of the alkaloids over a long period proceeds through fibrosis of the liver to cirrhosis, which is indistinguishable form cirrhosis of other etiology.

Associated Foods

The plants most frequently implicated in pyrrolizidine poisoning are members of the Boraginaceae, Compositae, and Leguminosae families. Consumption of the alkaloid-containing plants as food, contaminants of food, or as medicinals has occurred.

KEY DEFINITION: PYRROLIZIDINE ALKALOIDS OF *SYMPHYTUM* SPP.

Toxin produced by plants from the Boraginaceae, Compositae, and Leguminosae families.

KEY DEFINITION: PYRROLIZIDINE ALKALOIDS OF *SENECIO LONGILOBUS* BENTH

Toxin produced by plants from the Boraginaceae, Compositae, and Leguminosae families.

Phytohaemagglutinin (Kidney Bean Lectin)

This compound, a lectin or hemagglutinin, has been used by immunologists for years to trigger DNA synthesis in T lymphocytes, and more recently, to activate latent human immunodeficiency virus type 1 (HIV-1, AIDS virus) from human peripheral lymphocytes. Besides inducing mitosis, lectins are known for their ability to agglutinate many mammalian red blood cell types, alter cell membrane transport systems, alter cell permeability to proteins, and generally interfere with cellular metabolism.

Nature of Acute Disease

Red Kidney Bean (Phaseolus vulgaris) Poisoning, Kinkoti Bean Poisoning, and possibly other names.

Nature of Disease

The onset time from consumption of raw or undercooked kidney beans to symptoms varies from between one to three hours. Onset is usually marked by extreme nausea, followed by vomiting, which may be very severe. Diarrhea develops somewhat later (from one to a few hours), and some persons report abdominal pain. Some persons have been hospitalized, but recovery is usually rapid (three to four hours after onset of symptoms) and spontaneous.

Diagnosis of Human Illness

Diagnosis is made on the basis of symptoms, food history, and the exclusion of other rapid onset food poisoning agents (e.g., *Bacillus cereus*, *Staphylococcus aureus*, arsenic, mercury, lead, and cyanide).

Associated Foods

Phytohaemagglutinin, the presumed toxic agent, is found in many species of beans, but it is in highest concentration in red kidney beans (*Phaseolus vulgaris*). The unit of toxin measure is the hemagglutinating unit (hau). Raw kidney beans contain from 20,000 to 70,000 hau, while fully cooked beans contain from 200 to 400 hau. White kidney beans, another variety of *Phaseolus vulgaris*, contain about one-third the amount of toxin as the red variety; broad beans (*Vicia faba*) contain 5 to 10 percent the amount that red kidney beans contain.

The syndrome is usually caused by the ingestion of raw, soaked kidney beans, either alone or in salads or casseroles. As few as four or five raw beans can trigger symptoms. Several outbreaks have been associated with slow cookers or Crock-Pots, or in casseroles which had not reached a high enough internal temperature to destroy the glycoprotein lectin. It has been shown that heating to 80° C may potentiate the toxicity fivefold, so that these beans are more toxic than if eaten raw. In studies of casseroles cooked in slow cookers, internal temperatures often did not exceed 75° C.

Grayanotoxin

Grayanotoxin was formerly known as andromedotoxin, acetylandromedol, and rhodotoxin. It is honey intoxication caused by the consumption of honey produced from the nectar of rhododendrons. The grayanotoxins cause the intoxication. The specific grayanotoxins vary with the plant species. These compounds are diterpenes, polyhydroxylated cyclic hydrocarbons that do not contain nitrogen. Other names associated with the disease are rhododendron poisoning, mad honey intoxication, or Grayanotoxin poisoning.

Nature of Disease

The intoxication is rarely fatal and generally lasts for no more than 24 hours. Generally the disease induces dizziness, weakness, excessive perspiration, nausea, and vomiting shortly after the toxic honey is ingested. Other symptoms that can occur are low blood pressure or shock, bradyarrhythima (slowness of the heart beat associated with an irregularity in the heart rhythm), sinus bradycardia (a slow sinus rhythm, with a heat rate less than 60), nodal rhythm (pertaining to a node, particularly the atrioventricular excitation), and complete atrioventricular block.

Diagnosis of Human Illness

The grayanotoxins bind to sodium channels in cell membranes. The binding unit is the group II receptor site, localized on a region of the sodium channel that is involved in the voltage-dependent activation and inactivation. These compounds prevent inactivation; thus, excitable cells (nerve and muscle) are maintained in a state of depolarization, during which entry of calcium into the cells may be facilitated. This action is similar to that exerted by the alkaloids of veratrum and aconite. All of the observed response of skeletal and heart muscles, nerves, and the central nervous system are related to the membrane effects.

Because the intoxication is rarely fatal and recovery generally occurs within 24 hours, intervention may not be required. Severe low blood pressure usually responds to the administration of fluids and correction of bradycardia; therapy with vasopressors (agents that stimulate contraction of the muscular tissue of the capillaries and arteries) is only rarely required. Sinus bradycardia and conduction defects usually respond to atropine therapy; however, in at least one instance the use of a temporary pacemaker was required.

Associated Foods

In humans, symptoms of poisoning occur after a dose-dependent latent period of a few minutes to two or more hours and include salivation, vomiting, and both circumoral (around or near the mouth) and extremity paresthesia (abnormal sensations). Pronounced low blood pressure and sinus bradycardia develop. In severe intoxication, loss of coordination and progressive muscular weakness result. Extrasystoles (a premature contraction of the heart that is independent of the normal rhythm and arises in response to an impulse in some part of the heart other than the sinoatrial node; called also premature beat) and ventricular tachycardia (an abnormally rapid ventricular rhythm with aberrant ventricular excitation, usually in excess of 150 per minute) with both atrioventricular and intraventricular conduction disturbances also may occur. Convulsions are reported occasionally.

Prions and Transmissible Spongiform Encephalopathies

Prions are normal proteins of animal tissues that can misfold and become infectious; they are not cellular organisms or viruses. In their normal noninfectious state, these proteins may be involved in cell-to-cell communication. When these proteins become abnormally shaped (i.e., infectious prions), they are thought to come into contact with a normally shaped protein and transform that protein into the abnormally shaped prion. This process causes a geometric increase of abnormally shaped prion proteins until the number of abnormally shaped proteins causes overt illness. When consumed by animals, prions are thought to be absorbed during digestion into the body, where they begin the process of changing their normal protein counterparts into abnormal proteins; however, infectious prions from one species of animal have less of a potential of causing the abnormal shape in the normally shaped prion proteins of another species (the "species barrier"). While the "prion theory" of transmissible spongiform encephalopathies (TSEs) is widely accepted, there are other theories of the cause of these illnesses.

Nature of Acute Disease

Prions are associated with a group of diseases called transmissible spongiform encephalopathies (TSEs). In humans the illness suspected of being foodborne is variant Creutzfeldt-Jakob disease (vCID). The human disease vCJD and the cattle disease, bovine spongiform encephalopathy (BSE), also known as "mad cow" disease, appear to be caused by the same agent. Other similar but not identical TSE diseases exist in animals, but there is no known transmission of these TSEs to humans. Included among these is chronic wasting disease (CSE) of deer and elk, and the oldest know of these diseases—scrapie—which occurs in sheep and goats. No early acute clinical indications for TSEs have been described. After an extended incubation period of years, these diseases result in irreversible neurodegeneration.

Nature of Disease

The neurodegenerative phase of vCJD in humans typically involves the formation of "daisy-shaped" areas of damage in the central nervous system. There is also, in common with other TSEs, vacuolization (formation of holes) that gives brain tissue a spongy appearance when examined under a microscope. It is thought that the buildup of the abnormally shaped prion proteins causes the observed neurodegeneration.

Diagnosis of Human Illness

The most reliable means for diagnosing any TSE is the microscopic examination of brain tissue—a postmortem procedure. Preliminary diagnoses of vCJD are based on patient history, clinical symptoms, electroencephalograms, and magnetic resonance imaging of the brain.

Associated Foods

The major concern for consumers is the potential contamination of meat products by BSE-contaminated tissues or the inclusion of BSE-contaminated tissues in foods, including dietary supplements. High risk tissues for BSE contamination include the cattle's skull, brain trigeminal ganglia (nerves attached to the brain), eyes, tonsils, spinal cord, dorsal root ganglia (nerves attached to the spinal cord), and the distal ileum (part of the small intestine). The direct or indirect intake of high-risk tissues may have been the source of human illnesses in the United Kingdom and elsewhere. Bovine meat (if free of central nervous system tissue) and milk have, to date, shown no infectivity in test animals. Gelatin, derived from the hides and bones of cattle, appears to the very low risk, especially with adequate attention to the quality of source material and effectiveness of gelatin-making process. Based on many studies, scientists have concluded that forms of CJD other than vCJD do not appear to be associated with the consumption of specific foods.

IMPORT SAFETY

Tom Raum, of the Associated Press, reported that President Bush on July 18, 2007, established a Cabinet-level panel to recommend steps to better guarantee the safety of food and other products shipped into the United States.

"It's important for the American people to know their government is on top of this situation and constantly reviewing procedures and practices," Bush said after his first meeting with the Import Safety Working Group.

REFERENCES

Raum, T. 2007. *Consumer Products.* Associated Press Release.

Ray, K. J., and C. G. Ray, eds. 2004. *Sherris Medical Microbiology.* 4th ed. New York: McGraw-Hill.

USDA. 1992. *Bad Bug Book*, at http://www.cfsan.fda.gov/~mow/intro.html. Includes regular updates.

USDA. 2002. *2002 Farm Bill Provisions*, at http://www.ams.usda.gov/cool/ (accessed July 11, 2007).

USDA. 2007. *Image Gallery.* USDA Agricultural Research Service, at http://www.ars.usda.gov/is/graphics/photos (accessed July 11, 2007).

Index

About the Author

Frank R. Spellman is assistant professor of environmental health at Old Dominion University, Norfolk, Virginia, and author of 55 books.

Spellman's book titles range from *Concentrated Animal Feeding Operations (CAFOs)* to several topics in all areas of environmental science and occupational health. Many of Spellman's texts are listed on Amazon.com and are available at Barnes and Noble. Several of his texts have been adopted for classroom use at major universities throughout the United States, Canada, Europe, and Russia; two are currently being translated into Spanish for South American markets.

Spellman has been cited in more than 400 publications, serves as a professional expert witness for three law groups and an accident investigator for a northern Virginia law firm, and consults on homeland-security vulnerability assessments (VAs) for critical infrastructure including water/wastewater facilities nationwide.

Spellman receives numerous requests to coauthor with well-recognized experts in several scientific fields. For example, he is a contributing author for the prestigious text, *The Engineering Handbook*, 2nd ed.

Spellman lectures on homeland-security and health and safety topics throughout the country and teaches water/wastewater operator short courses at Virginia Tech.

Spellman holds a B.A. in public administration, B.S. in business management, M.B.A., M.S. in environmental engineering, and Ph.D. in environmental engineering.